THE BIBLE AND SOCIAL REFORM

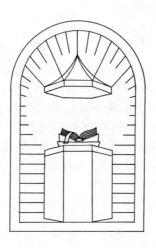

SOCIETY OF BIBLICAL LITERATURE

The Bible in American Culture

General Editors:

Edwin S. Gaustad
Professor of History
University of California, Riverside

Walter Harrelson
Distinguished Professor of Old Testament
Vanderbilt University

1. *The Bible and Bibles in America*
   Edited by Ernest S. Frerichs

2. *The Bible and Popular Culture in America*
   Edited by Allene S. Phy

3. *The Bible in Letters and the Arts*
   Edited by Giles Gunn

4. *The Bible in American Law, Politics, and Rhetoric*
   Edited by James T. Johnson

5. *The Bible in American Education*
   Edited by David Barr and Nicholas Piediscalzi

6. *The Bible and Social Reform*
   Edited by Ernest R. Sandeen

THE BIBLE AND SOCIAL REFORM

edited by

ERNEST R. SANDEEN

FORTRESS PRESS
Philadelphia, Pennsylvania

SCHOLARS PRESS
Chico, California

SOCIETY OF BIBLICAL LITERATURE

CENTENNIAL PUBLICATIONS

Library of Congress Cataloging in Publication Data

Main entry under title:

The Bible and social reform.

(The Bible in American culture)
Includes index.
1. Bible—Influence—Addresses, essays, lectures.
2. United States—Social conditions—Addresses, essays,
3. Church and social problems—United States—History—
Addresses, essays, lectures. I. Sandeen, Ernest Robert,
1931-   . II. Series.
BS538.7.B54   1982   261.8′0973   81-71386
ISBN 0-8006-0611-6   AACR2

9412E82   Printed in the United States of America   1-611

CONTENTS

Editor and Contributors

CHARLES CHATFIELD of Wittenberg University has published, among many works, these dealing with problems of peace: *For Peace & Justice: Pacifism in America, 1914–1941* (1971); and, *Kirby Page & the Social Gospel: Pacifist & Socialist Aspects* (1974).

WILLIAM M. KING completed his doctoral work at Harvard University in 1978, writing his dissertation on "The Emergence of Social Gospel Radicalism in American Methodism." He teaches at the University of Virginia.

WILLIAM D. MILLER, professor at Marquette University, is the author of *A Harsh and Dreadful Love: Dorothy Day and the Catholic Worker Movement* (1972).

PETER J. PARIS of the Divinity School at Vanderbilt University has written *Black Leaders in Conflict: Joseph H. Jackson, Martin Luther King, Jr., Malcolm X, Adam Clayton Powell, Jr.* (1978).

JAMES P. RONDA, who teaches at Youngstown State University in Ohio, is the author (with James Axtell) of *Indian Missions: A Critical Bibliography* (1978).

ERNEST R. SANDEEN, editor of this volume, is the author of *The Roots of Fundamentalism: British and American Millenarianism, 1800–1930* (1970); he teaches at Macalester College in Saint Paul, Minnesota.

JAMES B. STEWART, also of Macalester College, has written *Holy Warriors: The Abolitionists & American Slavery* (1976).

BARBARA BROWN ZIKMUND, Dean and Professor of Church History at the Pacific School of Religion, is co-editor (with Clyde L. Manschreck) of *The American Religious Experiment: Piety & Practicality* (1976).

Preface to the Series

To what extent are Americans a "people of the book"? To what degree is the history of their nation intermixt with the theology and story and imagery of the Bible? These and other questions are addressed in the several volumes of our series, The Bible in American Culture.

Initially conceived as part of the 1980 centennial celebration of the Society of Biblical Literature, this series explores the biblical influence—for good or ill—in the arts, music, literature, politics, law, education, ethnicity and many other facets of American civilization in general. It is the task of other series to examine biblical scholarship per se; these books, in contrast, search out the way in which the Bible permeates, subtly or powerfully, the very fabric of life within the United States.

The undersigned heartily commend the individual editors of each volume. They have persisted and pursued until all authors finally entered the fold. We also gladly acknowledge the wise counsel of Samuel Sandmel in an earlier stage of our planning, regretting only that he is not with us at the end.

Finally, we express our deep appreciation to the Lilly Endowment for its generous assistance in bringing this entire series to publication and wider dissemination.

EDWIN S. GAUSTAD
WALTER HARRELSON

As this volume went to press, we received with deepest regret the unwelcome word of its editor's death. Ernie Sandeen was a respected teacher, a sensitive scholar, a treasured colleague, and a human being of great heart. We miss him and mourn him.

Introduction

Ernest R. Sandeen

> Next Sunday we all went to church, about three mile, everybody a-horseback. The men took their guns along, so did Buck, and kept them between their knees or stood them handy against the wall. The Shepherdsons done the same. It was pretty ornery preaching—all about brotherly love, and such-like tiresomeness; but everybody said it was a good sermon. (Clemens: 90)

Within a few hours, the Grangerfords and the Shepherdsons were killing one another again; Huck Finn "was powerful glad to get away from the feuds" and back onto the Mississippi (96). Mark Twain's bitter characterization of the futility and hypocrisy of religiously inspired moral reform in this episode from *The Adventures of Huckleberry Finn* serves as an illustration of one stereotypical judgment upon the role of American religion in social reform. On the other side there are a thousand pious sources that attribute every blessing enjoyed by Americans to the potent influence of the Scriptures. When one turns from the ambiguous judgment of the conventional wisdom to more scholarly sources, the ambiguity appears again, but what strikes one most forcibly is the slim list of authors who have been willing to look at the ambiguity seriously.

In celebration of the centenary of the Society of Biblical Literature, the authors of the seven chapters that follow have examined the role of the Bible in a series of archetypal reform movements. It was not the aim of the volume to provide a summary of social reform nor even to summarize the history of specific movements (although some of the authors do achieve that result incidentally). And, of course, the authors do not attempt to judge whether the Bible was properly appropriated by the many reformers discussed. Since each of the chapters was written independently of the others, the volume lacks the coherence of a monograph, but in this case the variety of treatment ultimately provokes conclusions that might not have been so plain if one writer had attempted to cover the whole subject.

An Overview of This Volume

Indian missions at first glance would not appear to be a likely movement for inclusion in a volume devoted to social reform, but as James Ronda points out, the aim of the early American Indian missions was nothing less than the transformation of Indian culture into an idealized version of the Euro-American social order represented by the Puritan and Jesuit missionaries. Especially among the Indians evangelized by the Puritans, the Bible functioned as the agent of dramatic and rapid social change. Three hundred years after the fact, most historians (including James Ronda) view that attempted transformation as a regrettable disaster. We hesitate to refer to it as a reform in part because we prefer to label as reforms only changes of which we approve.

In his chapter on the impact of the Bible upon the abolitionist movement, James Stewart explains that early nineteenth-century reformers committed to the emancipation of the slaves were agreed in the early stages of their movement that the "moral suasion" of the Bible would be sufficient authority to rout the slave power and free the blacks. Opposition to slavery allowed idealistic young reformers to purify their Christian commitment and to break free from the fear that true reform was impossible. Unhappily for them, the nation-wide campaign to convert everyone to immediate emancipation backfired, especially after the killing of Elijah Lovejoy and the "great postal campaign" of 1835. The abolitionist movement, in danger of complete collapse, broke into factions none of which continued the early emphasis upon biblical warrant so characteristic of the first phase of its history. The Garrisonian splinter group abandoned both the Scriptures and the constitution for a higher law. The Liberal party, as the conservatives came to be known, turned increasingly to practical political strategy. Almost none of the abolitionists survived the Civil War with faith intact.

Shailer Mathews, Francis Greenwood Peabody, and Walter Rauschenbusch, the three social gospel representatives whose work is discussed in detail in Chapter III, were fully aware of the collapse of antebellum reform; they were also convinced from their own experience that something more than moral suasion was required if the late nineteenth-century crisis of the cities was to be resolved. The strength of the social gospel, William King argues, lay precisely in its recovery of a biblical ethic that was pertinent to the reformers' dilemma. Social gospel apologists recognized that the new liberal theology allowed them to see Jesus and his teaching about the kingdom with fresh eyes and to apply his vision to their own social situation with prophetic power. Yet, King admits, these three social gospel proponents and their few disciples were not able to carry the day either within their own churches or in society as a whole. In contrast to the antebellum reformers whose biblicism was shared widely in the culture, Mathews, Peabody, and Rauschenbusch were relatively isolated voices for a biblical reform ethic in the face of an increasingly secular America.

By treating both sides of the controversy over women in ministry in the nineteenth century, Barbara Zikmund illustrates another difficulty besetting reform. Both those favoring the traditional restraints placed upon women's participation in the Protestant denominations and those attempting to upset the male applecart appealed to the Bible for support. Elizabeth Cady Stanton and those who helped her edit *The Woman's Bible* were convinced that the Bible had proven a significant stumbling block in the path of female emancipation. But many other feminists—both male and female—disagreed with them, and their ingenious arguments may give pause to twentieth-century observers of the contemporary struggle for women's emancipation who are accustomed to accepting the stereotype that all defenders of the Bible must necessarily be conservatives if not male chauvinists.

In contrast to the episodes of reform treated in earlier chapters, Charles Chatfield provides a survey of the impact of the Bible upon the peace movement during the past two hundred years. Thus, Chapter V recapitulates some of the conclusions reached by authors in earlier chapters—especially Stewart and King—and carries the story into the twentieth century. The Bible has continued to exert its influence upon the twentieth-century peace movement, but the problems of reform have become more complex and more difficult to handle. The testimony of the historic peace churches (Quakers, Mennonites, Moravians, Church of the Brethren) has been consistently proclaimed, but the character of that witness has shifted significantly as the cultural isolation of these denominations has diminished. Just war thought, once virtually identified with Catholic theology, began to attract Protestant defenders, especially because of the influence of Reinhold Niebuhr; but simultaneously some Catholics, such as Dorothy Day, began to preach a pacifism that resembled the teaching of the historic Protestant peace churches.

Because of their unique freedom from white control, the black churches have served as the focus of most black reform efforts. In Chapter VI Peter Paris examines the sermons of five black preachers of the twentieth century and finds, not surprisingly, that the Bible is important to each. However, these black leaders—Joseph H. Jackson, William Holmes Borders, Martin Luther King, Jr., Adam Clayton Powell, and Albert B. Cleage, Jr.— do not agree with one other; their positions are discussed under four rubrics: pastoral, prophetic, reform, and nationalist. In spite of their differences there is a unifying impulse to all black reform thought, which Paris names the "black Christian tradition." In this tradition he discovers a distinctive hermeneutic that joins certain biblical assumptions about human nature with the struggle against racism. This black Christian tradition unifies the black churches and provides the yardstick against which to measure even the Scripture itself.

In the last chapter William Miller describes the character and career of Dorothy Day, leader of the Catholic Worker Movement. As one reads the preceding chapters in this volume, the role of the Bible in social reform becomes more and more difficult to understand. It is not a simple problem; but through Miller's eloquent and moving account of the life of Dorothy Day, one can grasp the fact that the Bible still retains its power to move Americans to challenge and possibly to change their society for the better.

The Problem of Protestant Bias

Dorothy Day is virtually the only Catholic reformer treated in this volume; Jewish reform thought is entirely omitted. Let me hasten to add that the Protestant slant is not the product of sectarian blindness on the part of the editor but of the way in which the question has been posed and, ultimately, of the character of the American past. Most Catholic and Jewish scholars who were invited to contribute to this volume have been unable to understand how their scholarly interests could fit into this project.

Protestant and Catholic reformers have based their movements upon clearly contrasting authorities. For example, John Ryan, the Catholic advocate of the social gospel, might be considered representative of Catholic reformers; his arguments relied primarily upon papal authority and pragmatic considerations. So clear was the nineteenth-century Protestant-Catholic alternative that conversions from one denomination to the other were frequently based upon that issue. The Catholic church provided an escape for some Protestants who found that exclusive dependence upon biblical authority in their denominations left no room for tradition and historical argument; Orestes Brownson and Isaac Hecker are two examples of this kind of Catholic convert. Dorothy Day is an unusual case of a Catholic reformer with a strong dependence upon the Bible; ironically, she too was a convert from Protestantism, but her concern with Scripture, as William Miller points out, was especially strong in her later years.

Jewish reform movements have often sprung directly from religious inspiration; one would imagine that it would not be difficult to find examples of Jewish reformers who were moved and motivated by the Scriptures. That no suitable chapter could be obtained for this volume may be owing to the present state of the historiography of Judaism rather than to contrasting bases of authority as was true of Catholicism. In comparison with the historiography of Protestantism, the history of American Judaism is still in its denominational phase, and it is not surprising that its historians turn their eyes inward.

The Historical Controversy over Social Control

Beyond the denominational context, a volume entitled *The Bible and Social Reform* cannot escape the influence of recent historical controversy over the nature of reform itself. In part this debate was generated by the American political climate of the late 1960s and 1970s, which undermined confidence in the motives of the most highminded. In addition to reflecting the general mood of cynicism about the motives of reformers, however, historians have wondered whether reform itself was not tainted—whether all attempts to improve the condition of the poor or provide for the unfortunate have not also been, consciously or unconsciously, attempts to control society.

The controversy began as early as 1954 with a series of books devoted to antebellum reform groups such as the American Bible Society, the American Tract Society, and the American Sunday School Union /1/. The historians of these movements had discovered that the clergy and laity who organized these societies were frightened by a vision of the future that they could characterize only as immoral (since it would not be regulated by their moral code) and unlawful (since it would not be governed by members of their class). They concluded that rather than being applauded for good intentions in distributing Bibles and tracts the reformers ought to be criticized for promoting their own interests and for attempting to perpetuate their own social control.

When reviewed in the light of the 1980s, these monographs of the late 1950s and 1960s seem to be the product of outraged innocence. In his recent magisterial survey, *Urban Masses and Moral Order in America, 1820–1920*, Paul Boyer has provided a more dispassionate view of social reform. There is an inescapable element of manipulation in all reform movements, Boyer argues, and we should not expect to be more successful in locating a pure reformer than was Diogenes in finding an honest man. More significantly, reform must be sparked by a vision. Most often reformers aim to restore a social equilibrium that they have experienced in the past or that they have discovered imaginatively. The success of the reform is often directly proportionate to the extent that the reformer's vision is shared by those who are addressed. Boyer finds little evidence to support the picture of upper class reformers forcing their values upon a hostile working class. Furthermore, the reformers themselves were often marginal members of the reforming class, attempting through the Sunday school or YMCA, for example, to stabilize their own lives. Those to whom they ministered characteristically did not greet the reformers with hostility but often with despair. They often shared the aims and values of the reformers but could not conceive of the possibility of their being able to affirm them.

James Stewart's essay on the abolitionists (Chapter II) illustrates the controversy aptly. The abolitionist movement was fundamentally concerned with the eradication of slavery, and Stewart's explanation of the complexity of the movement is not intended to denigrate that concern. But underlying the antislavery attitudes there was a utopian vision of America which the reformers assumed was shared by all citizens and which the reformers themselves were affirming by their antislavery activity. The abolitionists were not attempting to reform the slave, of course, but the slave owner and those who sympathized with slave owning. No gulf of social class separated the reformers and their potential converts; the reformers' assumption of an identity of values with their potential converts gives special poignancy to the collapse of the antislavery movement. As the possibility of reform disappeared, the possibility of real conflict began to loom ominously.

Similarly, the missions to the Indians seem to have been founded with the expectation that the Indians could be reformed—that is, that white and

Indian through the preaching of the gospel could be brought into the same community, or to use Boyer's terminology, be brought into social equilibrium. But as James Ronda makes clear in his description of Natick and Sillery, two Indian "praying villages," physical coercion was necessary in order to obtain acquiescence and even the coercion was unsuccessful. The vision of reform degenerated into dictatorship. The use of the Bible did not guarantee that John Eliot and the Puritans would approach the Indians with respect and an appreciation of Indian values. In fact, Ronda provides evidence for arguing that Indian religion was more capable than Christianity of providing the context of tolerance necessary for any real Indian-white accommodation.

In terms of this analysis of social reform, the history of the peace movement becomes the archetypal reform. The vision of the perfect society in the minds of peace advocates is one in which reform and not coercion is the means of social control. Chatfield's discussion of the dialectic of the peace movement can be read as a contribution to the historians' debate on social control. The pacifism of the historic peace churches is difficult to define as reform at all, since the aim of these believers seems to be to maintain such a distinct separation between the church and the world that the social disequilibrium of secular politics cannot penetrate the precincts of the sacred community. The aim of that kind of pacifism is not the control of violence in the world but the protection of an exclusive spiritual utopia. The formation of antebellum peace societies by Worcester and Dodge initiated a genuine reform phase of the peace movement and inaugurated the American debate on the legitimate use of force in dispute settlement—just war theory, nonviolent social action, and Niebuhr's pragmatic politics.

The Role of the Bible in Social Reform

A series of questions about the Bible also springs from the essays contributed to this volume. Let us address the easiest question first: In the reform movements discussed in this book, is the Bible an agent in effecting dramatic social change? Apologists for the Bible have frequently cited its influence for good in transforming human institutions, but on the strength of these seven chapters there is little evidence that the Bible exerts this kind of influence independently of other cultural forces. Peter Paris and Barbara Zikmund, for example, describe situations in which the authority of the Bible is acknowledged but the effect of the Bible is ambiguous. Women in ministry are both criticized and supported on the strength of the Scriptures. Accommodation, toleration, nonviolent social action, and separatism all are advocated by black ministers on the authority of the Bible. And in one case in which biblical authority is not accepted by all the parties—the case of Indian missions—biblically justified customs are forced upon the Indians. Whatever impact the Bible has had upon social reform, its effect is not predictable, one-dimensional, certainly not magical.

It is also clear that the Bible cannot be defined simply as either a conservative or progressive force in social reform. The social gospel reformers were advocating a liberal transformation of attitudes among Protestants as were the abolitionists, but the Bible was also being used to defend slavery and to oppose labor unions. Both just war theories and the indefensibility of war were taught on the authority of Scripture.

Lastly, it is clear that the Bible does not exist in isolation from its culture, but in community. Peter Paris argues this thesis directly and forcibly, making the point that the Bible cannot be expected to proclaim a racist doctrine to black Christians. He is unflinching in his willingness to allow the implications of that position to stand clear. But the same lesson emerges from Ronda's treatment of European attitudes toward the Indians. Neither Puritans nor Jesuits could comprehend a Christianity which did not reflect community standards. When the community itself was divided—as was true concerning slavery, women's rights, and war—the biblical message itself seemed unclear.

Nineteenth-century Protestantism carried the Reformation doctrine of *sola scriptura* to lengths that left the believing community with little except the King James Version as the ostensible authority for all thought and action. But those, such as the abolitionists, who attempted to build a reform movement upon biblical authority found that they leaned upon a broken reed. Ironically, then, this volume may not be devoted to so exclusively Protestant a subject as previously indicated. Dorothy Day's dependence upon the Scripture in relation to other authorities makes an interesting comparison with the theories of scriptural warrant developed by social gospel proponents such as Walter Rauschenbusch or a black spiritual leader such as Martin Luther King, Jr. In spite of the theology of *sola scriptura,* in practice Protestan. depended upon communities of definition to interpret the Bible as much, if not as openly, as Catholics.

These are a few of the conclusions that I have drawn from the study of these seven chapters. I have found each of them stimulating and provocative, although I am not convinced by them all. My aim has been not to produce uniformity but to present essays that would point out the complexity of issues that are too frequently treated superficially.

NOTES

1. The best discussion of this controversy is found in Banner. The most commonly cited works in this controversy are Griffin, Bodo, Cole, and Foster.

WORKS CONSULTED

Banner, Lois W.
     1973   "Religious Benevolence as Social Control: A Cri-
                       tique of an Interpretation." *Journal of American
                       History* 60: 23–41.

Bodo, John R.
     1954   *Protestant Clergy and Public Issues, 1812–1848.*
                       Princeton: Princeton University Press.

Boyer, Paul
     1978   *Urban Masses and Moral Order in America,
                       1820–1920.* Cambridge: Harvard University Press.

Clemens, Samuel Langhorne
     1961   *The Adventures of Huckleberry Finn.* Ed. by
                       Bradley, Beatty, Long, and Cooley. New York:
                       W. W. Norton.

Cole, Charles C., Jr.
     1954   *The Social Ideas of the Northern Evangelists,
                       1820–1860.* New York: Columbia University Press.

Foster, Charles I.
     1960   *An Errand of Mercy: The Evangelical United
                       Front, 1790–1837.* Chapel Hill: University of
                       North Carolina Press.

Griffin, Clifford S.
     1960   *Their Brothers' Keepers: Moral Stewardship in
                       the United States, 1800–1865.* New Brunswick:
                       Rutgers University Press.

I

The Bible and Early American Indian Missions

James P. Ronda

In the past two decades there has been a not-so-quiet revolution in the writing of American Indian history. Spurred partly by a renewed sense of Indian cultural tribalism and a scholarly commitment to present a fuller picture of the American experience, a growing number of historians are now engaged in what has been called "the new Indian history" (Berkhofer, 1971, 1973; Prucha; Washburn). These scholars labor to destroy the invidious, time-worn stereotypes that have long dominated both Hollywood and academe. Revisionist historians are not suggesting that we reverse the good guy/ bad guy scenario and make all Indians into selfless patriot chiefs and all whites into genocidal murderers. *Little Big Man* and *Soldier Blue* might have been fine vehicles for advancing the careers of Dustin Hoffman and Candice Bergen, but they are history of a questionable and misleading nature. Massacre history with the roles switched is still massacre history, and playing the politics of outrage will never get us closer to understanding the complex events of culture contact. At the same time, sensitive scholars realize that they cannot abrogate the responsibility to make moral judgments. That those moral judgments are now more fully grounded in an awareness of both European and native American cultures is one of the most exciting features of the new Indian history.

The reevaluation of Indian life and culture has touched all facets of tribal history and Indian-white relations. Tribal military societies are being restudied as is the role of the United States Army. Native American literature, long only the province of the folklorist, has now gained the attention of a number of literary historians. While these arenas of Indian experience are being examined with fresh methods, one central point of encounter is only now beginning to feel the hand of revision. The Christian mission to native Americans has been, since contact, one of the primary points of meeting between indigenous and European peoples. For many tribes the missionaries and the literature they brought along served as the major source of information about Europeans—their values, behavior, and material culture. The Christian mission served as a unique stage for the clash of cultures. Missionaries challenged, in the name of the Christian God, all elements of Indian culture. That challenge provoked arguments and debates between Europeans and Indians unparalleled in other contact situations. The contemporary mission literature produced by those encounters is a precious source for reconstructing an essential chapter in American history. The element of ideology and the missionary insistence on radical culture change made the Christian mission distinctive among contact situations. Yet the writing of Indian mission history has remained until recently very much the domain of the missionaries themselves and their denominational apologists. Only now are we beginning to see a concerted reevaluation of the mission and Indian responses to its challenge. A careful study of Indian mission literature is an especially useful way to probe the mission in culture contact.

We can appreciate the radically new direction of Indian mission studies if we look briefly at the course of mission historiography over the past three and one half centuries. For most of that time the image of the mission and Indian response to its efforts remained much the same. Because the missionaries were usually dedicated and self-sacrificing in the pursuit of Indian souls as well as skilled propagandists, their words—in mission reports, relations, letters, pamphlets, and autobiographies—have long dominated our view of the mission. The classics of mission writing such as *The Jesuit Relations*, the John Eliot tracts, Father Nicholas Point's words and paintings in *Wilderness Kingdom*, and the *Life, Letters, and Travels of Father Pierre-Jean De Smet* all offer essentially the same interpretative slant (Thwaites; Eliot, 1647, 1655; Donnelly; Chittenden and Richardson). Missionaries consumed with holy passion, so runs the old argument, struggled against nearly overwhelming odds to bring the joys of Christian salvation and the benefits of Western civilization to pagan savages. Those Indians who opposed the mission and its divine blueprint were branded as either agents of the devil or, as in the case of Indian religious leaders, men jealous of their own personal influence. Such a perspective with all its harsh overtones of racism and cultural arrogance dominated Indian mission writing from the time of the first missions until well into this century. Whether in a mission report drafted for home consumption or a tract written for a congregation of converts, the mission message was the same—the story of the mission is the epic of valiant soldiers of the cross laboring to do good and overcome evil while always staring holy martyrdom squarely in the face (Riggs, 1869, 1880). The influence of the civilization-versus-savagery motif (ever present when one culture imposes its will on another and then writes the history of that imposition) has surely left its mark on mission history.

It has been only in the past twenty years that history has begun to replace hagiography in the study of Indian missions. Using the methods of ethnohistory, scholars are now beginning to look beyond missionary rhetoric to probe the mission as a crucial arena for culture contact and change (Sturtevant; Thomas). An awareness of Indian religions as well as a knowledge of the means employed by missionaries to promote radical social change has made the newer studies a dramatic departure from the traditional formulation. Revisionist mission history is characterized by the application of two arresting ideas. First, building upon the culture contact and acculturation studies done by anthropologists in the 1930s and 1940s, students of the mission have begun to understand the function of the mission in social change. The missionary was a social revolutionary bent on transforming Indian life on European patterns (Heise). Christian missions in North America, as elsewhere, were dedicated to the invasion of the savage body and the conquest of the heathen soul. To become a Christian, Indians were first to become purified Europeans. What the mission really demanded from native Americans was cultural suicide (Salisbury). Conversion for *Europeans* did not require such radical denial of the cultural past. Native converts were called upon to renounce tradition, past, and identity.

Perhaps the most exciting development in recent mission studies is the second theme—that of Indian responses to the mission invasion. The traditional histories simply ignore native American responses to and criticisms of the mission. A mission-centered analysis consistently argues that mission history is about missionaries and never mind about anyone else. Whether critical of the mission or not, conventional historical wisdom has been that missionaries are the featured players while Indians remain offstage providing only the necessary souls for salvation and bodies for Europeanization. The mission offers a unique vantage point from which to observe Indian peoples coping with an increasingly European world. On the mission stage both Indians and Europeans were actors—active, not passive, in the execution of their roles. Indians dealt creatively with the mission assault. The spectrum of response ranged from genuine conversion to accommodation, fierce theological debate and criticism, and finally physical violence. More than thirty years ago anthropologist Ralph Linton reminded us that culture contact is a two-way street (Appendix: Culture Contact Questionnaire). So far most mission history has served to map only one side of that street; mission history needs to be liberated from that historiographical bias. By listening to the native voices in mission literature we can recover something of the inner life of Indian missions.

Those two ideas make it possible for us more precisely to evaluate mission literature. Missionaries brought to their encounter with native Americans an exclusivist religion that proclaimed a universal truth for all people regardless of culture. That truth was to be propagated with an intense zeal. Mission workers, because they were uncritically proud of their Euro-Christian heritage, entered the mission dedicated to the notion of European cultural, if not racial, superiority. Missionaries tended easily to define Christianity in European cultural terms, confusing farm life with faith and trousers with the means of grace. The elements of exclusivist Christianity and cultural superiority produced a lasting commitment to the proposition that genuine Christian conversion required first an acceptance of secular European habits, customs, and institutions. Mission literature was to be an essential weapon in the battle to transform or, as the missionaries would put it, "reform" Indian life. To paraphrase the Bible, the new wine of Christian conversion could be entrusted only to newly Europeanized bottles.

Native Americans brought to the mission arena a very different set of perceptions about religion and cultures. Native American theologies were as culture-bound as European Christianity but with one fundamental distinction: they represented an inclusivist tradition that was ready to borrow bits and pieces from other sacred ways. Indian religions simply did not contain any evangelistic impulse (Richards: 263–64; Wax). As one Huron observed to a French Jesuit: "Do you not see that, as we inhabit a world so different from yours, that there must be another heaven for us, and another road to reach it?" (Shea: 2:79). And a Navajo medicine man said much the same three centuries later, declaring, "All different tribes have their own religion, so you can keep your own religion and I can keep my own religion too" (Rapoport: 86). With theologies rooted in profoundly divergent assumptions and with political power often slipping into unfriendly hands, Indians and missionaries acted out a turbulent part of culture encounter.

Mission Literature in New England and New France

Missionaries who worked in colonial New England and New France soon realized that unless their new converts were placed in carefully controlled environments, backsliding would quickly take place. Thus the mission was forced by necessity as well as by tradition to produce a substantial body of biblical and instructional literature. While primarily designed to nurture Indian converts in the faith, mission literature also served to spread the mission story among the European faithful. This literature, in both Indian and European languages, ranged from brightly colored pictures with simple Bible texts to complete catechisms and full-scale translations of the Bible. As this essay will suggest, such material had a profound impact on both converted Indians and their traditionalist kin. While missionaries and their Indian assistants were writing and translating these works, the same people were also looking to the Bible as a blueprint for Indian convert communities. In both New France and New England missionaries struggled to build such villages where the new believers might lead European-styled lives, follow Christian teachings, and be shielded from the attractions of the unconverted. Villages such as Sillery in New France and Natick in Massachusetts Bay had their roots in the missionary concept of what the Bible defined as the good and moral life. Town regulations and even political structures were closely linked to biblical (especially Old Testament) injunctions. Even more than printed literature, the mission towns are vivid examples of the impact of the Bible and the missionary venture on the daily lives of native Americans.

Both Puritan and Jesuit missionaries did produce literature for Indian consumption. Yet it is important to bear in mind the basic differences between the Protestant and Catholic approaches to the use of such material. Puritans such as John Eliot, Thomas Shepard, and Thomas Mayhew were schooled in a tradition that stressed preaching and Scripture study as marks of the true faith. If Indian converts were to participate fully in the Christian life, they would have to become literate in their own language if not in English. The rejection of ritual and the equally strong affirmation of hearing the word preached placed an especially heavy burden on the Puritan mission enterprise. Puritan missionaries were compelled to engage in arduous translation and composition ventures for which they were poorly prepared. The distrust of communal ceremonies and ritual healing rites further served to seal off Puritan evangelists from the very center of the Indian mental world. Catholics, on the other hand, were able to use effectively their processions, vestments, symbols, and rites. Catholic mission workers had an entrance into the Indian religious universe and a functional role in the Indian daily world almost wholly denied to Protestants. However, the Catholic dependence on the spoken catechism (almost always in an Indian language) and the ceremony of the Mass as mission tools meant that literature would not be as important as it surely was for Puritan Protestants. In New France the problem was compounded by the lack of printing facilities, necessitating the importation of all books and other mission materials from France.

At the very heart of the Indian mission literature movement in New England was one man—John Eliot. This zealous Puritan divine and his dedicated Indian assistants produced over a period of about fifty years a vast body of translations and compendiums in both the Massachusett and the English language. The centerpiece of the Eliot achievement was his Indian Bible, first published in 1663. It should be noted that Indian assistants did all the actual translating. Because students of the mission have focused so much attention on the Indian Bible, other and perhaps more influential works have been largely ignored. Those other works range from his *Logick Primer* (1672) to the very important *Indian Primer* (1669) and *The Indian Grammar* (1666) and his fascinating and imaginative *Indian Dialogues* (1671). While frequently overshadowed by the linguistic achievement of the Bible undertaking, the lesser-known Eliot mission pieces deserve our careful attention, for they illuminate both missionary expectations and convert realities.

John Eliot surely wanted his treasured Indian Bible to be in the hands of every literate convert. Yet it is probable that another of his books had far greater circulation among the Indian faithful of southern New England. Published in 1669, *The Indian Primer* was designed by Eliot as a tool for promoting Indian-language literacy and a means of propagating the essentials of the faith. The subtitle of the book, *The way of training up of our Indian Youth in the good knowledge of God, in the knowledge of the*

Scriptures and in an ability to Reade, reveals Eliot's dual aim. Eliot began the *Primer* with a spelling lesson in both English and Massachusett coupled with the injunction that Indian scholars "Wise doing to read Catechism; first, read primer; next read Repentance Calling [a probable reference to Baxter's *Call,* published in an Indian version in 1664] next read Bible." After offering Indian and English versions of the Lord's Prayer, Eliot composed in Massachusett a series of twenty questions and answers that explained the major tenets of the prayer. A second set of questions and answers expounded the doctrines contained in the Nicene Creed. Of greatest interest to us is the middle section of the book entitled "Degrees of Christian Duties for several estates, collected out of the holy Scripture." It is no longer possible to capture the nuances of word choice and composition in the Eliot translation, but we can regain some sense of missionary expectations for Indian converts by carefully noting the proof texts that Eliot selected for illustration of the major Christian duties. The missionary evidently used the sermon structure he most commonly employed when preaching as the outline for his exposition.

Eliot began that exposition by exhorting Indian children scrupulously to obey their parents. Using biblical illustrations drawn from the Gospels as well as Old Testament texts, Eliot stressed love and obedience as marks of the Christian family. While requiring obedience from children, the *Primer* did not neglect the responsibilities incumbent on Christian Indian parents. Drawing texts from Proverbs, Deuteronomy, the Psalms, and especially Ephesians 6:4, Eliot taught that convert parents had a special instructional duty toward their children. The Puritan missionary sensed, as did later mission workers, that the success of the mission depended in many ways on strong and stable convert families. A careful examination of conversion patterns from one generation to the next reveals that Eliot's emphasis on the family as a teaching tool was well justified.

From consideration of the right relations between parents and children, Eliot carried the readers of his *Primer* to the duties of young men and women. Again Eliot drew texts from throughout the Bible to instruct his readers. Those young converts could not have missed Eliot's message that they ought to be subject to the opinions of their elders, humble before their betters, and in all things sober minded. Eliot's selection of 1 Peter 2:17 ("Honor all men. Love the brotherhood. Fear God. Honor the king") fully reflected the political, theological, and social virtues he sought to teach. Some of those virtues paralleled indigenous values but the requirement of absolute obedience to parent and king was quite outside the pre-contact Indian experience.

Throughout the history of Indian missions there had been a constant struggle to impose European standards of courtship and marriage upon native Americans. Eliot was no exception. He, like other Europeans, was scandalized by what seemed "loose and irregular" Indian sexual and marriage customs. If the convert family was to flourish as a little Christian commonwealth, it had to be "stable and regular." In his *Indian Primer* Eliot laid great stress upon marital fidelity and peaceful relations between husbands and wives; he was clearly bent on reforming Indian family life according to patterns acceptable to seventeenth-century European tastes. Interestingly, Eliot selected nearly half of the biblical quotations from those verses that demanded obedience and submission from wives. Indian women were to be, like their idealized European sisters, "meek and quiet."

By the time Eliot composed the *Primer* in the late 1660s, an increasing number of native Americans were working for English folk as paid laborers. Sensing that Indian converts would long be dependent on the English for both protection and employment, Eliot gave over a substantial section of the *Primer* to the obligations of servants to masters. Texts from Timothy, Titus, and Ephesians were brought forth to illustrate the bond of faithful obedience that was to characterize the relationship of servant to master. Eliot was here applying concepts of obedience, obligation, and service quite familiar to the English mind but quite outside the Indian experience. The missionary surely knew that some Indian servants, whether converts or not, would be treated harshly by their English masters. Yet Eliot was careful to include at the end of the section a translation of 1 Peter 2:18: "Servants be subject to your masters with all fear; not only to the good and gentle but also to the froward." Ill-used Indian servants, often denied justice in colonial courts, were not going to find solace in the church either.

All these Christian duties were to culminate in the creation of godly Indian families. Puritan divines had long sought to make the family the cornerstone of a Holy Commonwealth. Eliot took those ideas and applied them to an Indian culture that also valued family but manifested that attitude in ways strange to English eyes. The good and godly household, Eliot declared, was to be marked by order, stability, hard work, submission, and faith. In the concluding section on Christian duties, Eliot offered a list of what he perceived as the marks of a Christian household. Reflecting his own commitment to hard agricultural work, private property, and self-sufficiency, the missionary quoted verses from Timothy and Proverbs urging Indians to keep a good house, be diligent in labor, and provide for themselves. Like other missionaries, Eliot held that the traditional habit of sharing food in time of want was dangerous to the virtues of self-sufficiency and personal integrity. Drawing his text from Exodus 20:8 and 10, Eliot called upon converts to avoid labor on the Sabbath. Almost as an afterthought he reminded masters in Christian households that as God was no respecter of persons they ought to be just and equal in all their dealing with servants.

The system of social behavior offered by Eliot in *The Indian Primer* demands our careful attention. It contains Eliot's image of what a good Indian convert ought to be, and the ideas in the *Primer* became the stock-in-trade for much of the rest of Indian mission history. On one level it seems clear that Eliot and his co-workers were bent on fomenting a radical revolution in Indian life. Eliot viewed traditional Indian culture as a vile and disgusting spectacle produced by lost souls. That culture had to be destroyed before Indians could even begin the conversion process (Eliot, 1801:222–28, 1647:14). The ethic proposed by this mission literature was surely negative in both intent and consequence. It weakened tribal cohesion, undermined sachem authority, and eroded belief in the traditional ways—all this at a time when Indian people were undergoing an unprecedented assault on their very existence. Yet on another and equally important level, the mission literature written by Eliot and other Puritans had a very positive effect on a considerable number of southern New England Indians. By the time the *Primer* was published, traditional indigenous life was rapidly changing. Those changes in mental outlook and material culture were caused by the full force of European contact. As the old ways decayed or were transformed, a growing number of Indians began to search for a new faith, a new ideology that could order their lives in an increasingly European world. For these people the rules of behavior and social intercourse propounded by the mission were a means of coping with an alien world while still remaining Indian. The subculture of Christian Indians in New England needed guidance and nurture. Eliot's mission literature provided those converts with both rules for daily living and inspirational thoughts for their education and illumination. That the Christian Indian world was too dominated by English secular interests and too frail to withstand the violence of the 1670s is part of the larger mission failure in North America.

Eliot's Jesuit contemporaries in New France had a significantly different view of mission literature. The Catholic position, suggested earlier in the essay, meant that missions in New France would not produce the rich variety of mission literature that flourished in New England. Jesuit mission planners, like Father Paul Le Jeune, depended upon Indian language preaching, extended live-in visits with tribes, and the powerful force of daily ritual to convey the Christian message. The Jesuits themselves became perhaps the most gifted missionary linguists in early America. The Jesuit position did not preclude a literate Indian convert group. Indeed the Jesuits struggled throughout the 1630s to found a seminary for the education of Indian children. Their efforts were thwarted by disease, Iroquois raids, and intense parental resistance to the deculturation in mission education. Those early failures convinced mission planners that education, literacy, and by extension the production of a body of mission literature were a poor investments of mission energy and money.

Nonetheless, a small and very ephemeral body of literature was circulated in New France. Perhaps the most common form was the small, brightly colored picture card with appropriate text—a teaching tool vividly described by Father Le Jeune: "Here is a picture of those who would not believe; see how they are bound in irons, how they are in the flames, how mad with pain they are; those others who go to heaven, are the ones who have believed and obeyed Him who made all things." The Jesuit Superior admitted that the illustrations were "half the instructions that one is able to give the savages" and argued that "fear is the forerunner of faith in these barbarous minds" (Ronda, 1972; Thwaites: 11:87-89). In the Jesuit missions it was the village experiments that most fully exemplify the impact of the Bible on both the missionaries and their Indian charges.

Mission Literature in Convert Communities

The study of Indian mission literature can easily slip into an antiquarian chronicle of authors, variant titles, and publication dates. Perhaps the best way to avoid that pitfall is to select specific mission situations that illustrate, for both missionaries and Indians, the impact of the Bible and mission literature on culture contact. In the history of early North American missions this can best be done by a thorough analysis of mission towns. The ordering of those towns and Indian lives within them provides us with a rare glimpse into the inner world of the mission. A close look at convert communities gives, as the analysis of literature content cannot, exciting human dimension to culture encounter in the mission arena.

John Eliot once wrote, "The work which we now have in hand will be as a pattern and copy before them, to imitate in all the country, both in civilizing them in their Order, Government, Law, and in their Church proceedings and administration, and hence great care lyth on me to set them right at first, to lay a sure foundation" (Whitfield, 1652:171–72). The creation of Christian Indian villages was at the heart of that "sure foundation." The village would provide converts with an urban, agricultural life— with civilization as both Le Jeune and Eliot defined it. As its native residents began to live the lives of purified Europeans, the village would become a showpiece of the cultural revolution missionaries so devoutly desired. Within the village missionaries could best exercise political, social, and ideological control while conserving mission manpower and financial resources. The controlled environment of the village would also protect new converts from the temptations of their former ways. "For what more hopeful way of doing them good would there be," declared Eliot's co-worker Thomas Shepard, "than by cohabitation in such towns, near unto good examples, and such as may be continually wheting upon them and dropping into them the things of God?" (39). Jesuit Paul Le Jeune clearly believed that village life and piety were synonymous. "It is the same thing in a savage," he wrote, "to wish to become sedentary and to wish to believe in God" (Thwaites: 14:217). Convert villages were to be a missionary Marshall Plan providing Indians with a stable economic base and a sure spiritual foundation.

In his *Relation* of 1634, Father Le Jeune began to develop plans for a village to be settled by Montagnais Indians. Chapter Three of the *Relation*, aptly titled "On the Means of Converting the Savages," outlined his basic strategy. The Jesuit realized that it would be difficult to make town life attractive to the seminomadic Montagnais. He suggested that workers be sent from Quebec to help the Montagnais clear farm land and build a town. The missionary also hoped that the presence of a few pious French families would serve as a good example to the Montagnais and woo more of them into the experiment. Le Jeune and his fellow Jesuits had been deeply influenced by the example of mission towns in Paraguay as well as their understanding of biblical imperatives concerning the godly life. The missionaries envisioned orderly and peaceful Indian communities founded on true religion and following sanitized European ways. Once the Montagnais were made village folk, they "could be more easily won and instructed" (Thwaites: 6:145–55).

In the spring of 1638 sufficient funds and land were finally found and work began on the village of St. Joseph de Sillery. By summer, Le Jeune's project boasted a crowded one-room house and an unknown number of bark cabins. The enterprise seemed well under way when a smallpox epidemic in 1639 forced the Jesuits to order the village abandoned. It was not until the following year when the disease subsided and Sillery was reestablished that Le Jeune and his converts were able to turn their full attention to the material and spiritual transformation of the Montagnais. Working through a small group of Christian Indians, Le Jeune and his successor Barthelemy Vimont developed a system of village regulation designed to change Indian life dramatically (Thwaites: 12:161–67).

The village rules drafted by the Jesuits reflected the experience of the Society in Spanish America. But equally significant was the role played by the Bible in Le Jeune's law system. Life in Sillery was to follow Franco-European patterns as well as the dictates of the decalogue. In many ways Sillery was to be a Bible commonwealth comparable with that created by the Massachusetts Bay Puritans. The regulations touched every aspect of native life, from political leadership to marital relations. Just as the rules touched every part of Indian life, so too did they touch off considerable dissent among the residents of Sillery. The regulations that provoked the greatest controversy were those devised to outlaw traditional sex, courting, and marriage practices. To Le Jeune's dismay, premarital experimentation, group sex, and polygamous marriage were not unknown among the Montagnais. The Jesuit convinced his small band of converts that Christianity required absolute fidelity to European manners and morals. Soon after their election—an action unprecedented in traditional life—Christian Indian town officials rounded up the youth and women of Sillery to scold them for supposed sexual transgressions. "Now know," declared the officers, "that you must obey your husbands and your parents and our captains, and, if any fail to do so, we have concluded to give them nothing to eat" (Thwaites: 18:105–7).

Despite such threats there was great uproar, confusion, and open resistance when the Christian minority in Sillery moved to enforce their stringent moral code. Most Sillery residents wanted to enjoy the security of village life without giving up their customary freedoms. The Montagnais Christians, urged on by the missionaries, became still more militant in their crusade for piety and decided to use prison sentences and even the threat of execution to force adherence to the regulations (Thwaites: 20:143–55). In 1642 a special prison was built at Sillery and public floggings of young women became a common sight (Thwaites: 22:117–27, 24:47–49). Significantly, there is no record of any male being disciplined for alleged sexual misconduct; apparently both the Montagnais converts and their French instructors agreed that only women would bear the burden of guilt. Despite these forceful measures the mission revolution failed in Sillery. Traditionalist resistance and the Iroquois invasions of the mid-1640s destroyed Le Jeune's dream. Father Vimont once described Sillery as "the seed of Christianity amid this great barbarism" (Thwaites: 23:303). The village seed was planted to grow European Indians. Its failure to bear fruit was part of the larger Christian mission failure in North America.

The Jesuit commitment to village building for social change was matched in southern New England by the efforts of John Eliot and his assistants. Like Le Jeune, Eliot viewed the village as a prime weapon in the war for Indian souls. Within the village, or "praying town" as Eliot styled it, the missionary could exercise all the necessary moral and political controls required to produce genuine converts. "I find it absolutely necessary," he stressed, "to carry on civility with Religion" (Winslow: 88). The principal features of Eliot's village plans can be discerned in his long theological and political treatise *The Christian Commonwealth*, first published in 1660. The essay was originally addressed to the political concerns of English Puritans in the aftermath of the Civil War, but it also contained Eliot's basic plan for a holy society—a plan he would try to implement among the Indian peoples of southern New England. Even the most cursory reading of *The Christian Commonwealth* reveals that its plans were deeply rooted in Eliot's extensive Old Testament reading. Eliot's good and godly society was to be a highly structured and regimented organism. Inspired by the Old Testament judges and patriarchs, Eliot fashioned Christian magistrates who were to regulate all aspects of life. The tribes of Israel were to become God's tribe of sanctified Indians. Eliot's politics were far more biblical in origin than English in practice. The missionary hoped that the native peoples of North America would be the raw material for the creation of the biblical commonwealth and that their glorious new society would be a model of true religion, social harmony, and productive labor. Biblical injunctions were to weigh far more heavily on Indians—and with far greater cultural consequences—than on any English folk.

Massachusetts Bay gave Eliot its blessing and support in 1647 with a series of Indian control laws. All Indians were required to live in praying towns and cease worship of traditional gods. Town regulations in turn assumed the Europeanization of resident Indians (Shurtleff: 2:166, 176–79). In the years that followed, Eliot established a network of praying towns which eventually contained fourteen villages with about eleven hundred inhabitants. At Natick, Eliot's most successful village, the missionary labored to mold life "according to the holy pattern" set forth in the Bible-influenced *Christian Commonwealth*. To nurture God's tribe he appointed Christian Indian "rulers" to oversee groups of ten individuals each. This strategy both boosted the influence of converts and subverted loyalty to those sachems who opposed the mission. Eliot ordered, with the full weight of the Bay government behind him, the abandonment of all traditional sacred rites and required the adoption of English dress styles. Eliot drafted an elaborate set of statutes designed to regulate the sex and marriage patterns, geographical mobility, and work habits of the villagers. Fines were imposed on the nonconforming, ranging from five pence for bared female breasts (a traditionally acceptable aspect of dress among Indians) to twenty shillings for premarital intercourse (Eliot, 1655:271–76; Whitfield, 1652:171–72). As Indians had little money except that earned working within the English colonial economy, the fines and debts actually made Indians increasingly dependent on their foreign masters. But Eliot was enthusiastic. He joyfully described the efforts at Natick as "the sprinklings of the spirit and blood of Christ Jesus in their hearts" (Eliot, 1647:20–21).

One of the most important and revealing pieces of Indian mission literature to come out of Eliot's praying towns was *Christiane OOnoowae Sampoowaonk*. This *Christian Covenanting Confession* was first printed as a bilingual (Massachusett/English) broadside in 1660. It represents the model for establishing Indian congregations and praying towns instituted by Eliot throughout the Bay Colony. Because an English text has not been readily available for nearly a century, the following is provided. The *Confession* demonstrates both the biblical theology to which converts were repeatedly exposed and the village design so central to Eliot's mission.

A Christian Covenanting Confession
I believe with my Heart and Confess with my mouth Rom. 10:10.
1. There is but one, onely, liveing and true God. Deut. 6:4 Jer. 10:10 But he is Father, Son, holy Spirit. Matt 28:19 I John 5:7.
2. In the Beginning God made Heaven and Earth very Good Gen. 1:1,31.
3. He made Adam to rule this Lower world. Gen. 3
4. Adam quickly sinned, and was punished. Gen. 3
5. Adam conveighed to us his sin, and also his guilt and punishment. Rom. 5:12
6. For this cause, we are all born in sin. Psal. 51:5
7. Our sin is two fold
    1. Origenal sin Rom. 3:10
    2. Actual sin Matt. 15:19
8. By these wee desarve Damnation in Hell for ever Rom. 6:23
9. I believe we shall all rise again to Judgement at the last day. I Cor. 15
○ ○ ○ ○ ○

1. Jesus Christ is the Son of God. Psa. 2:6,7. He became a man, and is both God and man in one person. Heb. 2:16,17.

2. Jesus Christ hath Three offices, Priest, Prophet, King. Heb. 7:1,2,3. Acts 3:32. Isa, 33:22.

3. Jesus Christ obeyed perfectly for us, He payed his Death for us when He dyed for us, and hereby He deserved pardon for all our sins. Rev. 1:5. Matt. 3:15.

4. Now by the Gospel New-Covenant Jesus Christ calleth us all to repent, and believeingly to turn unto God. Acts 17:30.

5. For these causes, wee that dwell in this towne called _____ are gladly willing to bind our selves to God, to Remember the Sabbath day to keep it holy, so long as we live. And also to bind our selves to each other, to meet together every Sabbath day (when it may be done) to doe all our Sabbath day Services, prayers etc., according to the word of God, the holy Spirit of God helping us.

By this gospel covenant, we doe give our selves and our Children to Jesus Christ, to walk with Him in Church order so long as we live.

O Lord Jesus Christ, by thy Pardoning free grace and mercy Graciously receive us.

We compel not any, but meekly say to all let us joyne together to doe all this.

The Impact of Mission Literature on Native Americans

This missionary theology and the tactics used to propagate it were vigorously applied in the Concord, Massachusetts, experiment of Thomas Shepard, and from his writing we have what is perhaps the fullest account of Bible-based village law for social change. Shepard's "Orders and Regulations" also betrays the rather unsubtle intentions of the English to dispossess the Massachusett Indians of their land as well as their culture. It was no accident that one of the signer-administrators of the rules was Captain Simon Willard, an influential Bay Colony land speculator who later established a number of English towns in the Concord-Merrimack River valley region. In his preaching to Indians around Noonanetum in 1646, Shepard told his listeners that they should give up their "surplus" land to the deserving English as a precondition to accepting Christianity. Most Indians were understandably reluctant to take such harsh medicine, but one young sachem and his band decided to break with the majority of the tribe and accept the faith. They were required to give up all material signs of Indian identity. The new believers were ordered to cut their hair "as the English do," to refrain from body painting, and to halt all powwow disease-healing ceremonies. The traditional mourning rites were also strictly forbidden. These regulations, clearly a synthesis of English customs and biblical decrees, plainly implied that the Massachusett were now under alien political and cultural control (38–40).

By its very nature, the content of Indian mission literature constituted a direct threat to indigenous religious and political leadership. Both Jesuit and Puritan missionaries cultivated younger Indian politicians, urging them to challenge the authority of their elders. Mission workers knew that to eliminate resistance they had to topple certain sachems and religious leaders from power. They understood that they were locked in a very deliberate battle for the loyalties of the flock. In Sillery the struggle took a form that would be repeated throughout the history of the Indian missions. A faction of Montagnais politicians—some of whom converted—made a very pragmatic and secular alliance with the Jesuits. The Indian politicians were convinced that village life under the military protection of the French was the last chance for survival since it would afford some defense against the dreaded Iroquois raids and supplement an ever-dwindling food supply. Father Le Jeune used this pro-village faction to harass native priests and those Montagnais politicians who branded the village a front for French domination. In his sermons and daily teachings, Le Jeune personally derided the Montagnais shamans and commanded the destruction of all Indian sacred objects. As the competition played itself out, both the mission and the Montagnais were weakened. Le Jeune's persistent abuse of ancient ways made it easy to mark him as a power hungry and sacrilegious man. Jesuit tactics simply strengthened traditionalist zeal. However, the band as a whole experienced unprecedented *ideological* factionalism. With the vital cultural link of a shared religion strained and probably weakened beyond repair, the Montagnais were further fragmented in the face of the fatal Iroquois invasion (Ronda, 1974).

In the praying towns Eliot and his co-workers employed similar tactics to change Indian loyalties. Eliot first tried to convert Cutshamoquin and other powerful Massachusett sachems. When they resisted, he decided to pursue the politically ambitious non-sachem males of the tribe. In 1646 this approach paid off with the conversion of Waban. Waban was a politically eager man, and Eliot satisfied the Indian's ambition by making him "the Chief Minister of Justice." Waban used his office in God's new tribe to build and strictly discipline an Indian church (Eliot, 1647:3, 19; Jennings: 205; Shepard: 37–38).

It is clear from Eliot's *Indian Dialogues* that the sachems readily understood this aspect of mission strategy. In the third of Eliot's dialogues a prominent sachem complains that the refusal of Christian Indians to make the customary tribute payments to him was undermining his position and dividing his people. He would continue to resist Christianity, he resolved, until such matters of authority were settled. This sachem was certain that Christianity had nothing to offer him. "In the way I am now I am full and potent, but if I change my way and pray to God, I shall be empty and weak. . . . My tribute will be small and my people few, and I shall be a great loser by praying to God." The sachem insisted that the new friends and allies of conversion might bring him were simply not worth the sacrifice (46-50; Whitfield, 1651:139). But the Massachusetts Bay missionaries continued to encourage factional and ideological disputes in the hope of raising up a new Christian leadership elite. Through that new elite the mission sought to undermine the sachems and the powwows. By weakening the old bonds of deference and authority, the missions helped make native Americans easy prey for those who would strip them of all political strength (Jennings: 205–7; Salisbury: 35–39).

Missionaries did not demand the destruction of Indian ways out of some sinister desire to inflict suffering and confusion. They wholeheartedly believed that God required native peoples to forsake their former identities and become radically new people. The act of conversion itself implied a decisive change of heart, whether the convert be English, French, or native American. All mission literature pounded home that becoming a Christian meant casting off the old identity and putting on the new. For Le Jeune and Eliot, the language of conversion became the language of the mission revolution: as God had promised to transform the individual in the miracle of salvation, so would God transform Indian society by the efforts of the mission. Le Jeune and Eliot failed to realize that because Indians were expected to renounce their own ethnic past as something vile and disgusting, conversion took on an entirely new and terrifying dimension. The Indian Christians (especially in the first generation of mission contact) were required to confess *as sin* their very heritage, their very Indian identity. The potential converts were called upon to deny not only their own personal past but that of their ancestors as well. In this spirit one of Eliot's converts testified that he had abandoned "all the works of darkness, our old Indian customs, laws, fashions, powwowings, and whatever that is contrary to the right knowledge of the true God and of Jesus Christ our Redeemer" (Eliot, 1671:25). Another Indian found conversion to be an agonizing experience. "I know not what to do" (Eliot, 1671:20). This man sensed that despite the physical surroundings of praying towns and the theological trappings of Indian mission literature the mission would be hard pressed to grant converts any meaningful new identity. Indian Christians could no longer be Indians, at least in the eyes of their unconverted kinsfolk, because the faith was inextricably bound to the terms and value of its European representatives. Indian Christians knew as well that they would never be fully accepted in the white colonial world. Neal Salisbury has aptly described the convert's dilemma: "The converts were left suspended between two cultures, with their own cultural expression carefully controlled from without" (46).

While the challenge of mission literature produced a sizable number of converts and native preachers, it also called forth a powerful Indian initiative sharply critical of missionary teachings. That traditionalist movement was especially visible and vocal in Sillery. From the very beginning of the Sillery experiment the Christian minority faced strong and determined resistance to change. Mission opponents successfully portrayed Christian Indians as petty, power hungry traitors and French missionaries as foreign devils bent on dividing and destroying the Montagnais. They effectively argued that Christian doctrine was too complex to grasp and ill-suited to Indian needs. Since the Jesuits frequently baptized those on the verge of death, traditionalists were easily able to claim that Christianity was in fact hazardous to the health of converts. The fact that feared European diseases accompanied the missionaries provided considerable support for that belief. It was not difficult for Montagnais shamans to depict Christianity as a strange, complicated, and potentially dangerous ideology. To the Jesuits' consternation, shamans were able to operate a flourishing religious underground in Sillery throughout most of the village's existence (Thwaites: 18:95–105; 20:157–59; 24:25–27).

Puritan missions inspired similar opposition. John Eliot's first foray into mission work, at Dorchester Mill in 1646, met with considerable resistance. He was compelled to admit that "when I first attempted it, they gave no heed unto it, but were weary, and rather despised what I said" (Shepard: 50). In the following years Eliot encountered strong opposition from both political and religious Indian leaders. Perhaps the fullest account of Indian objections to Christianity can be found in Eliot's *Indian Dialogues*. In the first of three dialogues, a Natick Christian Indian and an unconverted relative discuss the merits and demerits of accepting the Christian faith and English ways. The new Christian contended that the Indian way was a "deep pit and filthy puddle." In response the relative asked if accepting Christ brought great prosperity not possible with traditional religion. When told that the Christian life did not guarantee wealth, he pointedly asked the value of such conversion. The skeptical relative cited the wisdom of those Indians—past and present—who valued the Indian way: "Our forefathers were (many of them) wise men, and we have many wise men now living. They all delight in these our Delights: they have taught us nothing about our Soul, and God, and Heaven, and Hell, and Joy, and Torment in the life to come." Englishmen invented those terror stories, he charged, to "scare us out of our old customs, and bring us to stand in awe of them." Perceiving the connection between the mission and the political goals of Massachusetts Bay, the Indian attacked Christianity as a method designed to "wipe us of our lands and drive us into corners." The Christian's response was a rather lame defense of the English presence in America and a brief discourse on the universality of the Christian faith. Unimpressed, his kinsman sighed, "You make long and learned discourses . . . which we do not well understand. I think our best answer is to stop your belly with a good supper. We are well as we are and desire not to be troubled with these new wise sayings." That "good supper" did not prove effective in stopping the preaching. Finally, the Indians assembled for the meal offered their objections in a most pragmatic and telling reply. "It is an ill time for you to come to perswade us to pray to God, when praying to God is so opposed, hated, and hindered; you may be more like to prevail with us when praying to God is of credit, honor, and good esteem" (2–10, 50; Ronda, 1977).

Despite their best efforts, Le Jeune, Eliot, and the native converts never prevailed—never convinced a majority of native Americans that praying to the Christian God was noble. Many Indians agreed with the sachem in Eliot's third dialogue. Christianity, he said, is "a bitter pill, too hard for me to get down and swallow" (Eliot, 1671:50). Native Americans understood that behind the seminaries, praying towns, Bibles, and long hours of instruction lay a profound impulse to deculturate them and transform them into passive tractable converts. Primers and praying towns, confessions and covenants might sustain a dependent Christian Indian subculture, but they could not protect native peoples from the erosion promoted by self-appointed apostles. By the eighteenth century there were many Indian preachers and elders in southern New England, but those preachers were part of a colonized culture and they were reminded of their inferior status daily. Mission literature probably contributed to Indian literacy, a key to coping with the colonial world of bureaucracy, written treaties, and impersonal courts of law. But literate Indians counted for little in a white world growing steadily more hostile. Whatever the immediate "Marshall Plan" benefits of places like Sillery and Natick, they remained ghettos in the wilderness where Indians could be watched by ever-suspicious colonial governments. When missionaries surveyed the task of saving Indian souls, they envisioned mission literature as a sharp tool to level the native house of culture. When those same missionaries ventured to rebuild the Indian house with Christian materials, mission literature proved to be bricks without straw.

WORKS CONSULTED

Axtell, James
1978   "The Ethnohistory of Early America: A Review Essay." *William and Mary Quarterly*, 3d Ser., 35: 110–44.

Berkhofer, Robert F.
1971   "The Political Context of a New Indian History." *Pacific Historical Review* 40: 357–82.

1973   "Native Americans and United States History." In *The Reinterpretation of American History and Culture*, ed. W. H. Cartwright and R. L. Watson. Washington, DC: National Council for the Social Studies.

Bolton, Herbert E.
1936   *Rim of Christendom: A Biography of Eusebio Francisco Kino, Pacific Coast Pioneer.* New York: Macmillan.

Brown, G. Gordon
1944   "Missions and Cultural Diffusion." *American Jour-
                        nal of Sociology* 50: 214–19.

Chittenden, Hiram M. and Richardson, A. T., eds.
1905   *The Life, Letters, and Travels of Father Pierre-
                        Jean De Smet.* New York: Francis P. Harper.

Clancy, James T., ed.
1973   "Native American References: A Cross-Indexed
                        Bibliography of Seventeenth-Century American
                        Imprints Pertaining · to American Indians." *Pro-
                        ceedings of the American Antiquarian Society* 83:
                        287–341.

Donnelly, Joseph P., ed.
1967   *Wilderness Kingdom: Indian Life in the Rocky
                        Mountains 1840–1847, the Journals and Paintings
                        of Nicholas Point.* New York: Holt, Rinehart, and
                        Winston.

Eames, Wilberforce
1890   *Bibliographic Notes on Eliot's Indian Bible and
                        on His Other Translations and Works in the Indi-
                        an Language of Massachusetts.* Washington, DC:
                        Government Printing Office.

Eliot, John
1647   *The Day-Breaking, if not the Sun-Rising of the
                        Gospell with the Indians in New-England.* Lon-
                        don: Richard Cotes. Reprinted in *Collections of
                        the Massachusetts Historical Society*, 3d Ser., 4,
                        whose pagination is followed here.

1655   *A Late and Further Manifestation of the Progress
                        of the Gospel amongst the Indians in New Eng-
                        land.* London: M. Simmons. Reprinted in *Collec-
                        tions of the Massachusetts Historical Society*, 3d
                        Ser., 4, whose pagination is followed here.

1660a   *Christiane OOnoowae Sampoowaonk: A Christian
                        Covenanting Confession.* Cambridge, MA: Samuel
                        Green.

1660b   *The Christian Commonwealth: Or, The Civil Pol-
                        icy of the Rising Kingdom of Jesus Christ.* Lon-
                        don: Livewell Chapman.

1663	*The Holy Bible containing the Old Testament and the New. Translated into the Indian Language.* Cambridge, MA: Samuel Green and Marmaduke Johnson.
1666	*The Indian Grammar.* Cambridge, MA: Marmaduke Johnson.
1669	*The Indian Primer; or, The way of training up of our Indian Youth in the good knowledge of God, in the knowledge of the Scriptures, and in an ability to Reade.* Cambridge, MA: Marmaduke Johnson.
1671	*Indian Dialogues, for Their Instruction in that Great Service of Christ.* Cambridge, MA: Marmaduke Johnson.
1672	*The Logick Primer.* Cambridge, MA: Marmaduke Johnson.
1801	"Dedications to the Old and New Testaments of the Indian Bible." *Collections of the Massachusetts Historical Society,* 1st Ser., 17: 222–28.

Heise, David R.
1967   "Prefatory Findings in the Sociology of Missions." *Journal for the Scientific Study of Religion* 6: 49–58.

Jennings, Francis
1971   "Goals and Functions of Puritan Missions to the Indians." *Ethnohistory* 18: 197–212.

Linton, Ralph
1940   *Acculturation in Seven American Indian Tribes.* New York: Appleton-Century.

Pilling, James C.
1891   *Bibliography of the Algonquian Languages.* Washington, DC: Government Printing Office.

Prucha, Francis P.
1976   "Books on American Indian Policy: A Half-Decade of Important Work, 1970–1975." *Journal of American History* 63: 658–69.

Rapoport, Robert N.
1954   "Changing Navajo Religious Values: A Study of Christian Missions to the Rimrock Navajos." *Papers*

*of the Peabody Museum of American Archae-
ology and Ethnology* 41, pt. 2.

Richards, Cara
   1972   *Man in Perspective: An Introduction to Cultural
                        Anthropology.* New York: Random House.

Riggs, Stephen Return
   1869   *Tah-koo Wah-kan; or, The Gospel among the Da-
                        kotas.* Boston: Congregational Sabbath-School and
                        Publishing society.

   1880   *Mary and I: Forty Years with the Sioux.* Chicago:
                        W. G. Holmes.

Ronda, James P.
   1972   "The European Indian: Jesuit Civilization Planning
                        in New France." *Church History* 41: 385–95.

   1974   "The Sillery Experiment: A Jesuit-Indian Village in
                        New France." Unpublished manuscript.

   1977   "'We Are Well As We Are': An Indian Critique of
                        Seventeenth-Century Missions." *William and Mary
                        Quarterly*, 3d Ser., 34: 66–82.

Salisbury, Neal
   1974   "Red Puritans: The 'Praying Indians' of Massachu-
                        setts Bay and John Eliot." *William and Mary
                        Quarterly*, 3d Ser., 31: 27–54.

Shea, John G.
   1900   *History and General Description of New France
                        by the Rev. P. F. X. De Charleviox.* 6 vols. New
                        York: Francis P. Harper.

Shepard, Thomas
   1648   *The Clear Sun-Shine of the Gospell. Or an His-
                        toricall Narration of Gods Wonderfull Workings
                        upon sundry of the Indians.* London: Richard
                        Cotes. Reprinted in *Collections of the Massachu-
                        setts Historical Society*, 3d Ser., 4, whose pagina-
                        tion is followed here.

Shurtleff, Nathaniel B., ed.
   1853–1854   *Records of the Governor and Company of the
                        Massachusetts Bay in New England.* 5 vols. Bos-
                        ton: W. White.

Sturtevant, William C.
    1966   "Anthropology, History, and Ethnohistory." *Ethno-*
                    history 13: 1–51.

Tanis, Norman E.
    1970   "Education in John Eliot's Indian Utopias, 1646–
                    1675." *History of Education Quarterly* 10: 308–
                    323.

Thomas, Keith
    1963   "History and Anthropology." *Past and Present* 24:
                    3–24.

Thwaites, Reuben G., ed.
    1896–1901   *The Jesuit Relations and Allied Documents,*
                    1610–1791. 72 vols. Cleveland: Burrows Brothers.

Washburn, Wilcomb
    1971   "The Writing of American Indian History: A Sta-
                    tus Report." *Pacific Historical Review* 40: 261–81.

Wax, Murray
    1968   "Religion and Magic." In *Introduction to Cultural*
                    Anthropology, ed. James Clifton. Boston: Hough-
                    ton, Mifflin.

Whitfield, Henry
    1651   *The Light Appearing More and More Towards*
                    the Perfect Day. Or, A Farther Discovery of the
                    Present State of the Indians in New England,
                    Concerning the Progresse of the Gospel amongst
                    them. London: T. R. & E. M. for John Bartlet.
                    Reprinted in *Collections of the Massachusetts*
                    Historical Society, 3d Ser., 4, whose pagination is
                    followed here.

    1652   *Strength out of Weaknesse; Or a Glorious Mani-*
                    festation of the Further Progresse of the Gospel
                    among the Indians of New England. London: M.
                    Simmons. Reprinted in *Collections of the*
                    Massachusetts Historical Society, 3d Ser., 4, whose
                    pagination is followed here.

Winslow, Edward
    1649   *The Glorious Progress of the Gospel amongst the Indians in New England.* London: Hannah Allen. reprinted in *Collections of the Massachusetts Historical Society*, 3d Ser., 4, whose pagination is followed here.

II

Abolitionists, the Bible, and the Challenge of Slavery

James Brewer Stewart

Late August 1831 found the citizens of Charleston, South Carolina—the deep South's most vocal slave state—in a frenzy of anxiety. News had just arrived that in Southampton County, Virginia, a bloody revolt led by the slave Nat Turner had claimed the lives of at least thirty-seven whites. Other rumors, soon confirmed, spoke of yet another massive black insurrection in the British sugar colony of Jamaica. As the South Carolina legislature assembled, members warned that these terrifying events were but the first fruits of a far-flung abolitionist conspiracy, directed from New England which would attempt to free all the slaves by inciting racial holocaust. Soon the delegates were debating a special message from the governor which decried incendiary abolitionist newspapers. South Carolina's senior senator, Robert Y. Hayne, received authorization to consult with the mayor of Boston about how best to silence the "dangerous fanatics" who resided in his city. Outraged Charleston citizens formed a vigilance committee, hoping to ferret out abolitionist plotters and rebellious blacks (Freehling: 301–60).

In retrospect it is clear that the behavior of these South Carolinians was far out of proportion to the actual threat. Yankee abolitionists had nothing to do with Turner's insurrection or with any other slave rebellion. The abolitionists disavowed Turner's deeds, reaffirmed their own pacifism, and insisted that voluntary emancipation constituted the only way to achieve harmony between warring races. Yet for all its paranoia the South Carolina response was understandable and in certain ways accurate. The practice of slaveholding had been largely unquestioned in much of the South and throughout the rest of the nation for the better part of 150 years. During this long period the moral validity of owning slaves had sometimes been debated, but doubts had impeded neither the rapid spread of slavery in the South nor its ever-increasing importance in the nation's economy. Most of the South's planter class had concluded long before the American Revolution that slavery was not only profitable as a business but also wholly compatible with America's republican institutions and Christian character.

The vast majority of northerners too had displayed no uneasiness about southern slavery, except for a time during the American Revolution. While

gradually emancipating the handful of slaves found in their states and decrying the horrors of the African slave trade, most Yankees had remained content
after the 1780s to segregate local blacks while letting the remote South
manage its own peculiar institution. A handful of zealous Quakers protested
the sin of slavery, but even northern antislavery-minded leaders such as
Benjamin Franklin, Alexander Hamilton, and Albert Gallatin, supported
constitutional devices that protected slavery. These individuals emphasized
modest voluntary approaches to reforming slavery, which leading planters
like Thomas Jefferson, John Marshall, and George Washington could also
endorse. Gradual, compensated emancipation had become the popular
program of that day, coupled with impractical colonization schemes designed
to ship unwanted blacks to far away West Africa. Meanwhile, from the 1790s
through the 1820s the South's slave population had more than doubled,
surpassing two million; the number of acres devoted to cotton and tobacco had
expanded as rich bottom lands were opened on the Mississippi-Georgia-
Alabama frontier (Davis, 1974:213–326). It is hardly surprising that the white
citizens of Charleston, South Carolina—like most other white Americans,
North and South—had come to assume that owning black slaves was a routine
and profitable enterprise that one was no less an American for perpetuating.

However, in the 1830s Yankee abolitionists began zealously proclaiming
just the opposite: "Woe to this guilty land unless she speedily repents her evil
doings," declared William Lloyd Garrison, one of the important early agita-
tors. "The blood of millions of her sons cries out for redress! IMMEDIATE
EMANCIPATION can alone save her from the vengeance of Heaven" (*Liberator*, Sept. 3, 1831). Such volcanic phrases announced the sudden appearance of the radical abolitionists, one of the most controversial and important
groups of reformers to be found in American history. The conventional
reaction, North and South, was one of outrage: "Why so sudden and savage
an outburst of mania and rant?" demanded an angry John C. Calhoun, a
principal defender of slavery and South Carolina's most prominent politician
(Calhoun: 6). Though laced with disdain, Calhoun's question offers a useful
starting point for understanding why these Bible-inspired men and women
felt so compelled to challenge American slavery, what they achieved, and
what their efforts meant to the evangelical Protestantism that spawned the
movement in the first place. To find an answer to Calhoun's petulant query
one must return first to the 1820s when pious New Englanders felt keenly
beset by powerful challenges to their evangelical creeds.

The Roots of Religious Radicalism

During the 1820s American society posed formidable problems for
many pious New Englanders, including those who were soon to become
abolitionists. For most of the decade Protestant voices had denounced the
nation's obsession with wealth, geographic expansion, urbanization, and party politics. Vice, ignorance, and infidelity, they warned, flourished on the

frontiers and in the eastern cities. Numbed by alcohol and illiteracy, hundreds of thousands of Americans were being transformed into the tools of heartless politicians who now denied the Christian character of government and insisted on popular rule. Unless someone imposed stringent correctives the nation would slide into moral anarchy, thereby inviting God's righteous retribution (Thomas, 1965:71–93).

Despite their shrillness these warnings reflected undeniable realities. The nation's population was, in fact, growing and moving with unprecedented speed. People spilled across frontiers as never before; city populations increased at a rate never since matched in American history. Meanwhile new forms of mass communication such as inexpensive books, pamphlets, newsprint, and (soon) the telegraph as well as new types of transportation such as canals, steamboats, and (soon) the railroads began to shatter old bonds of religious community and moral consensus. Regional economic systems became more sophisticated and interdependent, and mass political parties matched their transformation with popular appeals to the ordinary citizen's material interests. New England Protestantism, in short, faced its own form of future shock, beset on every hand by the dynamic forces of secularism and economic modernization.

Yankee ministers met the challenge by mounting an impressive counterattack that emulated the techniques of their irreligious foes. The printing presses of many newly-founded organizations such as the Tract Society, Temperance Society, and Bible Society spewed forth thousands of pamphlets exhorting repentance. Efficient bureaucrats in many denominations commissioned itinerant preachers whose task it was to recover lost souls in the backcountry and in the urban slums. All these activities envisoned the reassertion of older Protestant values on a national scale. At the same time, though unintentionally, such efforts began provoking pious young abolitionists-to-be to religious and social rebellion.

All of these programs of Christian restoration drew inspiration from religious revivalism with its emphasis on the conversion experience. The great revivals of the 1820s, led by powerful evangelists like Lyman Beecher and Charles G. Finney, proclaimed that human beings, though sinners, possess God-given power to convert, that is, to choose redemption from the voluntary selfishness of sin. Each person should seek God's redemptive grace, embrace a new life of sanctification, and then apply this new holiness in efforts to expand Christ's earthly domain. Here was a creed that deemphasized original sin, stressed people's responsibility for their own salvation and the creation of a better society. The imperatives of spiritual individualism and social activism had never before been so strongly fused within American Protestantism, and Yankees responded with alacrity. They flocked to the temperance, Bible and tract societies. They tithed to spread God's word among native Americans, blacks, sailors, hoboes, convicts, and paupers. They subsidized the divinity schools and added to scholarship funds (Barnes,

1933:1–28). All the while, these ambitious evangelicals glimpsed a glorious new era: purged of liquor, atheism, prostitution, and the lust for mammon, the sanctified public would soon live peacefully in a truly Godly society. From this clearly defensive setting a radical crusade against slavery was quick to take form.

In one sense the outcome hardly seems surprising. The revivalists' conviction that their dedication alone prevented the unleashing of God's vengeful wrath contained strong overtones of alienation and sudden activism. From this perspective, all American institutions and social customs could seem vulnerable to corruption. The urge to dedicate one's life to a Christian struggle against this all-consuming sin often became too intense to ignore. Meanwhile, young men and women who harbored these urges found unprecedented opportunities to act on them. By the mid-1820s careers in the ministry no longer remained restricted, thanks to the rapid expansion of the seminaries. In addition the benevolent agencies themselves, which were highly developed bureaucracies by the standards of their day, were in need of agents, editors, and fund-raisers. For the first time in American history social reforming was considered a legitimate and popular professional career. Earnest ministerial candidates and pious laypersons began taking positions as circuit riders, temperance lecturers, editors, and school teachers with salaries underwritten by the benevolent agencies. Among them were many notable abolitionists-to-be (Wyatt-Brown, 1970). William Lloyd Garrison, whose newspaper the *Liberator* was soon to trumpet the first sustained call for immediate emancipation, spent part of the 1820s editing a temperance magazine. Other incipient radicals like Elizur Wright, Jr., Henry C. Wright, Samuel J. May, Amos A. Phelps, Stephen S. Foster, and Joshua Leavitt began as seminarians who either managed evangelical publications or rode the circuit. Theodore Weld, soon to become abolitionism's most effective grass-roots organizer, spent his early years helping to organize Charles G. Finney's revival meetings.

Many more examples could be cited, but the crucial point is this: unprecedented numbers of morally intense young Americans had dedicated themselves to rooting out sin. They were taking their responsibilities seriously and were fully expecting to realize their goals. Further, as recent research has shown, the parents of most abolitionists had raised their children to adhere to the highest standards of uprightness and social awareness. These were people bred to a strong sense of individuality, who were sure of their ability both to master themselves and to lead others to obey God's will. Yet their suspicion of existing practices and institutions was also unmistakable. Religious inspiration, social alienation, and a heightened sense of self thus conjoined to create an unmistakable potential for radicalism. (Stewart, 1976:37–40). As these young people responded to the complexities presented by the 1820s, these feelings were quick to develop.

As they set about America's spiritual renewal, future abolitionists suddenly discovered that the same Protestant establishment upon which they placed their hopes was hardly free of the very materialism and bureaucratic staleness that they had been bred to reject. To their dismay young ministers like Samuel J. May, Charles T. Torrey, Henry B. Stanton, Henry C. Wright, and Elizur Wright, Jr., found themselves ensnared in denominational intrigues and surrounded not by God-fearing congregations but by unstable groups of rootless individuals. In politics aspiring evangelical people in business like Lewis Tappan, his brother Arthur Tappan, and the pious young attorney William Jay struggled in vain to replace the urban political machines with pure Christian leaders. Throughout New England young evangelicals began to sense that the day-to-day routine of their most cherished institutions—the denominations, the benevolent associations, even revivalism itself—fell sinfully short of God's requirements (Wyatt-Brown, 1971:316–41). A disappointed Theodore Weld expressed these widespread feelings perfectly, complaining bitterly to his mentor, Charles G. Finney, that "revivals are fast becoming with you sort of a trade to be worked at so many hours a day. . . . The machinery all moves on; every wheel and chord in its place; but isn't the *main spring* waxing weaker?" (Barnes and Dumond: 1:15).

As such misgiving began to surface, young evangelicals grew increasingly unsure of the authenticity of their own commitment as Christians. The formulas for Protestant renovation so dear to their parents now seemed fatally flawed. If so, then society was far more deeply stained with sin than anyone had ever suspected, and the individual reformer also needed reforming. A genuine commitment to God's will was required, a fresh dedication to creating a truly Christian nation. The powerful combination of conservative Yankee revivalism, the social dislocations of economic growth, and personal impulses for redemption thus led young men and women to the radical religious vision that initially characterized abolitionism. Opposing slavery certainly allowed one to affirm with unprecedented intensity one's dedication to personal purity and to a lifetime of combat against sin. Young reformers thus seized upon all of the features commonly associated with slaveholding—irreligion, economic exploitation, sexual abandon, drinking, duelling, gambling, and the undermining of family ties—and used them, by contrast, to fashion a purer sense of Christian commitment. Suddenly the primal source of the nation's degradation seemed absolutely clear. Slavery was the cause of it all, the original sin from which all others flowed. God's warrant to the true Christian was thus unmistakable—one must demand that the institution be abolished immediately. As newly converted abolitionist Theodore Weld exclaimed, the cause of emancipation "not only overshadows all others, . . . but *absorbs* them into itself. . . . Revivals, moral Reform, etc., etc., must and will remain nearly stationary until the Temple is cleansed" (Barnes and Dumond: 1:244).

As young reformers began sensing these predispositions, the ominous course of public events seemed to confirm that slavery was to blame for the nation's wretched state. Like so many other Americans abolitionists expressed genuine alarm over the notes of black violence and southern militancy upon which the decade of the 1830s opened. The Nat Turner and Jamaica slave insurrections of 1831 appeared to these receptive souls as harbingers of God's avenging justice. Worse still, these bloody occurrences seemed the logical consequences of a pamphlet first published in 1829 in Boston by an ex-slave, David Walker, which was already causing shudders of fear as it circulated throughout the white South. In no uncertain terms Walker called as a last resort for armed rebellion: "I do declare," he wrote, "that one good black man can put to death six white men" (Walker: 25).

Accompanying these radical explosions came intemperate statements from whites in South Carolina, threatening armed secession from the union during the Nullification Crisis of 1829–32. Dismayed by federal tariff policies and distraught lest outsiders begin subverting their peculiar institution, John C. Calhoun and others defied national authority, proclaimed states rights, and risked occupation by federal troops. Abolitionists pondered these events and with wrenching suddenness concluded that divine judgment upon a guilty land was imminent; without a speedy abolition of slavery, anarchy, and bloodlust, civil and servile insurrection would surely engulf all. In 1831 Garrison prophesied final judgment: "What we have long predicted . . . has commenced its fulfillment. The first step of the earthquake which is ultimately to shake down the fabric of oppression, leaving not one stone upon the other, has been made" (*Liberator*, Sept. 10, 1831). One by one, young activists cast aside the last of their self-doubts and prayerfully dedicated their lives to the immediate overthrow of slavery. One such person, John Greenleaf Whittier, captured the spirit of commitment well: "By our duty as Christians, by our duty to ourselves, our neighbors and our God," abolitionists must now "give slavery no resting place . . . , tear it root and branch from the soil of this domain" (Whittier: 5).

The Crusade for Immediate Emancipation

The abolitionists' sudden demand for immediate emancipation may be partially understood as a tactical device. After all, previous generations had paid lip service to gradualism with but little practical result. Yet as Whittier's remarks suggest the most important meaning of immediatism was a personal religious one. By embracing the doctrine the young reformer experienced a spiritual transformation closely akin to a conversion experience. Suddenly pangs of self-doubt vanished before the spirit of sanctification. Reborn in holiness, abolitionists affirmed their fitness to take God's side in a righteous war to reassert biblical authority and to redeem a fallen nation (Loveland: 172–88). "By the help of Almighty God," as a group of them promised, they would struggle against slavery, "come what may to our persons, our interests or our reputations." Gladly would they "perish as martyrs in this great, benevolent and holy cause" in order to "overthrow the most exorable system of slavery that has ever been witnessed on earth" (American Anti-Slavery Society: 180). Here was romantic radicalism of the most daring and disruptive sort. Abolitionists now placed their entire faith in the people's ability to cast the sin of slavery from their heart and then to combat the institution ceaselessly throughout the land. No timid regard for tradition, no reflexive loyalty to inherited institutions should be allowed to limit the demands of conscience. These young men and women were capable of challenging the very foundations of established social order. At the same time, embedded in the demand for *"immediate, unconditional, uncompensated emancipation"* was a daring affirmation that black people and white could live with each other in justice and harmony, freed of the burdens of racism and exploitation. Never before and seldom since have groups of Americans taken their nation's traditions of liberty as highmindedly or attempted to apply them as consistently.

As individuals converted to immediatism, they quickly established the framework of a formal movement, following the example of the benevolent associations. By 1833 abolitionists had founded state-wide societies in Massachusetts, New Hampshire, Vermont, New York, Pennsylvania, and Ohio. Late that same year delegates from all over the North convened in New York City to found the American Anti-Slavery Society, whose task was to direct a national campaign against all who condoned or practiced slave owning. Garrison presided, and the familiar bureaucratic shape that the organization adopted was unmistakably that of the benevolent societies. Yet despite its well-defined structure the American Anti-Slavery Society's basic character was clearly that of a spontaneously gathered religious movement. Those who joined sensed their acceptance into a spiritually purified circle, united in a holy quest to witness for Christ in ways that their memberships in recognized denominations had never satisfied. For abolitionists, the movement and the church had suddenly taken on nearly interchangeable meanings. Elizur Wright, Jr., a charter member of the society, captured this religious mood perfectly in 1833 declaring that "the doctrine of the immediate abolition of slavery asks no better authority than is offered by Scripture. It is in perfect harmony with God's word" (Wright: 65).

The society's *Declaration of Sentiments* also reflected this heightened sense of biblical sanction and holy community. Those who signed this document explicitly rejected as un-Christian "the use of all weapons" either by abolitionists or by slaves. Instead, members of the society promised to rely on the conversion experience, or "moral suasion" as they called it, to convince their fellow Americans to cast out sin by espousing immediate emancipation. Slave holders were to be warned that they faced damnation, convicted by Scripture of "usurping the prerogative of Jehovah." All non-slaveholders were likewise to be exhorted that their sin matched that of the foulest slave driver so long as they upheld black bondage. All Americans must instead be made to realize that slaves had every moral right to instant freedom and equal protection under the law. Even more, these abolitionists also declared it their duty to oppose racism in all its forms, to make others realize that all blacks in America—whether slave or free—must be granted at once "all rights and privileges that belong to them as men and as Americans" (American Anti-Slavery Society: 178–80). In simplest terms, then, these were the two demands that characterized moral suasion—immediate uncompensated emancipation and the complete abolition of all legally sanctioned discrimination.

The measures adopted by the delegates for promoting moral suasion only reinforce the impression that abolitionism constituted a form of nondenominational religious expression. Immediatists agreed to commission agents who would travel from town to town, conducting lectures, starting up newspapers, and founding local antislavery societies. The parent society would also circulate handbills and tracts, hoping especially to convert editors, clergy, and other leading citizens who presumably exercised pronounced influence over public opinion. Abolitionists felt especially eager to purify the churches of their willingness to tolerate slave owning. If members of the clergy all over the nation endorsed immediatism, their parishioners, it was assumed, would flock to the emancipationist banner. As they realized the enormity of their sin, churchgoing masters throughout the South would quickly release their slaves. In the North, meantime, racists and other apathetic citizens would heed their ministers' warnings and repent of their sinful complicity. In this way, the "dam of prejudice" would soon crumble, abolitionists believed, unleashing "one deep, still, mighty current" of conversion and emancipation. "Oh," exclaimed one young convert, "how it will sweep away those refuges of lies!" (Antislavery Collection: Elizur Wright, Jr., to his spouse, Apr. 12, 1833). Such, they fully believed, would surely be the results of moral suasion. Certain that full emancipation was but a few short years away, abolitionists embarked on projects that they fully expected would, as one of them put it, "overthrow prejudice by the power of love" and "abolish slavery by the spirit of repentance" (Antislavery Collection: Arnold Buffum to Garrison, Jan. 9, 1833).

Recalling the enormous loss of life that the Civil War finally exacted as the price of emancipation, such expectations must appear stupefyingly naive. Yet without these glowing hopes and sense of scriptural certainty abolitionists could have mustered neither the courage nor the incentive to challenge so formidable a problem as slavery in the first place. Besides, it seemed to them obvious that God's holy word spoke with such unequivocal authority against slave owning that no sincere Christian, whether minister or lay person, could fail to be persuaded. In this manner the conviction that "slavery is prohibited by the Book of Inspiration" became central to the religious tenets upon which the movement acted (Rankin: 73). Certain that they possessed a purer understanding of Scripture, abolitionists announced confidently that "religious professors of all denominations must bear unqualified testimony against slavery" (*Liberator*, July 30, 1831).

In so asserting, abolitionists displayed little inclination to debate fine points of Scripture. Wide-ranging moral agitation that evoked the spirit of the Bible, not formal academic disputation, characterized their use of Scripture. Garrison, as usual, captured the essence of this outlook: "Slavery," he wrote, "at a single blow annihilates THE WHOLE DECALOGUE" and "effectively excludes from the benefits of the Sabbath two and a half million of our countrymen" (*Liberator*, July 26, 1836). Simply put, abolitionists claimed that everything about slave owning stood in defiance of biblical injunction, and they eagerly elaborated these charges on rostrums, from pulpits, in newspapers, and in dozens of published testimonies. The litany was as extensive as it was obvious. Because slaveholders took every measure to perpetuate religious ignorance among their slaves, nearly three million souls remained untouched by God's word and mired in lives of debauchery. Because they sold husbands apart from wives, separated children from their parents, took sexual liberties with helpless black women, and forced slaves to breed with the hope of selling their offspring, slaveholders made perverse mockery of the Golden Rule. In the process they also violated every biblical injunction against covetousness, greed, and licentiousness. By waxing fat upon labor coerced with whips and chains, the slaveholders flouted commandments that prohibited theft. And finally it was charged that because they possessed total power over their slaves, slaveholders could (and all too often did) resort to murder to satisfy their passions.

In support of these claims abolitionists ransacked Scripture for appropriate analogies. They drew parallels between slaves in the South and the Israelites in Egypt, between the fate of the Sodomites and the judgments that awaited a nation of slaveowners, between Adam's original defiance of the Almighty and the planter's disdain for God's injunctions. Worst of all, Scripture demanded "thou shalt not have any gods before me," yet the slaveholders were clearly trying to play God, shaping the lives of other humans even as they defied biblical precept at every turn. This belief more than any other confirmed abolitionists in their insistence that Scripture and slave owning were wholly at war with one another and that all Christians must embrace immediatism. As Theodore Weld put it so clearly to Garrison, slaveholding actually reversed the biblically sanctioned order of creation, placing in human hands powers that only God should exercise.

> No condition of birth, no shade of color, no mere misfortune of circumstances, can annul that birth-right charter, which God has bequeathed to every being . . . by making him *a free* moral agent. . . . He who robs his fellow man of this tramples upon right, subverts justice, outrages humanity, unsettles the foundations of human safety, and sacrilegiously assumes the prerogative of God. (Barnes and Dumond: 1:98)

What Lucifer had failed to achieve slaveowners were also now attempting—total rebellion against God's supremacy. Little wonder, given such beliefs, that abolitionists expected Bible-professing Americans to enroll *en masse* in their crusade. Predictably, however, the future was to hold no such easy victory. Instead, abolitionists quickly discovered that they faced widespread, often violent opposition from all strata of the white social order.

Repression and the Failure of Immediatism

Recalling the behavior of the South Carolinians, general southern hostility to abolitionism hardly seems surprising. Historians have long recognized that aggressive justifications of slave owning were commonplace throughout the South even before the advent of radical abolitionism, so pervasive was slavery's impact upon the region's economy, customs, and social structures. In the North also, racial prejudice diminished class consciousness even as the disruption of economic growth increasingly separated rich from poor. Meanwhile, all the major institutions that united North and South were likewise dependent for their stability on the participation of powerful slaveholders. Candidates for national office faced sure defeat without the support of Southern politicians. Planters also ranked high in the councils of the Presbyterian, Methodist, Baptist, and Episcopal denominations. Much of New England's economic well-being was heavily dependent on southern cotton and southern markets (Brown: 7–24; Mathews: 3–110; Frederickson). Little wonder that influential politicians, ministers, editors, and business people joined with countless common folk in both sections to silence this jarring demand for immediate emancipation.

"Harsh words . . . stale eggs and brickbats and tar . . . indignities too gross to be printed. . . . A mob . . . broke the windows, doors, tore off the gate and attacked me." Reports such as these, filed by agents in the field, arrived regularly at the home offices of the American Anti-Slavery Society during the mid-1830s (for example, Barnes and Dumond: 1:256–62). Abolitionist organizers commonly encountered this sort of resistance in the small villages and hamlets of Ohio, Pennsylvania, Illinois, and Indiana. In large northern cities, meanwhile, abolitionist meetings became occasions for full-blown rioting. Leading citizens commonly united with the lower classes in declaring abolitionists subverters of the white social order and plotters against individual liberty. New York in 1833 witnessed a mob of fifteen hundred which dispersed an abolitionist gathering, hoping to lay hands on Garrison. The next year lower class whites ran amok in that city's black neighborhoods protesting what they perceived as abolitionist plans for amalgamating the races. Meanwhile, in Boston, Cincinnati, and Utica, lawyers, politicians, merchants, and even clergy members led mobs that broke up meetings, wrecked printing presses, and drove abolitionists into hiding. And in 1837 in the small southern Illinois river town of Alton the predictable finally happened. Here Elijah Lovejoy, an uncompromising abolitionist editor, refused to be silent even after mobs had repeatedly thrown his presses into the river. Prominent clerics, office holders, and private citizens then announced that they were no longer willing to protect him from harm. On May 7, 1837, the mob gathered once again and set Lovejoy's office afire. As Lovejoy emerged, gun in hand, he was suddenly cut down by several bullets. Abolitionism had enrolled its first martyr (Richards: 3–156).

Certainly the demand for immediate emancipation was in itself sufficiently radical to provoke this wave of illegal resistance; yet one specific abolitionist project stimulated most of this intransigence. Initiated in 1835, this enterprise became known as "the great postal campaign." A device of moral suasion modeled clearly on evangelical precedents, the campaign was designed, as Lewis Tappan explained, "to sow the good seed of abolition over the whole country" by flooding the mails with abolitionist literature. Budgeted at over thirty thousand dollars, this daring project attempted to convert hundreds of thousands of citizens by mailing them abolition tracts (Wyatt-Brown, 1969:143–45). Soon influential citizens throughout both sections began to find in their mailboxes such items as *The Slave's Friend, The Sin of Slavery and its Remedy,* and the most offensive title of all, *The Despotism of Freedom, or The Tyranny and Cruelty of American Republican Slave-Masters, Shown to be the Worst in the World.*

Once the mailings were completed abolitionists awaited a groundswell of emancipation. Instead the postal campaign became a principal stimulus to the northern mobs and sent waves of hysteria throughout the slave states. By June 1835 over one million pieces of abolitionist literature had been dispatched; by July angry southerners had broken into post offices, seized mailbags, and made bonfires out of the incendiary tracts. Clerics and members of Congress thundered against depraved Yankee conspirators, while leading planters formed vigilance societies to search incoming deliveries. In Washington representatives began demanding that abolitionism be suppressed; President Andrew Jackson made speeches that encouraged these suggestions. He also made it clear that federal authorities would not prevent citizens from rifling the mails (Wyatt-Brown, 1969:149–51).

As the waves of anger mounted, it became clear that the abolitionists' program was collapsing. Grave doubts had been cast on their hopes that slaveholders could be converted peaceably and that northern indifference could be overcome with the message of the Bible. The time of reconciliation between the races now seemed farther off than ever. Moral suasion was being emphatically repulsed; scriptural warrant was proving no guarantee of worldly success. But, as their hopes of imminent Christian victory began to falter, abolitionists also began to realize that their crusade was making a different sort of progress from what they had originally foreseen.

As it turned out, intransigence in the South and riots in the North were provoking new kinds of antislavery feelings among many previously unconcerned Yankees. The plain fact was that every attempt to silence the abolitionists only drew attention to the movement and publicized its principles.

As an excited colleague exclaimed to Garrison at the height of the violence, "Our opposers are doing everything they can to help us," for the subject of slavery was being debated everywhere (Antislavery Collection: Samuel J. May to Garrison, Sept. 2, 1835). Yet the emphasis of these discussions was significantly different from that of the debates that had taken place at early meetings of the American Anti-Slavery Society. Sectional opinions now expressed by previously silent portions of the northern population were clearly not prompted by the same religious inspiration that had inspired the immediatists to demand black freedom in the first place. Instead, the self-reinforcing interplay of agitation and repression was suddenly raising disturbing new questions about the safety of white civil liberties. The shift was apparent to major abolitionists like James G. Birney, who observed in 1835: "The contest is becoming . . . one, not alone of freedom for the *black*, but freedom for the *white*. It has now become absolutely necessary, that slavery should cease in order that freedom may be preserved to any portion of our land" (Dumond: 243).

A markedly secular legalistic concern over white civil rights, not the Bible-inspired power of moral suasion, was suddenly proving the more effective force in mobilizing northerners against slavery. Like the repression itself, here was another unforeseen development for which abolitionists had to account. How were they to reconcile their hopes for an immediatist triumph with the nation's violent rejection of moral suasion? How, too, might they square their biblical commitments to the conversion experience and to black emancipation with the fact that, as one abolitionist described it, "many . . . have their 'dander up' (as some express it) about their own rights. . . , but few really sympathize with the slave" (Barnes and Dumond: 2:735)?

The famous petition campaign launched by the abolitionists in 1836 highlighted all of these questions and made them even more pressing. As the tide of repression mounted, the American Anti-Slavery Society began encouraging local and state organizations to petition Congress for legislative action against slavery. Though this tactic had been used before, immediatists now employed it on an unparalleled scale. By 1837 a national campaign to flood Washington with antislavery remonstrances was in full swing. Most significant was the lack of religious focus in the petitions. Here was a clear indication that at least some abolitionists were starting to deemphasize the biblical absolutes of moral suasion in order to stimulate the more mundane forms of antislavery expression. The petitions demanded, for example, not immediate emancipation but requested that Congress take measures to end slavery in the District of Columbia, to repeal the Three-Fifths Compromise, and to prevent the admission of new slave states to the Union. Here were issues that all northerners who had their "dander up" about the South—not just dedicated immediatists—were willing to protest. In contrast to the postal campaign, moreover, the thrust of this campaign was entirely northward. It put no emphasis at all upon conversion of the slaveowners. Instead, as Elizur Wright, Jr., explained, the campaign aimed to raise issues upon which "all classes, abolitionists, colonizationists, Mongrels and Nothingarians can agree" (Barnes: 126).

In unmistakable ways the petition strategy suggested that some abolitionists were abandoning their hope for a religious conversion on behalf of peaceful emancipation. As the American Anti-Slavery Society central office instructed, petitions should "not be confined to abolitionists. All who hate slavery . . . should put their names to them without regard to their views on abolition" (Barnes: 137).

Considering the statistics, the success of this new approach was impressive. In May 1838 the American Anti-Slavery Society reported that over 415,000 remonstrances had been forwarded to various members of Congress in that year alone. The "petition flood," as it came to be known, testified to abolitionists' success in coalescing a broad antisouthern spirit throughout the North. The fact that a majority of congressional representatives from both sections regarded debate on the petitions as dangerous and divisive added powerful momentum to the petition effort. Thus, in 1836 the House of Representatives voted that antislavery memorials could not be debated and should be automatically tabled without a hearing. In force until late 1844 this "infamous gag rule," as its opponents termed it, only reconfirmed for many abolitionists their deeper suspicions about southern designs on white civil liberties. As dissenting representatives such as John Quincy Adams rose time and again to protest the gag rule, northern voters began to register their own disaffection at the polls. By the late 1830s representatives who opposed these southern abridgements of civil liberties were becoming ever more numerous. Gladly did they introduce the abolitionists' petitions as they hurled their own defiance at the gag rule and decried the prospect of admitting new slave states such as Texas into the Union (Barnes: 121-45; Gara: 5–18; Stewart, 1976:74–96).

Politicians, Political Action and Perfectionism

By the later 1830s abolitionists who contemplated these developments could only conclude that things had hardly turned out as first expected. Their initial efforts had led not to sectional and racial reconciliation. Instead, the results were increasing political friction between North and South. As the 1830s closed, members of the American Anti-Slavery Society clearly faced a fundamental reassessment of goals, tactics, and attitudes. Adding further to the complexity was the sudden demand by female abolitionists that they be accorded an equal status in the crusade. Driven by all of these pressures, abolitionists everywhere began to rethink the relationship between religion and reform. Soon bitter factional divisions began to surface within the American Anti-Slavery Society.

   William Lloyd Garrison, more than any other figure, prompted open
disagreement by suddenly espousing anticlerical, antigovernmental versions
of abolitionism. By 1837 he had clearly begun associating immediatism with
many other kinds of radicalism and opposition to all agencies of church and
state. Essays began appearing in his *Liberator* which denied the authority of
ministers, questioned the literal truth of Scripture, condemned denomina-
tionally organized religion, and even attacked the sanctity of the Sabbath,
"that pernicious and superstitious notion," as he termed it. His paper vigorously endorsed equality for women as part of a sweeping demand that
would overturn all corrupt churches and governmental agencies (Thomas,
1963:227-35).

   These unorthodox ideas attracted scores of people—dedicated feminist-
abolitionists like Angelina and Sarah Grimké, Abby Kelley, Lucretia Mott,
Elizabeth Cady Stanton, and Lydia Maria Child—who immediately took
Garrison's side. Here were women who during abolitionism's early years had
successfully tested their capacity for leadership, oratorical eloquence, and
editorial skill. Confident of their abilities and no longer willing to play sec-
ondary roles, they were making broad analogies between the subservient lot
of women and the oppressed condition of slaves. The most extreme male
practitioners of moral suasion (people such as Henry C. Wright, Charles C.
Burleigh, Steven S. Foster, and Wendell Philips) also allied with Garrison.
Some, like Wright and Philips, though unremarkable in bearing, were nonetheless drawn by temperament toward the most radical versions of reform.
Other adherents like the crude New Hampshireman Foster or the flamboyant Burleigh, combined bizarre behavior and appearance with unembar-
rassed doctrinal extremism.

   While the reasons for this outburst of radicalism are not well understood,
one fact remains clear. As Garrison and his supporters recalled the original
assumptions of moral suasion and as they contemplated the meaning of the
riots and repression, they drew some deeply disturbing conclusions about
American religious practices and political values. To these radicals the gag
rule, mail lootings, mobs, and clerical denunciation confirmed one thing
above all else—the nation had revealed itself as much more deeply mired in
infamy than anyone could have first imagined. Unlike many abolitionists who
were soon to oppose them, Garrison and his followers put little value upon
repression as a catalyst for generating antisouthern feelings among ordinary
northerners. Instead, these abolitionists concluded that the country deserved
"an avalanche of wrath, hurled from the throne of God, to crush us into
annihilation." Churches were condemned as "mean and corrupt," their
pastors as "blinded and foolish," their doctrines as "pernicious, jesuitical
malevolent." The two political parties of course were fully as apostate (*Liberator*, Jan. 9, 1838; July 6, 1840). Appeals to conscience thus had to be greatly
broadened to induce a complete reshaping of every religious value.
Consequently, all submission to the power of organized government, political

parties, ministers, denominations, received biblical dogma, and patriarchal husbands suddenly appeared no less sinful in God's sight than the master-slave relationship itself. "A slavish devotion to Scripture," as Garrison proclaimed in 1837, "is morally no less abominable than the whip or man-acle." The single object of reform, he continued, should now be the *"universal emancipation"* of all humanity from all forms of sinful coercion (Stewart, 1971:293–309; *Liberator,* July 28, 1837). Clearly, Garrison was redefining emancipation to encompass not only freeing the several million black slaves but also the millennial liberation of all humanity from evil through proclaim-ing God's perfect kingdom on earth.

The breadth of this radical vision was nearly limitless. Its goal, the peaceful perfection of the human race—a world-wide "moral revolution" as Garrison termed it—set him and his redeemed followers outside all agencies of church and state, for such "are all AntiChrist." These institutions, he ex-plained, "can never, by human wisdom, be brought into conformity with the will of God" (*Liberator,* Mar. 6, 1837). Instead, true Christians must heed the angel's injunction from Revelation 18:4 concerning Babylon's fall: "Come out of her, my people, that ye be not partakers of her sins, that ye receive not of her plagues." To separate oneself from all coercive institutions and relationships was thus to master spiritual perfection, to transfer one's al-legiance from the corrupt human government to the "divine ordination of God." This was the state of mind that Garrison attempted to convey when in 1838 he placed a new motto on the masthead of the *Liberator*: "No Union With Slaveholders." By 1838 a substantial portion of the American Anti-Slavery Society had begun to embrace some of these new doctrines. Others, feeling increasingly surrounded by dreamers and anarchists, began to recon-sider the relationship between religious imperatives and abolitionism.

Those most likely to despair at Garrison's course have since been desig-nated "clerical" or "conservative" abolitionists, and among them were the most active organizers of the petition and postal compaigns—Arthur and Lewis Tappan, John Greenleaf Whittier, William Jay, Elizur Wright, Jr., and Joshua Leavitt. Perhaps because these individuals had been involved so deeply in critical projects, they took profound exception to the Garrisonians' sweeping condemnation of American institutions and religious values. They pointed instead to the thousands of ordinary citizens, suddenly angered by slaveholding assaults on northern freedoms, who were signing petitions, protesting the gag rule, decrying the mobs, and insisting that no new slave states be added to the Union. Here, conservatives argued, was sure evidence that, as Joshua Leavitt put it, "Providence directs our course and urges the car of emancipation onward" (Antislavery Collection: Leavitt to David Lee Child, Oct. 6, 1838). They believed, in short, that abolition was indeed pro-gressing in a seriously flawed but nonetheless healthy Christian society. Ex-isting churches and governments were all proving susceptible to the reform-ers' influence. It would be a tactical disaster, they feared, as well as an errant abdication of Christian duty to confuse the slave's cause in the public mind with women's rights, anticlericalism, perfectionism, and other causes that aimed at "undermining the whole fabric of social relations," as Elizur Wright, Jr., once charged (*Liberator*, May 5, 1838; Kraditor: 41–117; Antislavery Collection: Wright to Amos Phelps, Jan. 22, 1839). Once convinced, conservatives began planning how best to purge Garrison and his radical followers.

Slowly the chasm between hopeful Christian reformers and alienated radicals grew unbridgeably wide. To conservatives like Elizur Wright, Jr., Christian duty now meant arousing a mass of sectionally conscious voters, whether religious or not, to protect the nation's "blessed liberties." But to Garrison and his cohorts, millennialism, perfectionism, and "No Union With Slaveholders" constituted the only godly response to a society whose every majority value and reigning institution reflected the antichrist. By late 1840 three years of volcanic debate and factional intrigue had left the American Anti-Slavery Society in shambles. Radicals, including nearly all the female leaders, finally retained control but only after conservatives had seceded to form their own American and Foreign Antislavery Society. Such veterans of moral suasion as James G. Birney, the Tappan brothers, Elizur Wright, Jr., John Greenleaf Whittier, and the upstate New York millionaire Gerrit Smith took charge of this new organization. The days of abolitionist unity had passed forever.

Departures from Biblical Radicalism

For the next two decades, as they traded endless charges both groups explored the religious implications and tactical necessities of their various new positions. Civil war, meanwhile, drew ever closer. Most conservatives soon concluded that the logic of experience and Christian duty led from the petition campaign to a direct involvement in national politics. Every year, they reasoned, greater numbers of northerners expressed their deep misgivings about the ominous implications of slaveholding for the future of the nation's republican institutions. This trend became ever more unmistakable as sectional debates quickened following Texas's annexation and the subsequent war with Mexico (1846–1848). In response, many conservative abolitionists decided that northern voters had to be given a truly Christian alternative to the two major parties. According to these political abolitionists, both the Whigs and the Democrats remained irredeemably tainted by the many slaveholding leaders and proslavery supporters within their organizations. "Bible politics" became the term these abolitionists adopted to describe a style of activism that would fuse immediatism with the process of campaigning and voting (Kraditor: 118–77). The Liberty party, as the new enterprise became known, first nominated James G. Birney to run for president against the Whig William Henry Harrison and the Democrat Martin Van Buren in the election of 1840.

Although Liberty party members such as Birney, Joshua Leavitt, Gerrit Smith, and Elizur Wright, Jr., were hardly conscious of it, their decision to enter politics constituted public recognition of how far they had traveled since the scripturally inspired days of moral suasion. True, they insisted repeatedly that it was "immeasurably wicked" to vote "for any other purpose than to furnish a true medium thro' which the throne of the Messiah may be reflected" (Dumond: 1143; Sewell: 43–170). They sincerely proclaimed themselves the Christian party, which allowed voters to withdraw from the corrupting taint of the Whigs and Democrats. Yet efforts to court sectionally aware voters inevitably meant deemphasizing the sin of slavery in order to accommodate that same legalistic concern with white liberties which they had originally been so anxious to stimulate as petition organizers back in 1837–38. Moreover, even though their totals each election day always remained small, Liberty party voters did sometimes obtain a critical balance of power between the two major parties. In such situations third party leaders inevitably found themselves drawn into the log rolling of workaday politics that was no less characteristic of that age than of the present. In such circumstances it often proved impossible not to sacrifice "first principles" for "the loaves and fishes of office," as people of that day described the process.

As the 1840s wore on, moreover, unmistakable signs of confusion increasingly characterized Liberty party affairs. By the election of 1848 most of its leaders had coalesced with the Free Soil party—a collection of dissident northern politicians from the two major parties—who now adamantly opposed slavery's westward expansion. Among many Free Soilers the racist desire to preserve western lands for whites only constituted the paramount consideration; the continued enslavement of three million black southerners scarcely troubled most Free Soilers. As hostile Garrisonians constantly pointed out, these doctrines were certainly a significant retreat from genuine abolitionism; in such an ideology the twin goals of slave emancipation and black equality could have little if any formal place (Foner: 1–72, 261–317; Stewart, 1976:119–23, 175–77). By the mid-1850s the conservative abolitionists' venture into Bible politics could thus be judged as ending in a sad mixture of political failure and spiritual collapse, a dismal declension from the righteous days of the 1830s. Candidate James Birney certainly felt this way. In despair he formally renounced politics, took up hermit's quarters in the Michigan wilderness, and during the 1850s counseled all blacks to flee the nation.

However, when judged by the criteria of black activists, the history of political abolition appears more productive. In the early 1840s as the American Anti-Slavery Society broke apart, black abolitionists began to appear as vital independent forces in the crusade against slavery. Some, like Frederick Douglass and William Wells Brown, had recently escaped from slavery; others, like Henry Highland Garnet, Martin Delany, and Jermain Lougen, came from well-educated northern backgrounds. Politically sophisticated and determined to resist slavery in every effective way, these leaders disagreed with one another on such vital points as separation versus integration, nonviolence versus resistance, and African emigration versus full American citizenship. Few of these voices sustained a permanent interest in millennial Garrisonian radicalism, becoming instead vocal supporters of white political abolitionism.

The reasons for this striking preference are several, but one fact deserves special emphasis. Precisely because of their tendency toward doctrinal moderation and secularism, the Bible politicians offered black abolitionists an increasing immediate means for combatting slavery and opposing northern discrimination. As Liberty party members bartered ideological purity for increased voter support, they—unlike the Garrisonian perfectionists—began to make day-to-day contact with influential elements in northern political culture. As practical-minded blacks quickly realized, here for all of their racism and conservatism were the only sources of power capable of actually destroying slavery and bringing some measure of bi-racial idealism into American politics. For this reason a black spokesman like editor Samuel E. Cornish rejected as irrelevant the Garrisonian programs as *"neither parts nor parcels"* of the struggle for black freedom. Instead Cornish endorsed both the Liberty party and the Free Soilers, urging blacks to make their influence in these parties count for as much as possible (Pease: 173–205).

At the same time, black activists also supported political abolitionism because third party issues often became directly involved with northern racial questions. In New York during 1846, for example, Gerrit Smith, Lewis Tappan, and other third party abolitionists headed a drive to repeal state laws that restricted black suffrage. Though unsuccessful, this effort forced major-party politicians to confront discrimination within their own states and prompted a temporary alliance against restriction between Whigs and members of the Liberty party. In Ohio a similar coalition between Free Soil party leaders (many formerly of the Liberty party) and Democrats resulted in the repeal of that state's noxious "black laws" in 1849.

The very process of secularization and doctrinal adjustment which obscured the Liberty party's original radicalism thus enhanced the political process in the eyes of militant blacks. Late in 1860, on the eve of the Civil War, it had become nearly impossible to make worthwhile distinctions between old-time third party abolitionists and a host of ambitious Republican party newcomers. To this extent, Bible politics had long ago expired as a distinctive abolitionist force. But in dying, third party abolitionism had generated forces that gave black radicals like Frederick Douglass reason to hope. In the aftermath of the Civil War, Republican-sponsored constitutional amendments—not the perfectionist predictions of the millennium—were finally to guarantee the slaves their emancipation. In this way conservative abolitionist forays into electoral politics finally helped to make the nation's government and its egalitarian ideals more closely identifiable with one another.

Throughout the 1840s and 1850s, as Douglass, Leavitt, Birney, and other conservative abolitionists pursued gradual reform, Garrison, Steven S. Foster, Henry C. Wright, and the rest of the religious radicals reaffirmed their steadfast obedience to perfectionism's "divine principles." They spurned denominational affiliation, refused to vote, and would neither hold office nor swear allegiance to America's "impious" form of government. From the early 1840s on their slogan, "No Union With Slaveholders," bespoke an increasingly sophisticated political style and a thorough-going desire to divorce radicalism from traditional Protestantism. While Liberty party leaders secularized abolitionism in the public sphere by seeking to make gains in politics, Garrisonian radicals were also separating Scripture from reform in a wholly different fashion by appealing to "higher self-evident" doctrines of perfectionism. Henry C. Wright once expressed the process in the simplest terms, exclaiming that the Bible had always proven his sternest foe in his campaign to obliterate slavery, warfare, and other forms of self-evident sin. Hence, he concluded, "The Bible if Opposed to Self-Evident Truth, Is Self-Evident Falsehood," and what applied to Scripture was also true for the constitution (*Liberator*, May 11, 1848). That document's support of slavery made it, according to Garrisonians, "A Covenant with Death, An Agreement with Hell," to which no true Christian would ever give assent.

As a religious system, perfectionism was subject to endless vagaries of doctrine and became a source of extended speculative disagreements among its adherents. But as a refreshingly iconoclastic rejection of secular history and religious tradition, it is an effective variation on the original form of moral suasion. Perched on lofty steeples of perfectionism, Garrisonians surveyed America's moral landscape from a perspective that was both sweeping and acute. In contrast to abolitionists within the Liberty party, they were stationed perfectly to leap upon every instance of proslavery behavior and to exercise unlimited freedom to berate, condemn, and expose. In keeping with perfectionist dogma, their aim during the 1840s and 1850s was to transform the values of northern voters, hoping thereby to force elected leaders into increasingly radical positions on slavery.

To this end, Garrison, Wendell Phillips, and many of their associates incessantly preached the need for "No Union With Slaveholders" to the constituencies of antisouthern politicians. At the same time they mercilessly criticized the politicians themselves, deplored their weaknesses, and jeered at their compromises. Phillips, for example, took special delight in rehearsing the pro-southern aspects of Abraham Lincoln's career, calling him repeatedly "the slavehound from Illinois." Meanwhile, during the later 1850s Phillips joined other prominent Garrisonians on western speaking tours aiming to rouse the voters by preaching antigovernment radicalism. Phillips's close friend, Edmund Quincy, once explained the tactic well, asserting that the Garrisonian approach to voters was to "make their conscience uncomfortable." "In nine out of ten cases," he averred, people thus affected would allay their guilt by demanding more radical actions against slavery from their elected representatives (*Liberator*, July 11, 1848; Stewart, 1969:197–209). In this way, Garrisonians remained wholly unfettered by compromise and explored to the fullest every chance to stimulate radicalism within the body politic. Even as racism became increasingly compatible with opposition to slavery's westward expansion, perfectionist Garrisonians played crucial roles thrusting before voters the undiminished ideals of black freedom.

The cry of "No Union With Slaveholders" also served other effective political purposes. As already mentioned, southern extremists were hardly reluctant before 1860 to threaten secession in order to protect slavery. Legalistic northern responses that simply affirmed the Union's perpetuity had the effect of leaving disunionist slaveholders with a considerable polemical advantage in political debates. Because of their rejection of human government, however, Garrisonians found themselves well positioned to correct this imbalance by reminding northern politicians and voters that querulous Unionism was no substitute for demanding the abolition of slavery. Garrison once again conveyed the radical position clearly, insisting that "it matters not what is the theory of government, if the practice of government be unjust and tyrannical." The slave-ridden American union, he charged, fostered "a despotism incomparably more dreadful" than that which had driven American patriots into rebellion. Since this constitutional oppression "which grinds [the slaves] into dust rests upon us," abolitionists must "struggle to overthrow it" (*Liberator*, May 31, 1844). By endlessly repeating such assertions, Garrisonians were able to demonstrate the necessity of appealing from the dry writ of lawyers to the truths of God's higher law. Here, then, was serious political activity on behalf of the slave which no vote-conscious political abolitionist could ever emulate. Yet as the sectional crisis ran its course, powerful Republican politicians like New York's William Seward, Massachusetts' Charles Sumner, and the more conservative Lincoln availed themselves of Garrisonian language, appealing to "higher law" and "self-evident truth" while warning of "irrepressible conflict" within "a house divided." Through perfectionist agitation Garrisonians thus contributed to the language of northern war politics words and concepts that enriched and sharpened the meaning of freedom.

Conclusion

Diverse and conflicting in approach and result, such were the major influences that moderate political abolitionists and radical Garrisonians brought to bear upon the sectional conflict after 1840. One clear tendency, however, characterized all of these efforts—an emphatic shift away from Scripture as the primary authority for abolitionists. Garrisonians and political abolitionists alike would have hotly denied that they had abandoned their individual devotion to the true spirit of Christianity. But by the early 1840s many of them, conservative third party members no less than radical Garrisonians, had joined the trend away from biblicism in American radical thought. Thus, while exploring new strategies in the years after 1840, abolitionists of all tactical persuasions carried on the spiritual pilgrimages, the first steps of which had brought them to immediatism.

Abolitionists might seem to have been moving in two paradoxical, if not contrary, directions. The first impulse was toward a utopian Christianity of the kind expressed by Garrison, which embraced anticlerical perfectionism in the name of true religion. Garrisonians deliberately fused such beliefs with new forms of radical agitation, but other abolitionists whose tactics remained much more moderate were no less receptive to this new kind of heterodoxy. Even as he entered presidential politics in 1840, Birney began to doubt the Bible's divine authorship and the reality of eternal punishment. Soon he had renounced his Presbyterian affiliation and was dabbling in Unitarianism. By 1850 he had decided, as a humanitarian Christian, that no organized religion could disappoint him, for he expected "so little—hardly anything, indeed, from it." Other prominent foes of Garrisonian radicalism such as Amos A. Phelps, Theodore Weld, and Gerrit Smith wandered down similar paths, hoping—as one put it—to become "less orthodox but more Christian" by rejecting any creed that thwarted pure humanitarianism (Walters: 47; Julian: 259).

Thus, some abolitionists were suggesting that spirituality could be measured wholly by the good measures that a person espoused. But such conclusions also pushed others toward skepticism and atheism, the second of those two significant new directions in the reformer's spiritual quest. Indeed such an outlook often proved capable of replacing all religious inspiration—old orthodoxy and new-style perfectionism alike—with a reliance on unaided human rationality. In such schemes God's sovereignty or the inspiration of the Holy Spirit retained little if any authority. Henry C. Wright and Elizur Wright, Jr., provide a striking example of this trend. The former was a most radical Garrisonian and the latter espoused moderate political abolitionism. They despised each other and for decades demeaned one another's views. Both, however, became freethinkers; toward the end of his life Elizur Wright announced his conversion to atheism. Henry C. Wright, for his part, declared the Bible "a lie and a curse to mankind" whenever it seemed to contradict rational human instincts for liberty. "Man is an appendage to nothing," he asserted in 1850, "not even to his creator" (Walters: 38–53).

Most abolitionists, however, were simply too inured in the culture of Protestantism to scrap piety itself for skeptical irreligion as the two Wrights

were doing. Most chose instead to embrace rational Christian humanitarianism while abandoning altogether their regard for organized religion.
Throughout the 1840s and the 1850s the frequency of coming out—that is,
of separating from tainted, coercive religious affiliations—became an excel-
lent measure of the drift toward heterodoxy and secularism within abolitionism. Extreme Garrisonians like Steven S. Foster witnessed for this doctrine in
ways so flamboyant that nearly all other abolitionists took exception. His
technique was to sit unnoticed in a New England congregation and then, in
the midst of the service, to interrupt with a spontaneous lecture that excori-
ated the clerical establishment as "thieves, blind guides and reprobates, a
cage of unclean birds." Outraged parishioners usually escorted him bodily
down the aisle and out of the door. Abolitionists like Lewis Tappan, Beriah
Green, and Birney chose quieter courses, renouncing their denominational
affiliations to form free churches which usually placed abolitionism,
temperance, and other humanitarian endeavors ahead of devotion to
Scripture. Gerrit Smith, exercising religious privileges open only to the
wealthy, simply purchased a building near his residence, declared it his
church and dedicated it to the "true religion of reform." For Smith as for so
many others the conscience of the reformer granted to itself the right to
judge all religion by self-evident standards. By such criteria institutional
Protestantism and the tenets of biblical orthodoxy had been deemed sadly
wanting. The gulf separating organized religion from organized reform
widened accordingly, and Baptists, Presbyterians, and Congregationalists
throughout the North experienced serious defections. Among Methodists
formal division and the secession of pro- and antislavery factions took place
in 1845 after several years of acrimonious debate (Walters: 38–53; Thomas:
316–37; Mathews: 148–282).

By 1861, as southern secession began in earnest and Lincoln called for
volunteers, the process of secularization was nearly complete; from then on,
piecemeal approaches to reform—not soul-inspired calls for moral revolution—were increasingly to characterize abolitionists' words and deeds. Early
in 1865 one long-standing Garrisonian explained the new mood particularly
well, declaring that "iconoclasm has had its day," that the "old antislavery
routine" of agitating moral absolutes was now passé. "For the battering ram
we must substitute the hoe and trowel," he advised, "for we have passed
through the *pulling down* stage of our movement" (J. Miller McKim to
Oliver Johnson, *National Anti-Slavery Standard*, May 3, 1862). Such
feelings, as it turned out, made some abolitionists particularly anxious to
work directly with the newly emancipated slaves. For most, however, this
attitude of secular practicality fostered new more mundane interests such as
women's suffrage, civil service reform, labor agitation, and improving the
morals of the immigrant classes. Abolitionists, in short, left behind no
enduring tradition that clearly linked Protestant evangelicalism and
Scripture to the ideal of racial justice. By the early 1960s, as the black drive

for civil rights began to take form, Dr. Martin Luther King was to face once again the task of educating an entire generation of whites to the gospel of black freedom (Stewart, 1976:178–203).

While abolitionists did not establish a legacy of Protestant radicalism that speaks directly to our age, they also proved unable in their own time to secure equality for the emancipated slave. Their failure, however, was not for lack of effort. During and after the Civil War many of them sponsored education for freed slaves, encouraged southern black political involvement, and helped to organize free labor experiments on lands abandoned by the planters. Others raised funds for black regiments and agitated for constitutional amendments to insure political equality for the former slaves. Yet it was Union soldiers, not immediate abolitionists, who finally intervened between slaveholder and slave. Emancipation came as a result of military necessity, not moral suasion, and throughout both North and South long-established patterns of white supremacy were to endure. Despite the best abolitionist efforts, the former slave was destined not to become an equal citizen but a segregated sharecropper, intimidated and coerced by vengeful whites. By the early 1870s, as abolitionism lost all coherence as a movement, whites in both sections found increasing areas of agreement concerning the subjugated position of the black race.

The fact that the abolitionists forged no enduring reform traditions and were unable to transcend the limits of their culture should hardly be surprising or depressing. Such failures do, however, suggest the importance of the movement for understanding the antebellum era itself. During the early 1830s, as we have seen, abolitionists reformulated Protestant revivalism into a strikingly radical egalitarian critique of long-accepted well-entrenched systems of race subordination. With the failure of moral suasion to achieve rapid immediate emancipation, the various factions began to redefine and secularize the religious assumptions and political tactics that had initially united them. The result during the 1840s and 1850s was an ever more divided movement but one which remained capable of prodding Americans to acknowledge some of the terrible inconsistencies of upholding slavery while living in a democratic society. In these ways, for all their obvious failures and tentative successes, abolitionists thus attempted to expand the boundaries for social justice permissible in their age.

WORKS CONSULTED

American Anti-Slavery Society

1833   "Declaration of Sentiments of the National Anti-
                          Slavery Convention. . . ." *The Abolitionist* 1 (De-
                          cember 1833): 178–80.

Antislavery Collection, Boston Public Library

> A major manuscript collection of abolitionists' private letters, including those of Garrison, Phillips, Elizur Wright, Jr., Amos Phelps, Henry C. Wright, Lysander Spooner, the Chapman, Weston, Child, and Jackson families. Referred to in text by specific letter, names of correspondents, and dates.

Barnes, Gilbert H.

1933   *The Antislavery Impulse*. Washington, DC: American Historical Association.

Barnes, Gilbert H., and Dumond, Dwight L., eds.

1934   *Letters of Theodore Dwight Weld, Angelina Grimké Weld and Sarah Grimké, 1822–1844*. 2 vols. Washington, DC: American Historical Association.

Brown, Richard H.

1966   "The Missouri Crisis, Slavery and the Politics of Jacksonianism." *South Atlantic Quarterly* 55: 7–24.

Calhoun, John C.

1836   *Speech on the Reception of Abolitionist Petitions*. Washington: Blair and Rives.

Davis, David B.

1966   *The Problem of Slavery in Western Culture*. Ithaca, NY: Cornell University Press.

1974   *The Problem of Slavery in the Age of Revolution, 1770–1823*. Ithaca, NY: Cornell University Press.

Dillon, Merton

1974   *The Abolitionists: The Growth of a Dissenting Minority*. DeKalb, IL: Northern Illinois University Press.

Dumond, Dwight L., ed.

1938   *The Letters of James G. Birney, 1831–1857*. 2 vols. Washington, DC: American Historical Association.

Foner, Eric

1970   *Free Soil, Free Labor, Free Men: The Ideology of the Republican Party before the Civil War*. New York: Oxford University Press.

Frederickson, George
 1971   *The Black Image in the White Mind: The Debate on Afro-American Character and Destiny.* New York: Oxford University Press.

Freehling, William H.
 1966   *The Nullification Crisis in South Carolina.* New York: Harper and Row.

Gara, Larry
 1969   "Slavery and the Slave-Power: A Crucial Distinction." *Civil War History* 15: 5–18.

Genovese, Eugene
 1967   *The Political Economy of Slavery.* New York: Random House.

Julian, George Washington
 1892   *The Life of Joshua Giddings.* Chicago: A. C. McClung.

Kraditor, Aileen
 1969   *Means and Ends in American Abolitionism: Garrison and His Critics on Strategy and Tactics.* New York: Random House.

Liberator
      January 1, 1833–December 31, 1865. The abolitionist newspaper owned and edited by William Lloyd Garrison.

Loveland, Anne C.
 1966   "Evangelicalism and 'Immediate Emancipation' in American Antislavery Thought." *Journal of Southern History* 32: 172–88.

Mabee, Carleton
 1970   *Black Freedom: The Nonviolent Abolitionists.* New York: Basic Books.

Mathews, Donald G.
 1965   *Slavery and Methodism: A Chapter in American Morality.* Princeton: Princeton University Press.

National Anti-Slavery Standard

New York Anti-Slavery Society
 1832   *Annual Report.* No publisher.

Nye, Russel B.
1949   *Fettered Freedom: Civil Liberties and the Slavery Controversy, 1830–1860.* Ann Arbor: University of Michigan Press.

Pease, Jane H., and Pease, William H.
1974   *They Who Would Be Free: Blacks' Search For Freedom.* New York: Basic Books.

Perry, Lewis
1973   *Radical Abolitionism: Anarchy and the Government of God in Antislavery Thought.* Ithaca, NY: Cornell University Press.

Rankin, John
1838   *Letters on American Slavery.* Boston: Garrison and Knapp.

Richards, Leonard L.
1970   *"Gentlemen of Property and Standing:" Anti-abolition Mobs in Jacksonian America.* New York: Oxford University Press.

Sewell, Richard H.
1975   *Ballots for Freedom.* New York: Oxford University Press.

Staudenraus, Phillip
1961   *The African Colonization Movement.* New Haven: Yale University Press.

Stewart, James B.
1969   "The Aims and Impact of Garrisonian Abolitionism, 1840–1860." *Civil War History* 15: 197–209.
1970   *Joshua Giddings.* Cleveland: Press of Case-Western Reserve University.
1971   "Peaceful Hopes and Violent Experiences: The Evolution of Radical and Reforming Abolitionism, 1831–1837." *Civil War History* 17: 293–309.
1976   *Holy Warriors.* New York: Hill and Wang.

Whittier, John Greenleaf
1834   *Justice and Experience.* Boston: Garrison and Knapp.

Wright, Elizur, Jr.

1833
The Sin of Slavery and its Remedy: Containing Some Reflections on the Moral Influence of African Colonization. New York: American Anti-Slavery Society.

Wyatt-Brown, Bertram

1969
Lewis Tappan and the Evangelical War against Slavery. Cleveland: Press of Case-Western Reserve University.

1970
"Abolitionists and New Leftists: A Comparison of American Radical Styles." *Wisconsin Magazine of History* 53: 6–19.

1970
"Prophets Outside Zion: Career and Commitment in the Abolitionist Movement." Unpublished MS.

1971
"Prelude to Abolitionism: Sabbatarian Politics and the Rise of the Second Party System." *Journal of American History* 58: 316–41.

III

The Biblical Base of the Social Gospel

William McGuire King

From the 1890s to the 1930s the social gospel exerted a major influence on American religious thought and practice especially within northern Protestantism. The popular appeal of the movement lay in its outlook on human beings and their place in society, an outlook that accorded well with the progressive spirit of the age. Social reform, the advocates of the social gospel insisted, must be vigorously pursued if such ideals as the worth of the human self and the solidarity of humanity in mutual love and service were to be preserved and extended. Although social gospel proponents differed among themselves regarding the degree and rapidity of reform that was desirable, they at least agreed that humanity can and should self-consciously direct the processes of social change.

A diverse array of social and cultural forces had converged during the last quarter of the nineteenth century to reinforce this assumption: the social activism and millennial optimism of antebellum evangelicalism; the increasingly modernist direction of postbellum theology; the interest in England and Germany in Christian Socialism; the intellectual revolution wrought by the newer social sciences, especially sociology; and, not the least important, the impact of the drive for national order and stability in a rapidly industrializing society. These trends all suggested humanity's ability, when inspired by religious ideals, to mold the social process for beneficent ends. Accepting the imperative of such a perspective, social gospel representatives argued that all individualistically-oriented points of view, including the traditional revivalistic theology of evangelicalism and the traditional laissez-faire ideology of American business, must be repudiated.

However, this reform orientation was only one aspect of the story. For many of the leaders in the movement the articulation of a distinctive religious vision was just as important as the achievement of practical reforms. This vision seemed to them to herald a reformation within Christianity. Consequently, proponents of a socially oriented Christianity displayed considerable interest in discovering biblical foundations for the social gospel. A study of the ways in which they appropriated the Bible is crucial for revealing how they perceived their own message. It is also significant because their interpretations dominated biblical studies in America during the first half of the twentieth century (Cadbury: 89–90). Since that time the social gospel's exegetical work has fallen into disrepute. It is therefore all the more critical that an analysis of the biblical base of the social gospel proceed in a dispassionate and orderly fashion. The key issues needing investigation are the social gospel's attitude toward the Bible in general, its focus on the historical Jesus, the major exegetical conclusions of its most representative spokespersons, its method of applying biblical materials to modern social problems, and the overall validity of its interpretive principles.

Search for Biblical Roots

Social gospel proponents wanted to develop a biblical foundation for social Christianity. The movement needed to demonstrate that it was rooted in the biblical word, that it was indeed a *gospel* and not merely a reflection of contemporary social and cultural anxieties. The legitimacy of the social interpretation of Christianity would thereby rest on traditional biblical sources of authority as well as on the practical necessity for Christian social action. The importance of this appeal to authority should not be minimized. Had social relevance and utility been the sole criteria of legitimacy, the social gospel viewpoint would probably not have received such widespread acceptance and support within the American churches. Its popularity lay precisely in its capacity to combine the modernist impulse of contemporary thought with the apparent rediscovery of the social dimensions of the biblical faith.

Social gospel advocates sincerely believed that they were not thereby introducing a foreign element into biblical theology or wrenching the biblical message from its context. On the contrary, one of the glories of the present age, they claimed, was the opportunity to recover the full import of the biblical word, which traditional Christian theology had missed. Such an attitude was not new on the American scene, and in this respect the social gospel stood in a long line of American religious movements that claimed to have disinterred from history the authentic religion of the Bible. Confident that the social interpretation was not a device of their own fancy but was embedded in the theology of the Bible, proponents of the social gospel felt exhilarated by their discovery. The social reinterpretation of the biblical record liberated them from the theological cul-de-sac into which the older evangelical viewpoint had seemed to lead them. Many social gospel representatives, for example, had been reared in strongly evangelical and revivalistic homes. Not wishing to reject what they deemed still valuable in their evangelical heritage, they nevertheless came in their adulthood to believe that the individualistic orientation of evangelicalism could not address the social needs and spiritual aspirations of an industrial civilization. When the social interpretation of the Bible appeared in the 1880s, it struck such individuals like a revelation; it resolved their internal conflicts between faith commitments and social commitments. It would certainly slight the personal significance of the social gospel's biblical exegesis to consider it merely a self-serving rationalization. Only a profound sense of awakening can possibly explain Richard T. Ely's exuberance in proclaiming that "as soon as we grasp this thought of the social character of Christianity, we find every page of the Scriptures illuminated with a new light" (158).

Walter Rauschenbusch has left a particularly vivid account of the way in which the new biblical interpretation bridged the gap in his own experience between revivalism and the social gospel. Rauschenbusch stated that he began his career with the traditional evangelical desire to become a missionary and to save souls. However, his early ministry in New York City impressed on him the extent of social misery in American society and the nature of the economic conditions responsible for it. For a while he suffered from an inability to resolve the conflict between his personal religious faith and the demands of his new social outlook. "How was I to combine the two things?" he asked. "I needed a unity of life—a faith. A real religion always wanted unity" (Handy: 266). He was "groping in the dark" during this period, while his older colleagues continued to advise a purely individualistic approach to the work of salvation.

> Such appeals were painfully upsetting. All our inherited ideas, all theological literature, all the practices of church life, seemed to be against us. There was no room in Bethlehem for this new-born interest of ours, and we young men were not yet ready to assert that this was the prince of the house of David coming to claim his ancestral home. (1912:92)

Retiring from the battle to the wilderness of German scholarship, Rauschenbusch awakened to the social perspective of the Bible. "When the forgotten social ideas of the Christian evangel did become clear to us, we felt like young Columbuses taking possession of a new continent" (1912:93). His soul "rejoiced" at finding "the social wealth of the Bible" (1912:42). "I felt a new security in my social impulses," he wrote. The social frame of reference

> responded to all the old and all the new elements of my religious life. The saving of the lost, the teaching of the young, the pastoral care of the poor and frail, the quickening of starved intellects, the study of the Bible, church union, political reform, the reorganization of the industrial system, international peace,—it was all covered by the one aim of the Reign of God on earth. That idea is necessarily as big as humanity, for it means the divine transformation of all human life. It alone can say without limitations, "Nil humani a me alienum" ["Nothing that is human is alien to me"]. (1912:93–94)

This reorientation had been made possible for the social gospel by recent advances in historical and biblical scholarship, particularly in Germany. The history-of-religions methodology, for example, by seeking to recover the cultural context of the biblical materials promised to shed further light on the social import of biblical traditions. Social gospel exponents, therefore, readily accepted the historical approach to biblical exegesis. Scholars like Shailer Mathews, Francis Greenwood Peabody, and Walter Rauschenbusch were thoroughly versed in German scholarship and declared themselves members of the "modern school of history" (Rauschenbusch, 1907:45).

In addition to its historical perspective the social gospel's biblical stand-point rested on the liberal theological assumption of a progressive revelation. According to this view the biblical text becomes revelatory only insofar as it speaks in progressively new terms to changing cultural situations. Revelation is progressive, not in the sense that older interpretations are wrong but in the sense that they are incomplete and always capable of being superseded. Thus Peabody could eloquently defend the possibility of fresh insights in biblical interpretation. Since "each period in civilization has had, in turn, its own peculiar interest and its own spiritual demands," biblical interpretation has ever been subject to the dominant cultural interests of its age. Such a circumstance, Peabody argued, does not mean that all interpretations are merely cultural projections but that all interpreters are merely "partial wit-nesses" who "stand in their own place and report that view of the gospel which presents itself to their minds." The result is not skepticism but a frank appreciation of the fact that the gospel "seems to each age to have been written for the sake of the special problems which at the moment appear pressing." No single interpretation will achieve finality until the consummation of history itself discloses the full dimensions of biblical revelation. In the meantime the teachings of the Bible manifest an "extraordinary capacity for new adaptations" (1900:71–73).

As a result of their acceptance of the doctrine of progressive revelation, the proponents of a social gospel felt justified in thoroughly reexamining the biblical record. The concerns of modernity would serve as the spade with which to attempt the unearthing of further biblical treasures. "Words and deeds which other generations have found perplexing or obscure," noted Peabody, "may be illuminated with meaning, as one now sees them in the light of the new social agitation and hope" (1900:73). Rauschenbusch ex-pressed the same outlook more succinctly. "The new present has created a new past," he said, and "the Bible shares in that new social interpretation" (1907:45). Once again one may marvel at the way in which a modernist impulse blended with traditional concerns in determining the social gospel's approach to the Bible.

The Preoccupation with Jesus

The focus of biblical interest for social gospel apologists was the teach-ings of Jesus, especially those teachings that dealt with the kingdom of God. They did not ignore the rest of the Bible, but they did not devote as much attention to it as they did to the Gospel materials /1/. Certain historical factors account for their concentration on the historical Jesus and his ministry as opposed to the Christ of the traditional christological dogmas.

The preoccupation with the centrality of Jesus' personality was itself deeply rooted in the American religious consciousness. Although the intellectual leaders of the social gospel were undoubtedly influenced by the Christocentric tendencies of German liberal theology, the social gospel as a whole did not need to import its brand of Christocentrism. The figure of Jesus had dominated American piety for over a century, whether Jesus appeared as the compassionate personality of the pietistic tradition, as the moral teacher of the rationalistic tradition, or as the representative man of romanticism.

The Christocentric preaching of the mid-Victorian American pulpit, moreover, may have prepared many people for the transition from evangelicalism to the social gospel. The popularity of preachers like Henry Ward Beecher at Plymouth Church, Brooklyn, and Phillips Brooks at Trinity Episcopal Church, Boston, was based in part on their abilities to bring the historical Jesus to life through word pictures and to make Jesus' ministry seem relevant to the personal and cultural concerns of the day. According to Beecher, Jesus "is the Architect, the Engineer, the Leader, the Guide, the Schoolmaster; he is the Friend; he is the Father and Brother; he is the Rescuer and Savior; he is the great Artisan and Artist of all the things which are required for the education of the race" (Cross: 190). Brooks went farther than Beecher in stressing Jesus' social relevance. Jesus' conception of human beings as children of God, said Brooks, "is the constructive power of the social life of man in all its various degrees" (76). In a popular address on "The Influence of Jesus in the Social Life of Man," Brooks explained that Jesus taught his disciples that such sonship—or self-realization—was possible "not in solitude, where character would be so much easier and so much more imperfect, but in contact with the world" (89). Through his ministry Jesus had demonstrated that sonship can be found only by means of brotherhood (103). The cross, Brooks maintained, must therefore be viewed as the completion of Jesus' ministry and not as an event separable from his historical life (100–111).

The liberal theology of the late nineteenth century in America demonstrated similar Christocentric tendencies by making the historical Jesus the norm of biblical revelation. Indeed what kept the liberal doctrine of progressive revelation from becoming merely a synonym for the spirit of the age was the liberal assertion that in the person of Jesus the highest and fullest revelation of truth for any age is to be found. The task of theology is to reflect continually on the person of Jesus. The historical Christ thus becomes the theological hinge by which liberalism retains its Christian integrity and identity.

It is here that we find the real meaning of the Bible. "The end," as Canon Mozley has so strongly shown, "is the test of progressive revelation." Jesus Christ, who is himself the Word ... is indeed the perfect Revelation of God. From his judgment there is no appeal; at his feet the wisest of us must sit and learn the way of life. (Gladden, 1891:369)

These words of Washington Gladden expressed the liberal theological viewpoint of the social gospel as a whole.

The early social gospel representatives, however, did not engage in a systematic exegesis of the teachings of Jesus. They tended to reduce Jesus' message to a simplistic law of love that could be self-evidently applied to personal and social relationships. In 1889, for example, Richard T. Ely, political economist at The Johns Hopkins University and later at the University of Wisconsin, explained social Christianity as "The Simple Gospel of Christ," which he equated with the second commandment (8). According to Ely, Jesus was referring to social as well as individual regeneration (149). Christ's conception of love must consequently include a "science of society" (4). In fact, said Ely, Christ demands that people be "in the fullest, completest sense of the word, philanthropists" and create by means of social science and social work a "wholesome environment" (17, 103).

Washington Gladden, the Congregationalist pastor in Columbus, Ohio, and the most important of the early social gospel voices, tied Jesus' teachings of "the law of love" to the postmillennial expectations of American Protestantism. In *Burning Questions* (1895) Gladden indicated that Jesus' concept of love was inseparable from his concept of the kingdom of God. This kingdom would be progressively realized on earth as both individual sin and social sin were transformed by universal obedience to Christ's law. The end result, as foreseen by Jesus eighteen centuries before, would be the production of a thoroughly Christian civilization maturing in America and spreading throughout all nations (183). However, the millennial process had only begun. "We are sure," declared Gladden, "that what we see is only the vanguard of the host that is coming; that teeming farms and noisy cities will soon line this thoroughfare" (189). Christ's law "has marked out the lines on which the King in His glory is to come to Zion, and it has gathered to itself some beautiful tokens of that kingdom of righteousness and peace which is by-and-by to fill the earth as the waters fill the sea" (189). The consummation awaits only "the reorganisation of industrial society" on the basis of good will rather than selfish competitiveness (192).

Gladden's sentiments were echoed by Josiah Strong, general secretary of the Evangelical Alliance for the United States. Strong felt that the law of Christ was *"a practical working principle, intended to control the organization of human society"* (121). Strong noted, furthermore, that the rationalistic skepticism regarding the life of Jesus, which had been propounded by thinkers like David Friedrich Strauss, had unwittingly stimulated historical interest in Jesus. Such widespread interest, he felt, had been providentially arranged in order to speed the fulfillment of the kingdom taught by Jesus. "This nearer and clearer vision of the Christ," wrote Strong in 1893, "this return to the study of his teachings, this discovery that he is the Savior of *man* as well as of men, that he laid down the fundamental laws of social relations on which the perfect society of the future is to be organized—all this is the timing of Providence that the new era of the near future may indeed be the fuller coming of the Kingdom" (113).

The social gospel could not subsist for long on such euphoria. The portrait of Jesus drawn by Ely, Gladden, and Strong was vague at best and certainly susceptible to the charge that it "reads into the Gospel ideas which properly belong to optimistic American philosophy and anthropology" (Lundström: 26). However, by the turn of the century many of the more scholarly exponents of the social gospel had become critical of the more simplistic interpretations of Jesus. Few of the earlier representatives had done careful exegetical work on the Gospels, but the later scholars attempted to draw a more sophisticated portrait of Jesus by means of serious biblical exegesis. They realized that the increasing popularity of social Christianity in the 1890s demanded a more discriminating defense of the social gospel and required an exposition of the ministry of Jesus that would stand up to the test of the best scholarly criticism of the day. Fortunately for them the massive critical work already done in Germany on the life of Jesus provided a basis on which the social gospel could build a more respectable theoretical edifice. This exegetical work probably kept the social gospel from becoming a passing fad rather than a legacy.

Exegetics of the Kingdom

The fundamental task of social gospel apologists at the close of the nineteenth century was to indicate how any sort of social gospel could legitimately be found in the teachings and mission of Jesus. The work of three scholars in particular laid down the lines of interpretation that the social gospel's exegesis of the Gospels would follow. The first attempt to supply this critical need was Shailer Mathews's *The Social Teaching of Jesus* (1897). Professor of New Testament history and interpretation at the University of Chicago, Mathews devoted a lifetime to the study of biblical history. His later efforts in this direction, namely, *The Messianic Hope in the New Testament* (1905) and *Jesus on Social Institutions* (1928), modified but did not negate his earlier conclusions. Francis Greenwood Peabody's *Jesus Christ and the Social Question* (1900) and his Lyman Beecher Lectures for 1904, published as *Jesus Christ and the Christian Character* (1905), were elaborate discussions of the Gospel accounts and the critical literature dealing with them. Despite the fact that Peabody was an ethicist and sociologist of sorts at Harvard University (Plummer Professor of Christian Morals), he read widely in the most recent German biblical scholarship and displayed a remarkable comprehension of the synoptic materials. Walter Rauschenbusch, professor of church history at Rochester Theological Seminary, made the final major contribution to the discussion of Jesus' teachings from the social gospel point of view. He produced a small textbook, *The Social Principles of Jesus* (1916), which was used extensively by Sunday School classes nationwide; but his most significant analysis came in the chapter on "The Social Aims of Jesus" in *Christianity and the Social Crisis* (1907). His discussion of Jesus profoundly influenced those who entered the movement after 1907.

Owing to the self-conscious nature of their attempts to justify the social interpretation of Jesus, Mathews, Peabody, and Rauschenbusch provide in their expositions a valuable insight into the exegetical methods of the social gospel at its best. One needs to determine (1) How did they attempt to show the validity of the social interpretation of Jesus' preaching? (2) How did they attempt to apply their conclusions to the social problems of modern society? These two questions are quite distinct. Not one of the three interpreted Jesus "as a social reformer of the modern type" (Rauschenbusch, 1907:47). Jesus, according to Rauschenbusch, was interested in moral (that is, religious) questions, not economic ones (1907:47). Peabody claimed that Jesus remained aloof from the major social problems of his day (1900:77–78). Mathews warned against construing what Jesus taught "in terms of to-day's thought" (1897:40). If Jesus' teachings have any social application, wrote Peabody, that fact is only a by-product of his main intention (1900:79). The application of his message to modern social problems can therefore proceed only by "inference," that is, by analogy and metaphor (Peabody, 1900:82–84). Given these disclaimers, one must ascertain why these commentators saw any social significance at all in Jesus' preaching before one can consider how they tried to apply these teachings to contemporary society.

The three scholars were in agreement on the answer to the first question. The social nature of Jesus' message lay less in what he said explicitly—at least as recorded in the Gospels—than in the historical context of what he was doing. The ministry and mission of Jesus, said Mathews, is just as crucial for interpretation as his isolated sayings (1897:14–15). "If we want to understand the real aims of Jesus," Rauschenbusch suggested, "we must watch him in his relation to his own times" (1907:49).

The demonstration that Jesus' ministry had a social as well as an individual dimension depended entirely on the social gospel's interpretation of Jesus' own understanding of the phrase "kingdom of God." "No other term," Mathews insisted, "unless it be Son of Man, is so characteristic of Jesus; none is more certainly his" (1897:42). Mathews pointed out that the phrase appears abundantly in the synoptic tradition and that even the Gospel of John, which tends to spiritualize Jesus' message, retains an occasional use of the term (1897:42–43). And even when the word was not explicitly used, it was the subject of Jesus' teachings. "The kingdom," Peabody thus noted, "was the one end to be desired; it was the pearl of great price for which all else might be sold; it was the piece of money to find which the house was diligently swept; it was to be the theme of daily prayer for the followers of Jesus: 'Thy kingdom come'" (1900:92).

The commentators agreed, however, that one should not form hasty conclusions about what the phrase meant to Jesus. Mathews argued that the critical issue was a historical one: to what was Jesus referring? He and Rauschenbusch conceded that "a hundred critical difficulties" stand in the way of determining Jesus' meaning, and both frankly admitted that considering the current state of scholarship "the results of this investigation are not at all completed" (Rauschenbusch, 1907:55). Nonetheless, both felt that nineteenth-century scholarship had advanced far enough to enable a recovery of a great deal of the historical usage of the term. It was linked to the traditional messianic hopes of the Jews, whether in their prophetic or apocalyptic forms. One thing was therefore certain, they thought: its reference was this-worldly. It involved the social and political redemption of the people of God through God's initiative in history or at the end of history (Mathews, 1897:55–57). Rauschenbusch maintained that the phrase, which he often preferred to translate as "reign of God," always referred to a collective hope, involving the restoration of a state of collective justice (1907:56–57; 1916:49).

If it could be shown that Jesus' preaching of the kingdom of God was in continuity with the Jewish eschatological hope, then these scholars believed that they had a firm basis on which to argue that Jesus' message was not simply limited to individual and otherworldly matters. Mathews supposed that the best single argument for Jesus' continuity with the Jewish eschatological expectation was the argument from silence. Jesus never defined what he meant because he did not need to; the people understood his meaning very well, even if future generations have not. Consider, he said, how the masses wanted Jesus for a national leader; "they hailed him as the successor of David and carried him in triumph to the Temple; while in the hopes of his followers the chief significance of his return from the tomb and his newly revealed life lay at first in the possibility of revolution and the reestablishment of a puissant Hebrew kingdom" (1897:41).

Rauschenbusch took a slightly different tack. Can it be without significance, he wondered, that Jesus' early ministry was so closely linked to the ministry of John the Baptist? John's preaching clearly presupposed the prophetic and messianic expectation, as his practice of baptism into the kingdom confirms. It was Jesus himself at the Jordan who self-consciously connected his own mission with John. "He took up the formula of John: 'The kingdom of God has come nigh; repent!' He continued the same baptism. He drew his earliest and choicest disciples from the followers of John. When John was dead, some thought Jesus was John risen from the dead. . . . To the end of his life he championed John and dared the Pharisees to deny his [John's] divine mission" (1907:52–53). If Jesus did not share the national and social hope of his people, why did he embrace the Baptist and use a traditional prophetic term like kingdom of God? "If he did not mean by it the substance of what they meant by it, it was a mistake to use the term. If he did not mean the consummation of the theocratic hope, but merely an internal blessedness for individuals with the hope of getting to heaven, why did he use the words around which all the collective hopes are clustered?" (1907:57).

Rauschenbusch further wondered how one could explain Jesus' crucifixion at the hands of the Roman government if his message lacked all social and political import. Would the authorities have crucified one whose message was merely one of simple other-worldly idealism? If such idealism was Jesus' intention, he was dangerously mistaken in emphasizing the kingdom of God, for "it unfettered the political hopes of the crowd; it drew down on him the suspicion of the government; it actually led to his death" (1907:57). A more reasonable hypothesis, thought Rauschenbusch, is that the social and political forces of the day correctly perceived something dangerous in Jesus' preaching. "All the great permanent forces of evil in humanity were strangely combined in the drama of his death: bigotry, priestcraft, despotism, political corruption, militarism, and the mob spirit. They converged on him and did him to death" (1912:68). Jesus was not at all misleading the people, Rauschenbusch concluded. He went to his death in order to redeem his people and that redemption was not only of individuals but of his society. The proclamation of the New Testament is that the authorities had executed Jesus, "but he is alive, and now it is their turn" (1912:68).

The social gospel commentators thus believed that modern historical scholarship had permitted for the first time a relatively accurate exegesis of Jesus' most characteristic phrase. In their minds, this recovery put to rest all attempts to interpret Jesus' teachings in a purely individual and otherworldly fashion or in a purely idealistic and timeless fashion. Jesus "was not a timeless religious teacher, philosophizing vaguely on human generalities. He spoke for his own age, about concrete conditions, responding to the stirrings of the life that surged about him" (Rauschenbusch, 1907:49). Mathews's agreement with this assessment was revealed by his repudiation of the idealistic interpretation of the kingdom advanced by Julius Kaftan, a prominent exponent of Ritschlian theology in Germany (1897:47–49) /2/. They concluded that the kingdom meant more than just an ideal; it referred to a concrete social reality. Presumably this seeming recovery of the core of Jesus' teaching had significant implications for Christian ethics. Because the early Christian community forgot the original meaning of the kingdom ideal, Rauschenbusch surmised, Christianity "lost its contact with the synoptic thought of Jesus" (1917:133). In fact, the ethics of Jesus have appeared relevant only to those who are able to get "the substance of the Kingdom ideal in their minds" (1917:134). The social gospel commentators therefore focused their attention on the synoptic Gospels, trying to find in them by comparative methods the form of kingdom sayings that seemed closest to the original teaching of Jesus.

Having argued that Jesus' message had some sort of social significance, Mathews, Peabody, and Rauschenbusch were aware that serious interpretive difficulties remained before they could draw any conclusions about what Jesus actually taught. They recognized the confusing variety of eschatological expectations current during Jesus' lifetime. And they were certain that Jesus had introduced some modifications of his own into the tradition. According to Rauschenbusch, Jesus accepted the traditional kingdom ideal; but "he accepted it, not as a slave, but as a son, and refashioned it with sovereign freedom" (1912:57). Both exegetical and ideological considerations helped the social gospel arrive at this assessment.

The three commentators were well aware of the work of Johannes Weiss and his argumentation for the consistent, futuristic interpretation of Jesus' eschatology—in direct contrast to liberal Protestant interpretations. Mathews felt that Weiss had permanently upset the idealist approach and that much could be said in favor of Weiss's position.

> Probably the recognition of the importance of the apocalyptic literature in the formation of the early Christian vocabulary, if not Christology, may yet be still further emphasized. Nor can it be denied that, especially in the latter part of his life, Jesus often used expressions which . . . would be sufficient to justify the sweeping statement that "the gospel entered into the world as an apocalyptic eschatological message, apocalyptical and eschatological not only in its form, but in its contents." (1897:51)

Peabody felt that the apocalyptic interpretation had been advanced "with ingenuity and learning," and he quoted Schnedermann to the effect that Weiss and his associates were to be commended for "the refutation of utterances of Ritschl" (1900:95). All agreed that Jesus usually referred to the kingdom as future, as coming, and that he even identified himself with the future Son of Man of that kingdom (Mathews, 1897:41; 49–53; Peabody, 1900:92–93, 97).

Yet the social gospel scholars could not accept the purely apocalyptic, futuristic interpretation of Jesus' expectation. Mathews was willing to concede that Jesus had employed some apocalyptic terminology. But they were far more willing to attribute the apocalyptic coloration of many kingdom passages to the influence of apocalypticism on the early church. The early church was responsible for giving Jesus' future expectation an apocalyptic connotation, claimed Rauschenbusch. Such alterations were inevitable since apocalypticism "was the hottest part of the faith of the primitive Church and anything coming in contact with it would run fluid" (1907:63). Peabody believed that, given a choice between conflicting kingdom statements, one should choose the more spiritual sayings as originally belonging to Jesus. The early church would not have spiritualized authentic apocalyptic sayings, but it would readily have done the reverse (1900:96). Of course they had no such problems accepting the authenticity of sayings in which the kingdom was spoken of as present. The kingdom was "near" (Mark 1:15) and "among you" (Luke 17:20) in the sense that it was being realized in Jesus' own preach-ing and ministry (Luke 4:17–21), exemplified by the good seed already scattered in the world (Matt 13:24–43)(Mathews, 1897:51–52; Peabody, 1900:92–93; Rauschenbusch, 1907:63–64). Peabody concluded that "we are brought, then, to the apparently paradoxical conclusion that the kingdom of God had to Jesus both significations, that of a future and that of a present state, that of a heavenly and that of an earthly society" (1900:99–100).

Several ideological reasons obviously predisposed the social gospel apol-ogists to reject the view of Jesus as an apocalypticist. For one thing, the apocalyptic perspective resembled too closely the premillenarian tradition that was gaining ground in American Protestantism at the turn of the cen-tury. The version of premillenarianism dominant at the time was sharply opposed to social action by the churches, and the social gospel was waging a major frontal assault on this teaching which they considered an "unsocial" gospel. An apocalyptic Jesus would have given too much aid and comfort to the opposition. Secondly, they were still constrained by the liberal assump-tion that Jesus must have been an original creative spirit whose unique per-sonality was the prime source of revelation. It was one thing to admit that Jesus was a product of his historical circumstances and limited by the context in which he worked, but it was quite another thing to admit that he was simply such a product and could not reshape current conceptions in accordance with his superior consciousness of God. The conclusion thus followed that since the apocalyptic expectation proved misguided, Jesus could not a priori have accepted it. Surely Jesus universalized the idea of the kingdom, removing it from the confines of a purely nationalistic hope of the Jews and thereby making it a subject applicable to twentieth-century Ameri-ca (Rauschenbusch, 1912:57–63).

These qualifications aside, the social gospel advocates did take seriously both the future and present components of the kingdom. Rauschenbusch proposed a "social de-mythologizing" of the apocalyptic hope. The early hope that Christ would return soon was significant, he insisted. "Expectancy was the true pose of Christians. Under the conditions of that time this was their way of declaring that the Kingdom of God is the highest good and that all our life should be concentrated on it" (1916:55). That sense of expectancy must be translated into a social hope. By so doing we can "still have a reli-gious sense of a great and divine future overhanging humanity which will give to our life the same value and solemnity which the first generation felt" (1916:55). Although he conceptualized the coming of the future kingdom as developmentally realized, he nevertheless urged that the future kingdom be seen as *God's* future coming to humanity on God's initiative.

The Kingdom of God, therefore, is miraculous all the way, and is the continuous revela-tion of the power, the righteousness, and the love of God. The establishment of a community of righteousness in mankind is just as much a saving act of God as the salvation of an individual from his natural selfishness and moral inability. (1917:139–40)

The Christian's hope, for Rauschenbusch, is not optimism in the essential goodness of human beings and humanity's ability to save itself. Christian optimism, as in the case of the early hope of primitive Christianity, is always a daring act of faith. Rauschenbusch was in fact far from saying that the consummation of the kingdom was near. For those without faith in the eschatological purposes of God, the kingdom may seem a futile hope in the midst of the woes of modern civilization. "It takes more moral daring today than for a century past to believe in the reemergence and final victory of God's social order. But this is the time for all true believers to square their shoulders and say with Galileo, 'And yet it moves'" (1916:60).

At the same time Rauschenbusch and the other social gospel advocates stressed that the kingdom must be seen as really present, not just as an ideal directing human energies but as a visible social reality. Their emphasis on the tangibility of the kingdom, which they refused to equate with the church or a spiritual community of Christians, deviated from Ritschlian liberalism; for Ritschl had stressed that "the presence of the kingdom of God within the Christian community is always invisible and a matter of religious faith" (Ritschl: 224). Rauschenbusch countered by saying that the social conception of the kingdom is plausible when love, which marks the presence of the kingdom, is no longer viewed as a personal sentiment or motive but as a "society-making quality" (1907:67). Wherever the kingdom is present, visible fellowship among people testifies to its reality, just as the messianic meals celebrated by Jesus gave tangible evidence of the presence of the kingdom of God (1907:67–70).

Rauschenbusch thought that the visibility of the kingdom was a cardinal factor in its transformative power. Only when it is experienced as a present reality can it bring freedom and release to individuals. Only by participating in its present reality can one find emancipation from the bondage of unsocial and antisocial forces through the revitalization of hope. Thus Rauschenbusch could maintain that Jesus' faith was an "emancipating faith" and the kingdom "the reality on which he staked all" (1917:163). He feared that the consistent eschatologists, such as Weiss, by stressing the interim character of Jesus' ethic, might reinforce the prevalent middle-class, bourgeois tendency to dismiss Jesus' radical understanding of the kingdom as an irrelevant imperative (1917:158).

The social gospel proponents struggled in attempting to solve the problem of how the kingdom could be both present and future. Mathews, Peabody, and Rauschenbusch abandoned the idealist solution without having an alternative theoretical formulation at hand. They therefore turned to a developmental theory to express their understanding of the kingdom. But this theory was awkward and led to confusion. The kingdom itself did not develop, but rather the "world" was gradually being conquered by it. This conceptual difficulty was what led Rauschenbusch to state that "any eschatology which is expressed in terms of historic development has no final consummation. Its consummations are always the basis for further development. The Kingdom of God is always coming" (1917:227). The later neo-orthodox interpretation of the kingdom as standing in opposition to all social and cultural realities was viewed by the social gospel exponents as a return to idealistic and spiritualizing modes of thought. Particularly after 1910, however, the eschatological interpretation of the kingdom increasingly dominated the social gospel's social theory. The result was a growing reluctance to identify the kingdom with the evolution of any particular cultural system but to view it instead as the effective power whenever justice and human solidarity were being realized, in whatever cultural context (Hutchinson, 1976; W. King).

The developmental explanation of the kingdom had a second disadvantage. It could not explain exegetically why the kingdom, even if it were accepted as a social reality, should be construed as applying to the existing social and political institutions of civilization. Why not formulate the relationship between the kingdom and existing institutions as one of continual conflict rather than as a matter of the gradual conquest of one by the other? Consistent eschatologists and neo-orthodox critics later drove this point home against the social gospel with fury. However, social gospel interpreters could not accept the perpetual conflict model. Their biblical exegesis emphasized the messianic principle that the kingdoms of this world are to become the kingdom of the Lord, interpreted noncatastrophically. For the social gospel apologists, the only alternative to accepting a developmental model was either doubting Jesus' proclamation of a final victory of the kingdom (the choice the social gospel later accused neo-orthodoxy of making) or accepting some version of millenarian apocalypticism. Since they could do neither, the developmental interpretation seemed the only reasonable reading of the kingdom expectation of Jesus. But what the social gospel exegetes often overlooked was the fact that the developmental theory remained just that: a theory to explain how the kingdom could be both present and future but not a social teaching explicitly stated in any biblical text.

Three Appropriations of the Teachings of Jesus

The developmental exegesis had a practical as well as a theoretical disadvantage. The developmental model assumed that Jesus' teachings could be applied to practical social problems, but it was unable to specify the procedure by which to determine precisely how this application might be done. Peabody spoke of the need to use inference and deduction. Rauschenbusch, on the other hand, took Jesus' explicit teachings literally while drawing principles from Jesus' ministry through the use of analogy and metaphor. The absence of any consistent interpretive rule by which to extend the teaching of the kingdom to cover practical social issues meant that each commentator was forced to supply his own norms. As a result the social gospel apologists arrived at no uniform set of conclusions regarding the contemporary relevance of the social teachings of Jesus. Of course they all accepted the general propositions regarding social justice, good will, nonviolence, and social solidarity; but they tended to diverge when it came to applying Jesus' teachings in a more concrete way to the complex problems of industrial civilization. These divergences are particularly evident in regard to economic issues. The social gospel exegesis of the kingdom could thus be used to buttress distinct reform tendencies *within* the movement, and these differences were discernible in the way each commentator represented Jesus' relationship to the social problems of his own age. At least three such characterizations were popular: Jesus, the transformer of culture; Jesus, the scientific philanthropist; and Jesus, the nonviolent radical. Mathews, Peabody, and Rauschenbusch conveniently exemplify these three approaches.

Shailer Mathews, in *The Social Teaching of Jesus*, asserted that the kingdom was to be consummated by the missionary and evangelistic activity of the church, albeit in a social mode (224). While the church itself is not identical with the kingdom, the life generated by the church has been "the most effective and historically about the only appreciable force that has been at work in the regeneration of society" (221). The kingdom's progress waits upon the expansion of Christian culture and the gradual assimilation of the total environment to it.

> The expanding Christian society, therefore, will consist of groups of men and women each possessed of the same spirit and method of life as that taught by their Master. These little groups of individuals Jesus likened to leaven which was thrown into the meal and there remained until it had leavened the meal. Though they are not of the world, yet they are to stay in it. Conquest, not flight, is to be their watchword. The progress of Christian society in the world will depend upon the power which each nucleus of Christian persons gathered into a society will have upon the surrounding social life. It can expand only by transforming and assimilating to itself this environment. (217)

This transformation occurs because the church is dedicated to the "replacing of bad men by good men" (225). Such good ones are those who have been "regenerated" to a personal awareness of their filial relationship to God in the kinship of the kingdom (189, 192). Such individuals become socially minded; and their personal influence permeates and transfigures the surrounding culture, creating harmony among all classes of people (191–95). Moreover, their benevolent impulses lead to an amelioration of all social misfortune.

This perspective accounts for Mathews's treatment of the problem of wealth. Jesus did not attack wealth per se, according to Mathews, but the wrong attitude toward wealth. Wealth must be subservient to social stewardship; indeed, Jesus' teaching meant the "making of friends [for the kingdom of God] by money" (144–45). Mathews clearly expected no radical alteration of the social order. He stated that Jesus believed that society would always be divided into social classes (167). Social action must be pursued to remove the antisocial inequities of every economic system, but the overall goal will be the creation of changed personalities. "Equality with Jesus," Mathews concluded, "was not to be attained by equalizing wealth or honor, but by the possession of a common divine life, the employment of equal privileges, and the performance of equal duties. It is moral, not material" (171).

Francis Greenwood Peabody would have accepted most of Mathews's conclusions. The social influence of Jesus lay less in what he said than in the supremacy of his character—the model for all who strove to participate in the kingdom (1905:chap. 3). Yet Peabody had far less faith in the church as such or in the assimilative capacities of the human personality. He had a greater appreciation for the role that social institutions and the social environment played in the development of character. This divergence from Mathews may have been the result of Peabody's stronger belief in the conflicts within the human will and of the ways in which "social sin" hinders people from the healthy development of their personalities. "The action of the will discloses an area of conduct in which are seen volcanic craters, threatening an outpouring of evil, from which one recoils with horror and alarm. Life, which had appeared a tranquill and orderly growth, seems disordered, divided, undermined" (1905:104). Environmental forces must be utilized to support spiritual forces. Hence the social control and manipulation of institutions is an essential strategy of the kingdom. For Peabody the Christian character must master more dimensions of social life than cultural attitudes alone; it must mean in addition "effectiveness, force, capacity, serviceableness, . . . a power by which things may be moved, or resisted, or overcome" (1905:149).

Peabody's Jesus demonstrated just such royal mastery and command of environmental forces in his ministry. Jesus taught that entrance into the kingdom girds one for social combat; it produces a social engineer. "The modern world," wrote Peabody, "is a vast mechanism which waits for power to do its work, and the form of power most applicable to the mechanism of the modern world is the Christian character" (1905:153). Peabody evidently saw a greater need than had Mathews for changing the social system itself. Jesus, Peabody observed, was not "so feeble a sentimentalist as to think that good will comes from within if the way is not prepared for it from without" (1900:111). External circumstances may not automatically bring about a change of heart, but they may make it more probable. Peabody therefore pinned his hopes less on the evangelistic activity of the churches than on the social power of Christian social engineers.

> The more perfected the social machinery becomes, the better trained must be its engineers. The external order calls for inward control. . . . [The teaching of Jesus] recognizes that the problem of adjusting the social environment must be a new problem with each age; it concerns itself, therefore, with the making of persons who shall be fit to deal with the environment which each new age in its turn presents. (1900:113)

Peabody's position appealed to those in the social gospel movement who were allied with the social work and social service professions. The elimination of unjust poverty was to be achieved by legislative restrictions on business practices and by "preventive" philanthropy, which sought the eradication of the causes of poverty (1900:29–30, 231–66; see also Ely: 87–90).

Walter Rauschenbusch would not have disputed the need for evangelism nor would he have minimized the importance of social service. But his analysis of the social problem struck deeper into the heart of the social system than the analysis of either Mathews or Peabody. According to Rauschenbusch, Jesus' ethic called into question all institutions and systems. Do existing social arrangements promote human solidarity or hinder it? That question, he said, was Jesus' "love-test" (1907:71). And Jesus applied that test with a righteous thoroughness. "Let us clear our minds forever," Rauschenbusch wrote in his Sunday school textbook, "of the idea that Jesus was a mild and innocuous person who parted his hair and beard in the middle, and turned his disciples into mollycoddles. Away with it!" (1916:72). Jesus was neither a dreamer nor a reformer but a revolutionary, and his ethical teachings were radical attacks on the social system of his time (1907:86). Jesus' liberation "from spiritual subjection to the existing civil powers" led him into a revolutionary confrontation with those institutions that dehumanized and degraded people. With "the keenest insight" Jesus went beyond the surface legitimization of institutions to test which human values they really espoused and fostered in their activities. His social teaching penetrated "into the masked selfishness of those who hold power," demonstrating thereby "a revolutionary consciousness" (1907:87). Rauschenbusch's conclusion as to the applicability of Jesus' ethic to modern man was clear and simple. "If a man wants to be a Christian, he must stand over against things as they are and condemn them in the name of that higher conception of life which Jesus revealed. If a man is satisfied with things as they are, he belongs to the other side" (1907:90). Those who belong to the kingdom ever demand a thorough reconstruction of the social system in accord with the values of Jesus.

Nowhere was Rauschenbusch's divergence from Mathews and Peabody more obvious than in his treatment of Jesus' teachings on wealth. He scorned expositors, like Mathews and Peabody, who tried to turn Jesus' advice to the rich young ruler into an object lesson on stewardship. "It gives a touch of cheerful enjoyment to exegetical studies to watch the athletic exercise of interpreters when they confront these sayings of Jesus about wealth. They find it almost as hard to get around the needle's eye as the camel would find it to get through" (1907:77–78). Jesus' meaning was rather the more straightforward one: "Equality will prevail only where substantial equality exists"

(1907:77). The Gospels do not relate this story to describe a mere private transaction between Jesus and one rich man but to show that all wealth involves a transaction "between man and God and the people" (1907:77). This story, Rauschenbusch insisted, reveals once again Jesus' central message that the kingdom always creates a "great reversal of values," a transvaluation of social values, expressed so eloquently in the Magnificat (1907:85). Jesus consistently sided with the poor and the oppressed, he maintained, not out of *noblesse oblige* but out of the certitude that they are indeed first in the kingdom of heaven; for it is the common people of the world who know what the stuff of human solidarity is. Jesus was himself made of such stuff, and his triumphal entry into Jerusalem was "a poor man's procession," with "the coats from their backs . . . his tapestry, their throats his brass band, and a donkey . . . his steed" (1907:84). Jesus' example thus provides the modern world with a manifesto. "Humanity is waiting for a revolutionary Christianity which will call the world evil and change it. We do not want 'to blow all our existing institutions to atoms,' but we do want to remould every one of them" (1907:91). Rauschenbusch's formulation must not be dismissed as rhetorical excess, for his writings on Jesus influenced an entire generation of social gospel radicals who dedicated themselves to prophetic action after the debacle of World War I.

Problems of Assessment

One may therefore conclude that the fabric of the social gospel's interpretation of Jesus, despite its rather uniform exegetical fiber, was not all composed of one weave. Its presuppositions were slender enough that they could snap from the tension of conflicting interests and the pressure of events or be severed by the cutting edge of modern scholarship. All three possibilities loomed large in the social gospel's future. World War I and the conservative mood of the country following the war destroyed the cooperative spirit on which the social gospel movement had flourished. The rise of totalitarianism brought into disrepute, although logically it could not refute, the developmental presuppositions of the social gospel's exegesis. And in the end further investigation into the apocalyptic background of Jesus' teachings and the rise of form criticism turned the social gospel's interpretation of Jesus into unfashionable goods /3/.

On the last point, many modern biblical scholars criticized the social gospel for modernizing Jesus—that is, to use Henry J. Cadbury's *bon mot*— for turning the Gospel of Matthew into the gospel of Mathews (203). An oft-repeated charge is that "there is throughout this movement little if any attempt to reach an exegetical understanding of what Jesus meant by the Kingdom of God, or to set this against its historical background" (Lundström: 17). Cadbury even accused the social gospel commentators of scholarly dishonesty,. implying that they really knew better. "For an age that boasts of scientific history, anachronism is a more unpardonable sin. To make of the scriptures mere echoes of our passing styles of thought . . . is to imitate the servile oracles of the pagans which answered to suit the wishes of the inquirers" (90). Since Mathews, Peabody, and Rauschenbusch claimed historical veracity as their chief ally, this charge is truly damaging. But is it just?

No absolute answer can be given, but some possible replies need to be suggested for the sake of fairness to the social gospel. The three interpreters reckoned with the peril of modernizing Jesus. Mathews began his most important chapter in 1897 with a warning.

> To speak of Jesus as anticipating a regenerate society may appear to some as savoring of literalism and to others as a mere modernizing of the simple records of the gospels. Both objections would not be altogether without foundation. There is constant danger that, in the attempt to restate the teachings of Jesus in the terms of to-day's thought, exposition may wait too subserviently upon desire. The first century, albeit surprisingly like the nineteenth, was nevertheless not the nineteenth, and Jesus the Jew was not a product of Greek syllogisms and German hypotheses. (40)

Peabody also cautioned against an anachronistic approach.

> [The social teaching of Jesus] was not the end toward which his mission was directed; it came about as he fulfilled that mission. To reconstruct the gospels so as to make them primarily a programme of social reform is to mistake the by-product for the end specifically sought, and, in the desire to find a place for Jesus within the modern age, to forfeit that which gives him his place in all ages. (1900:79)

Each of them believed that Jesus must be seen in the context of his own time and that anything less would be not only unscholarly but also impious. They therefore proceeded along the lines that they thought were consistent with the highest canons of scholarship and that reflected the conclusions of the best historical research available at the turn of the century. They would have conceded that the validity of their interpretation depended on its historical veracity. Nothing less than the real Jesus would confirm their claim to have recovered the full gospel of Christ.

At the same time they were quite confident that history did in fact support their contentions. Rauschenbusch criticized previous interpreters of Jesus for not being historical enough. "They had never undertaken to understand his life," he wrote, "in its own historical environment and his teachings in the sense in which Jesus meant them to be understood by his hearers" (1907:46). This confidence that the historical Jesus would be shown to be what they hoped he was meant that they may have somewhat selectively chosen their evidence. The willingness to cut short the full consideration of alternative historical possibilities was particularly evident in the way they handled Jesus' relationship with apocalypticism. Nevertheless, it is unfair to expect them to have arrived at a more modern viewpoint on an issue that was far from settled—and is far from being settled even today. It is itself an anachronism to judge the social gospel interpreters by the conclusions of later scholarship. Their failings may more appropriately be said to consist of a somewhat naive belief in the possibility of a presuppositionless historical science, which prevented them from giving due allowance to the fragility of their historical case. As they themselves would probably have admitted, the fact that they intended to avoid modernizing Jesus did not mean that they necessarily succeeded.

No matter how outdated their methods and conclusions may now appear, one should not overlook the important contribution that the biblical work of the social gospel made to American culture. The social interpretation of Jesus was the only serious competitor in America to the dominant evangelical portrait of Jesus, at least before the First World War. It stimulated a renaissance in biblical studies at the major universities and seminaries in America because it forced a thorough reevaluation of the New Testament materials. One could even argue that the social gospel exegesis of the kingdom prepared Americans to accept more consistently eschatological interpretations of the kingdom in theology and form-critical methods in biblical studies. The social gospel put the study of Jesus on the agenda of American biblical scholarship.

Finally, from a more contemporary perspective, the social gospel raised a challenging theological issue. Just how significant is the historical Jesus to the theological enterprise? How relevant is the ethic of Jesus? Francis Greenwood Peabody argued that in every age of rapid social change Christians invariably return to an "imitation of Christ." "As each new transition in human interest occurs," he wrote, "the teaching of Jesus seems to possess new value" (1900:72). The figure of Jesus provides Christians with a role model when other role models seem to have lost their cultural validity. Can Christian theology ignore this insight? Is the task of recovering the historical Jesus irrelevant to the concerns of theology? Can theology, as Rauschenbusch asked, proclaim the cross without proclaiming the historical ministry and mission of the man who died there? Or is the continual recovery of Jesus a perennial theological mandate? The social gospel obviously thought it was; and much of American theology has followed the lead of Peabody, who concluded that "the unexhausted gospel of Jesus touches each new problem and new need with its illuminating power, while there yet remain myriads of other ways of radiation toward other souls and other ages, for that Life . . . is the light of men" (1900:75).

NOTES

1. Hopkins's conclusion that after 1900 social gospel leaders "rationalized" their faith "in terms of the social teachings of Jesus rather than the kingdom ideal" does not seem justified (206). Washington Gladden, for example, wrote a series of books covering the entire biblical canon (1891; 1897); Lyman Abbott produced a social interpretation of Pauline theology (1898); Rauschenbusch displayed considerable interest in the Hebrew prophets and the primitive Church and desired a social interpretation of the Bible as a whole.

2. Albrecht Ritschl (1822–1889), influential liberal theologian at the University of Göttingen, used the doctrine of the kingdom of God as one of two foci in his exposition of the Christian faith (see Mueller). His influence on American liberal theology was great, but the exact relationship between his formulation of the kingdom ideal and the social gospel's formulation remains to be determined.

3. The social gospel interpretation of Jesus continued to be influential in liberal Protestant circles between the two world wars. See, for example: Luccock, Page, Poteat, Tittle, and Ward. Several defenses of the social viewpoint, however, tried to take into account the charges being leveled at its interpretation of Jesus by more recent biblical critics: Bennett, Macintosh, and— above all—McCown (1929; 1940).

WORKS CONSULTED

Abbott, Lyman

1892   *The Evolution of Christianity*. Boston: Houghton, Mifflin.

1896   *Christianity and Social Problems*. Boston: Houghton, Mifflin.

1898   *The Life and Letters of Paul the Apostle*. Boston: Houghton, Mifflin.

Abell, Aaron I.

1960   *American Catholicism and Social Action*. Garden City, NY: Hanover House.

Abell, Aaron I., ed.

1968   *American Catholic Thought on Social Questions*. New York: Bobbs-Merrill.

Averill, Lloyd J.

1967   *American Theology in the Liberal Tradition*. Philadelphia: Westminster Press.

Bennett, John C.
1935   *Social Salvation.* New York: Charles Scribner's
                       Sons.

Broderick, Francis L.
1963   *Right Reverend New Dealer: John A. Ryan.* New
                       York: Macmillan.

Brooks, Phillips
1879   *The Influence of Jesus.* New York: E. P. Dutton.

Cadbury, Henry J.
1937   *The Peril of Modernizing Jesus.* New York: Mac-
                       millan.

Carter, Paul A.
1956   *The Decline and Revival of the Social Gospel,
                       1920–1940.* Ithaca, NY: Cornell University Press.

Cauthen, Kenneth
1962   *The Impact of American Religious Liberalism.*
                       New York: Harper and Row.

Cross, Robert D., ed.
1967   *The Church and the City, 1865–1910.* New York:
                       Bobbs-Merrill.

Dombrowski, James
1936   *The Early Days of Christian Socialism in Ameri-
                       ca.* New York: Columbia University Press.

Dorn, Jacob Henry
1966   *Washington Gladden.* Columbus, OH: Ohio State
                       University Press.

Eighmy, John Lee
1972   *Churches in Cultural Captivity.* Knoxville, TN:
                       University of Tennessee Press.

Ely, Richard T.
1889   *Social Aspects of Christianity.* New York:
                       Thomas Y. Crowell.

Fine, Sidney
1956   *Laissez Faire and the General-Welfare State.* Ann
                       Arbor: University of Michigan Press.

Gladden, Washington
 1891   *Who Wrote the Bible?* Boston: Houghton, Mifflin.
 1895   *Burning Questions.* New York: Wilbur B. Ketch-
                              am.
 1897   *Seven Puzzling Bible Books.* Boston: Houghton,
                              Mifflin.
 1909   *Recollections.* Boston: Houghton, Mifflin.

Handy, Robert T., ed.
 1966   *The Social Gospel in America. 1870–1920.* New
                              York: Oxford University Press.

Hiers, Richard H.
 1968   *Jesus and Ethics.* Philadelphia: Westminster Press.
 1973   *The Historical Jesus and the Kingdom of God.*
                              Gainesville: University of Florida Press.

Hopkins, C. Howard
 1940   *The Rise of the Social Gospel in American Protes-
                              tantism, 1865–1915.* New Haven: Yale University
                              Press.

Hughley, J. Neal
 1948   *Trends in Protestant Social Idealism.* Morningside
                              Heights, NY: King's Crown Press.

Hutchison, William R.
 1975   "The Americanness of the Social Gospel." *Church
                              History* 44 (September 1975):367–81.
 1976   *The Modernist Impulse in American Protestant-
                              ism.* Cambridge, MA: Harvard University Press.

Hutchison, William R., ed.
 1968   *American Protestant Thought in the Liberal Era.*
                              New York: Harper and Row.

Jenks, Jeremiah W.
 1906   *The Political and Social Significance of the Life
                              and Teachings of Jesus.* New York: Young Men's
                              Christian Association Press.

Kent, Charles Foster
 1913   *The Life and Teachings of Jesus.* New York:
                              Charles Scribner's Sons.

1920   *The Social Teachings of the Prophets and Jesus.*
                        New York: Charles Scribner's Sons.

King, Henry Churchill
1910   *The Ethics of Jesus.* New York: Macmillan.

King, William McGuire
1978   "The Emergence of Social Gospel Radicalism in
                        American Methodism," Ph.D. dissertation, Harvard
                        University.

Leighton, Joseph Alexander
1907   *Jesus Christ and the Civilization of To-day.* New
                        York: Macmillan.

Lundström, Gösta
1963   *The Kingdom of God in the Teaching of Jesus.*
                        Trans. by Joan Bulman. Richmond, VA: John Knox
                        Press.

Luccock, Halford
1930   *Jesus and the American Mind.* New York: Abing-
                        don Press.

McCown, Chester Charlton
1929   *The Genesis of the Social Gospel.* New York: Al-
                        fred A. Knopf.
1940   *The Search for the Real Jesus.* New York: Charles
                        Scribner's Sons.

Macintosh, Douglas Clyde
1939   *Social Religion.* New York: Charles Scribner's
                        Sons.

Mathews, Shailer
1897   *The Social Teaching of Jesus.* New York: Macmil-
                        lan.
1905   *The Messianic Hope in the New Testament.* Chi-
                        cago: University of Chicago Press.
1928   *Jesus on Social Institutions.* New York: Macmil-
                        lan.

May, Henry F.
1949   *Protestant Churches and Industrial America.*
                        New York: Harper and Brothers.

Meyer, Donald B.
1960   *The Protestant Search for Political Realism, 1919–1941*. Berkeley: University of California Press.

Miller, Robert Moats
1958   *American Protestantism and Social Issues, 1919–1939*. Chapel Hill: University of North Carolina Press.

Mueller, David L.
1969   *An Introduction to the Theology of Albrecht Ritschl*. Philadelphia: Westminster Press.

Page, Kirby, and Eddy, Sherwood
1929   *Jesus or Christianity?* New York: Doubleday, Doran.

Peabody, Francis Greenwood
1900   *Jesus Christ and the Social Question*. New York: Macmillan.

1905   *Jesus Christ and the Christian Character*. New York: Harper and Row.

Perrin, Norman
1967   *Rediscovering the Teaching of Jesus*. New York: Harper and Row.

Poteat, Edwin McNeil, Jr.
1935   *The Social Manifesto of Jesus*. New York: Harper Brothers.

Rauschenbusch, Walter
1907   *Christianity and the Social Crisis*. New York: Macmillan.

1912   *Christianizing the Social Order*. New York: Association Press.

1916   *The Social Principles of Jesus*. New York: Association Press.

1917   *A Theology for the Social Gospel*. New York: Macmillan.

Ritschl, Albrecht
1972   *Three Essays*. Trans. by Philip Hefner. Philadelphia: Fortress Press.

Robinson, James M.
1959   *A New Quest of the Historical Jesus*. London:
                        SCM Press.

Schweitzer, Albert
1910   *The Quest of the Historical Jesus*. Trans. by W.
                        Montgomery. New York: Macmillan.
1968   *The Kingdom of God and Primitive Christianity*.
                        Trans. by L. A. Garrard. New York: Seabury Press.

Sharpe, Dores Robinson
1942   *Walter Rauschenbusch*. New York: Macmillan.

Smith, Timothy
1957   *Revivalism and Social Reform*. Nashville: Abing-
                        don Press.

Spain, Rufus B.
1967   *At Ease in Zion: Social History of the Southern
                        Baptists, 1865–1900*. Nashville: Vanderbilt Univer-
                        sity Press.

Strong, Josiah
1893   *The New Era*. New York: Baker and Taylor.

Tittle, Ernest Fremont
1932   *Jesus After Nineteen Centuries*. New York: Ab-
                        ingdon Press.

Ward, Harry F.
1929   *Our Economic Morality and The Ethic of Jesus*.
                        New York: Macmillan.

White, Ronald C. and Hopkins, C. Howard, eds.
1976   *The Social Gospel: Religion and Reform in
                        Changing America*. Philadelphia: Temple Univer-
                        sity Press.

Wise, Stephen S.
1949   *Changing Years: The Autobiography of Stephen
                        Wise*. New York: G. P. Putnam's Sons.

IV

Biblical Arguments and Women's Place in the Church

Barbara Brown Zikmund

The place of women in the church underwent a major shift in the sixteenth century Reformation. Instead of encouraging committed Christian women to find spiritual fulfillment in a convent, Luther and Calvin glorified women's role as wife and mother within the Christian family. Furthermore, as a Christian partner and important influence upon the development of the children, women needed enough education to understand the Bible. Young girls, therefore, were expected to study Scripture. They learned it well and embraced the Protestant assumption that all of life, private and public, could be appropriately regulated by God's word.

As American colonial history unfolded, new social and political circumstances gave women increased responsibilities. Biblically literate women looked to Scripture to justify their changing situation, especially in the churches. And as the nation developed, the use of scriptural logic to uphold past practices and/or promote radical changes in American church life was very common.

The nineteenth century was a period of dramatic change for American women. At the beginning of the century Protestant women founded Female Cent societies and organized themselves to support expanding missionary activities. By the end of the century thousands of church women were involved in every aspect of the American voluntary church. In fact, without the deep commitment and work of women, the history of American Protestantism would have developed quite differently.

Women's Place

It is my purpose to focus upon the great literary and theological debate that erupted repeatedly throughout the century and tried to define women's place in the church. To say that all Christian women were ministers by virtue of their baptism was inadequate. More and more church people tried to describe the ministry of women in specific categories related to the official organizational structures of their denominational traditions. As women took on new roles and worked for new causes, old assumptions were called into question. As many vocational areas expanded and embraced professional models, it was necessary to redefine women's role. Finally, as old authorities (especially Scripture) encountered new scholarship, past assumptions and customs were challenged.

The arguments that nineteenth-century writers offered to prepare the churches *for* change and to protect the churches *from* change were often biblical. Indeed, as the struggle of church women for recognition and power continues into the twentieth century, the same texts are examined over and over. It is a familiar scenario. Only within the last fifty years have most of the so-called mainline denominations moved to allow women the full rights and privileges of ordained leadership. Within Roman Catholicism this significant step has yet to be taken. In all cases social activists and ecclesiastical reformers have relied heavily upon biblical material and interpretations. Contemporary women have learned to build upon the work of past scholars who sought to expand women's role in the church. At the same time some of the logic used long ago to keep women in their "proper place" sounds very familiar. This examination of nineteenth-century literature has ongoing usefulness.

The movement of women into full equity in church leadership has been a step-by-step process. In quite regular sequence women have claimed the following rights: to speak in mixed church gatherings; to serve on the local church council or vestry; to be selected as lay delegates or representatives to regional and national church meetings; to exercise temporary pastoral or evangelistic leadership; to be ordained or given another form of permanent ministerial appointment; and, finally, in the connectional denominations, to achieve equity in conference membership. These six steps seem to have been followed in every major American denomination. The Congregationalists moved through the steps during the first half of the nineteenth century, whereas the Episcopal and Lutheran churches began the process much later. Several denominations have not reached the last steps until very recently. On occasion one can find debates about the role of women in the church that deal with several of these concerns during the same historical period. For example, in the 1880s and 1890s some Lutheran churches were debating the propriety of women having the right to vote in a local congregation, while the Methodist Episcopal Church, North, argued about whether women were eligible for membership in the General Conference, and the Presbyterians focused upon the propriety of women teaching in sabbath schools or preaching in a regular pulpit.

In this chapter we will examine the variety of nineteenth-century arguments surrounding the "woman question." I have chosen to present them thematically, not chronologically. Whether people are defending ongoing limitations upon female participation and power or justifying new options for female leadership the types of arguments used reflect patterns of logic

that continue into our own times. I believe that an awareness of these historical patterns can help church women today clarify their situation in many
denominations.

The Context

The nineteenth century was a period of rapid social change. It was also
a time of organizational consolidation for Protestant churches. As the new
nation upheld the constitutional separation of church and state, American
church life changed. From established institutions linked closely to the political order of New England towns, churches became independent voluntary
organizations. As the frontier pushed west Christians founded new churches
and took personal responsibility for their growth and health. And in these
frontier churches the volunteer energies of women were increasingly valuable. As a result of these changes women became more confident and concerned about their place in the churches. Women organized special ladies'
or female societies to enhance their mission work. Although at first these
organizations were closely linked to the care and outreach of the church, the
success of separate women's groups set a pattern for female involvement in
social reform. The antislavery crusade, educational reform, women's suffrage, and temperance were all causes that got started because some church
women cared. But as more and more women moved beyond their traditional
role, questions of propriety and authority arose. Eventually, serious concern
about the rights and obligations of women in the church confronted all religious groups.

The so-called woman question arose for many reasons: because an artic-
ulate woman such as Frances Willard shared her views in some large church
gatherings; because a national meeting of an antislavery organization refused to seat women delegates; because a gifted woman such as Jarena Lee
led a successful revival; because missionary women functioned as if they
were fully ordained; or because an ordained woman never received an appointment to serve anything but a marginal charge. In all of these cases the
questions emerged: What is the proper role of women in the church? What
does the Bible allow or encourage them to do? What is prohibited? Believing that the Christian religion was not irrational and arbitrary, many church
leaders sought biblical grounds to support or oppose change. In most in-
stances church groups had no specific legislation concerning women. Old
habits and customs within the denominations followed the generally
patriarchal patterns of church history. Christian women functioned in
supportive or separate arenas and the phrase "we've always done it that
way" seemed to suffice. However, the changing environment of nineteenth-
century America upset many unexamined assumptions about the proper role
of women.

Arguments for Change

As church populations increased throughout the nineteenth century the need for religious leadership grew apace (Scott). Historic methods of theological education grounded in classical learning and local parish experience· could not keep up with the demand for clergy. Most people "got religion" at some revival where they responded to the preaching of an itinerant evangelist. Furthermore, the revivalistic message was often skeptical of "book learning" and placed great emphasis upon a religious conversion experience. Women were active participants within this religious scene. They shared an evangelical enthusiasm that was especially appreciated in areas where male clergy were scarce. It was not long before some of these committed women claimed that they had received a call from the Lord to preach and teach the gospel. The first argument that developed to justify new roles and responsibilities for women in the church appealed to the work of the Holy Spirit.

Nineteenth-century literature resounded with the testimonies of women who had a conviction that God had called them to serve the church in new ways. The great temperance leader Frances Willard believed that she was once called by God to the ordained ministry, but she was too timid to respond without approbation from the Methodist Church. Later in life she encouraged "younger women who feel a call, as I once did, to preach the unsearchable riches of Christ." She beseeched "all Christian people, who grieve over the world's great heartache, to encourage every true and capable woman, whose heart God has touched, in her wistful purpose of entering upon that blessed Gospel ministry" (62). Women found it difficult to trust their call from the Lord and were ready to discount its power. The great Black preacher Jarena Lee remembered how she told the Reverend Richard Allen that she felt it was her duty to preach the gospel and how he had told her that the Discipline "did not call for women preachers." She was at first relieved "because it removed the fear of the cross—but no sooner did this feeling cross my mind, than I found that a love of souls had in a measure departed from me; that holy energy which burned within me, as a fire, began to be smothered." To some it might appear unseemly for a woman to preach, but she insisted that nothing was impossible with God. "If the man may preach, because the Saviour died for him, why not the woman? seeing he died for her also. Is he not a whole Saviour, instead of a half one?" (138–39). "Shall women preach? Certainly, if God calls them to preach. He cannot make a mistake. He is not the author of confusion. But will it not subvert the existing social order? If the existing social order is not in harmony with the divine plan, it will have to be subverted" (109).

At the ordination of Antoinette Brown to serve the Congregational church at South Butler, New York, on September 15, 1853, the Reverend Luther Lee followed the same logic: "We are not here to make a minister. It is not to confer on this our sister, a right to preach the gospel. If she has not that right already, we have no power to communicate it to her." Lee argued that all they could do was testify to their belief that Antoinette L. Brown was "one of the ministers of the New Covenant, authorized, qualified and called of God to preach the gospel of his son Jesus Christ" (22). In 1892 Mrs. Josephine Butler wrote: "Give us freedom; refuse us office if you like, though it would be more just in you to share all offices with women. But give us only freedom in the name and in the Spirit of Christ; and then you shall see what God may do with women, in the great work of the world's salvation." She believed that women's gifts in the spirit went beyond "offices in the church." She looked forward to a new day.

> When the Church or the Churches, become more deeply humble; when they have realized even more than they do now, their desperate need of the help of woman *as man's equal, absolutely,* in her relation to spiritual things, they will grant the freedom we ask; and then good gifts will no longer languish in a prison-house of conventionalities, and women's energies will not have to be folded in napkins and buried under the church floor. (32)

The second argument used to justify changed responsibilites for women in the church was pragmatic. Women were effective in new roles. Women were needed to get the job done. It was a new day. Writers who took this approach celebrated the results of women's work in the church and argued for their right to vote or their right to preach. In the *Lutheran Church Review* a progressive pastor, Ernst P. H. Pfatteicher, wrote, "Then there is so much to be done in the church, which would never be done if it were necessary to depend entirely upon the men." Women look after the sick and the poor; women care for the altar. "It is but just that these many, many people should be allowed to have a voice in the government of their own churches." Besides, women are often more businesslike than men in their transactions. He concluded, "We must remember that there is a growth even in Scriptures. . . . The sermons of a Luther would be very clumsy if preached to our people as he wrote them. . . . We are growing." Thus it was quite appropriate for the Lutheran Church to maintain its integrity by holding "to the rights of women as congregational voters" (474, 476, 478).

The same kind of logic was used by more liberal writers to argue for the expansion of female leadership in their churches. The Christian church confronted new problems, and the demands for laborers was urgent. One of the hopeful signs of the times, insisted John F. Humphreys, was that the true position of woman was being recognized more and more. Paul's words to the early church were not meant for women of all time and places. "The very spirit of Christianity has changed all this."

> The woman of to-day can enter some of the best universities and graduate with the highest honors; and the time may not be very distant when she will be admitted to all our theological seminaries, when she may be trained to serve God and humanity by

preaching the everlasting Gospel; and then, if she so desires, she can consecrate herself
to the Gospel ministry for the glory of God her Saviour; and when that time comes the
question about women speaking in churches, like many others of a limited nature, will
be settled forever. (495, 498)

Some people did worry that things might get out of hand. If women
were permitted in one thing, where would it stop? However, even persons
who were unwilling to support women preachers and pastors in the present
era agreed that practical consideration could change things. Charles W.
Torrey wrote, "It will not be what the old Greeks judged proper, nor what
the customs of the Jews allowed, nor what the Pilgrims of the Mayflower
tolerated, nor even what Christians of the nineteenth century may think
fitting, that will be standard of propriety for all time. Each age will and
must be its own arbiter of what is fitting, deciding according to its own light
and surroundings." It followed, therefore, that if it was ever really right and
fitting and proper for a woman to preach and if she considered it her duty
and God blessed her, not even the inspired direction to the Corinthian or
Ephesian churches would stand in her way (170). A noted male
denominational leader supported women in ministry because he believed
that they would bring more men to God. "Men ministers are converting the
women, as five women in the church to one man indicates; now let us have
a woman ministry and we shall see the men converted." And, he added,
"There is a profound problem here that we have too long overlooked"
(Willard: 76).

Other authors defended the ministry of women because it enriched the
entire church. They noted that many churches were weak in numbers and
would languish or die unless *all* took on the common work. Yet when pastors
were constrained "by the law of necessity" to break personal prejudice and
the letter of Paul's rule and allowed women to take new responsibilities,
they were "amazed at the opening of the mine of spiritual wealth, unknown
and unworked before." Many pastors continued to allow these things "not
compelled by necessity, but for the richness of the ore." This was a latent
power that would never be developed unless Christians recognized another
saying of Paul—that there was neither male nor female in Christ Jesus
(Torrey: 168).

A third argument took a pragmatic position, insisting that women were
already engaged in full ministry and therefore should be recognized. Writers of this persuasion wanted change to be celebrated rather than hidden.
They pointed out that many female missionaries were unable to share their
work in the mixed assemblies of American churches because of Paul's "alleged injunction of silence in the church on the part of women." It was an
awkward situation.

For while it is true that many Christians believe that women are enjoined from publicly preaching the Gospel, either at home or abroad, it is certainly true that scores of

> missionary women are at present doing this very thing. They are telling the good news
> of salvation to heathen men and women publicly from house to house, to little groups
> gathered by the wayside, or to larger groups assembled in the zayats. It is not affirmed
> that a majority of women missionaries are engaged in this kind of work, but that scores
> are doing it with the approval of the boards under which they are serving. If any one
> should raise the technical objection that because of its informal and colloquial charac-
> ter this is not preaching, we are ready to affirm that it comes much nearer the preach-
> ing enjoined in the great commission than does the reading of a theological disquisition
> from the pulpit on Sunday morning, or the discussion of some ethical or sociological
> question before a popular audience on Sunday evening. (Gordon: 910)

The question for A. J. Gordon was not whether the time was right for wom-
en to move into new forms of leadership; the question was whether the
churches would recognize existing ministries and celebrate their power. Just
as Peter was unable to accept the universality of the gospel until his vision of
a sheet descending from heaven showed him the oneness of God's people, it
was argued that "this extraordinary spectacle of ministering women" was
calling the church to recognize life under a new dispensation (921).

The fourth class of arguments to support the changing circumstances of
women reinterpreted the authority of Scripture. For some writers it was
especially important to explain how the specific prohibitions of Paul could
be interpreted alongside the emerging desires of women for full equality in
the church. For others a general reevaluation of all scriptural authority became necessary. Still others combed the Bible to find new ammunition and
specific support for the various ministries of women.

Many liberal thinkers directly challenged the validity of scriptural prohibitions for the nineteenth century. Although Paul did expressly say, "Let the
women keep silent in the churches," John F. Humphreys argued that Christians ought to look at Paul's words "in the light of those times in which they
were uttered." Attempts to solve the problem by implying that women could
speak in social meetings but not in regular assemblies would not do. "The
words are a direct prohibition for the women to speak in the churches." We are
forced to ask, therefore, whether Paul wrote these things "for reasons peculiar
to those times and places, or for reasons which hold good in all places for all
times?" Humphreys believed that a careful examination of the unique circumstances of Gentile women in the ancient world made it understandable that
women were forbidden to teach in the churches. "But no one can claim that
this rule was meant for all women of all time and places" (497–98).

Although Protestants have usually rejected the authority of the church
except as guided by Scripture, conservative church leaders, such as A. J.
Gordon, valued experience as an interpreter of Scripture. "To follow the
voice of the Church apart from that of the written Word has never proved
safe; but, on the other hand, it may be that we need to be admonished not
to ignore the teaching of the deepest spiritual life of the Church in forming
our conclusions concerning the meaning of Scripture." Every spiritual awakening in the history of Protestantism has honored the witness of Christian

women (e.g., Quakers, Wesleyans, and the Salvation Army). It may be that the spiritual intuition of the church has been "far in advance of its exegesis in dealing with this subject" (918–19).

W. S. B. Goodenow emphasized that Paul's understanding of the privilege of speech places responsibilities upon both men and women. Paul was neither "an old bachelor" nor a promoter of women. And Paul was not setting out rules for the Corinthians only, but for all. Christian women must live under the order of creation and should be subordinate to men. However, a woman "need not be shut up in her modest efforts to do good. Let her only keep to her divinely appointed position as the submissive helpmeet of man, and her loving lips, like her tender heart and her gentle hand, shall shed the dew of grace upon the church as well as the home."

> The gospel view of this subject is thus seen to be a plastic one, adaptable to changing times. . . . Scripture left this subject in such shape, that harsher times might keep less cultivated woman in the shade, as they have done; while still the advanced culture of these "last days" should have free scope to receive developed woman's aid in the church, just so fast and so far as developed man himself is ready to accept it as not exhibiting insubordination.

> The Scripture principle does indeed make women absolutely "keep silence," where the men insist upon this as the only sufficient token of their subjection. But whenever the men give express invitation to utterance, this certainly relieves the women from all risk or hindrance in speaking properly in their presence. When the men of the church themselves come forward, as in many little mission churches, and ask, even entreat women to aid them in their worship, then surely they cannot accuse themselves of the insubordination here condemned, if they kindly and helpfully do their part. (Goodenow: 130–31)

In the Methodist Episcopal Church, when a great debate developed over whether women were eligible for membership in the General Conference, several articles appeared to examine the authority of Scripture in this matter. Although some persons might look to Scripture for guidance, a strong case was made by the editors of the *Methodist Review* that Scripture had no authority on this issue. Other denominations might believe that a specific form of church government was found in the Scriptures, but not Methodism. "As a church we interpret the Scriptures on this point in a very liberal way, holding that no form is prescribed and any form is legitimate provided it have providential authority, and is adopted for the promotion of the interest of the divine Kingdom." The eligibility of women as delegates in the General Conference was a governmental question. Therefore, if Scriptures did not determine the question of church government, Scriptures could not be used as a guide in this ecclesiastical debate. "It is not a question of exegesis or interpretation that the Church is to decide, but a simple question of whether woman's eligibility shall be recognized by law, which the General Conference is competent to enact" ("Eligibility of Women": 288, 291). However, the authors of this argument were quick to point out that there were some issues surrounding women and the church that did relate to Scripture. "If such questions as woman's induction into the ministry, or woman's ordination to deacon's or elder's orders, or woman's appointment to the pastorate were before us, we should pronounce them scriptural" (289). "Woman's admission into the General Conference in no wise involves her admission into the ministry, though many antagonists are in self-torture over the prospects of woman's preaching the Gospel." The editors of the *Methodist Review* concluded that when women become part of the General Conference they should be satisfied, "and if not satisfied then the Church should teach [them] the New Testament" ("The Ground of Woman's Eligibility": 463).

Another tactic used to find a way around Pauline prohibitions against women speaking in the churches was to note that the Greek word used in all of these passages referred to a married woman. In the Greek world this was understandable, for most women were married, but there was reason to doubt whether Paul's words ever applied to unmarried women or widows. Perhaps in the nineteenth century the ministry of spinsters and widows did not need to abide by Paul's injunctions (Torrey: 169). Sometimes the examination of one or two words got very specific. Several writers presented detailed analyses of the Greek verbs to speak, tell, say, babble, prattle, preach, pray, prophesy, and exhort. They argued that Paul never prohibited women from preaching, praying, or prophesying in large or small assemblies in the churches. Rather, Paul was concerned that the women at Corinth keep out of all the babble and wrangling in the Corinthian church. Women were instructed to ask their husbands at home, because it was "a shame for a woman to prate and gabble to no profit or education in the assembly" (Loomis: 13). Another way of interpreting Paul's statements forbidding unveiled women to pray or prophesy was to reason that he was regulating a permissible activity. His concern was not whether women should speak but how they did it. "Why not understand that this was a permission to do it; only she must remember to avoid a scandal by continuing veiled" (Torrey: 169; see also Gordon: 914).

All efforts to relate biblical authority to the situation of women in the churches examined the usual texts and searched for new passages. Inasmuch as the conservative position grounded its defense of the status quo on biblical material, anyone seeking change had to do something with these passages. Thus, most progressive writers argued that certain Scripture passages were not binding—because they were not written for our times; because the Spirit spoke in the church as well as through the Bible; because, if modern men invited women to speak, women could preach and remain appropriately subordinate; because women's place in church government was not a scriptural issue; or because Paul's prohibitions were intended only for married women, or babbling women, or to regulate the manner of female preaching.

The Woman's Bible

Probably the most massive attempt to confront biblical authority occurred with the publication of *The Woman's Bible* in the late 1890s. Many
years earlier Elizabeth Cady Stanton, noted feminist, had anguished over the
way biblical material oppressed women. In her autobiography she remembered that in 1886

> the thought came to me that it would be well to collect every biblical reference to
> women in one small compact volume, and see on which side the balance of influence
> really was. To this end I proposed to organize a committee of competent women, with
> some Latin, Greek and Hebrew scholars in England and the United States, for a thor-
> ough revision of the Old and New Testaments, and to ascertain what the status of
> woman really was under the Jewish and Christian religion. As the Church has thus far
> interpreted the Bible as teaching woman's subjection, and none of the revisions by
> learned ecclesiastics have thrown any new light on the question, it seemed to me pre-
> eminently proper and timely for women themselves to review the book. As they are
> now studying theology in many institutions of learning, asking to be ordained as
> preachers, elders, deacons, and to be admitted, as delegates, to Synods and General
> Assemblies, and are refused on Bible grounds, it seemed to me high time for women to
> consider those scriptural arguments and authorities. (1898:390)

Stanton wrote to women to invite them to join such a committee but
could not "make the women understand what we wanted to do." Some of
those she asked said that "the Bible had no special authority with them," or
that "woman's sphere was clearly marked out in Scriptures, and all attempt
at emancipation was flying in the face of Providence." Still others wrote that
"the revisions made by men thus far, had been so many acts of sacrilege,
and they did hope women would not add their influence, to weaken the
faith of the people in the divine origin of the Holy Book, for, if men and
women could change it in one particular, they could in all" (1898:391). In
spite of this response Elizabeth Cady Stanton continued to work on the project. With her friend, Miss Frances Lord, and her daughter, Mrs. Stanton
Blatch, "We purchased some cheap Bibles, cut out the texts, pasted them at
the head of the page, and underneath, wrote out our commentaries as
clearly and concisely as possible" (1898:391). Some women consented to join
a revising committee, but later withdrew their names, "fearing the work
would be too radical." "Perhaps," Stanton wrote, "they feared their faith
might be disturbed by the strong light of investigation" (1898:452). However, by 1895 *The Woman's Bible* began to take shape. In reading many
commentators on the Bible, Stanton was surprised to see how little they had
to say about women. "The more I read, the more keenly I felt the importance of convincing women that the Hebrew mythology had no special
claim to a higher origin than that of the Greeks" (1898:452). She devoted all
of her time to "biblical criticism and ecclesiastical history, and found no
explanation for the degraded status of women under all religions and in all
the so-called 'Holy Books'" (1898:453).

When Part I of the book was published in November 1895, it created a "great sensation" (1898:453). The introduction, written by Stanton, summarized the Bible's position on women:

> Why is it more ridiculous for women to protest against her present status in the Old and New Testament, in the ordinances and discipline of the church, than in the statutes and constitution of the State? . . . Women have compelled their legislators in every state in this Union to so modify their statutes for women that the old common law is now almost a dead letter. Why not compel Bishops and Revising Committees to modify their creeds and dogmas? Forty years ago it seemed as ridiculous to timid, time-serving retrograde folk for women to demand an expurgated edition of the laws, as it now does to demand an expurgated edition of Liturgies and the Scriptures. Come, come, my conservative friend, wipe the dew off your spectacles, and see that the world is moving. (1895–98:10)

It was a controversial and unpopular book with the church-going public.

Alongside such efforts to counter or modify the power of biblical authority other writers used Scripture to support the contributions of women in the church. Barbara Kellison studied Scripture to lift up those stories and verses that specifically empowered women. She recalled and celebrated the prophetic work of Miriam, Deborah, Huldah, Nodiah, Ruth, and Anna. She remembered the preaching of the Samaritan woman and the company of women that followed Jesus throughout his earthly journeys. Kellison wrote that "there were female laborers in the gospel in the Apostles' day, and that they labored with men, and that they still have a right to continue their labor, and that in a public capacity as well as men." Some of those disciples whom Jesus sent two by two were women, "for he [Jesus] knew all their hearts and saw that it would be more prudent for her to go with her husband than alone." She would leave an example for future generations, "that other women might have the right" (21). Women must have been very active preachers in the early church, continued this argument, because Paul was always writing to churches giving "his brethren strict charge to help those women who labored with him in the gospel, as he knew they could not labor successfully unless they were assisted." If the work of the men was clearly preaching, why not say the same of the work of women? "No doubt there were more women preachers with him [Jesus] than men." If men are allowed to continue in this service, then women should be also (25–26). Furthermore, all of the Gospels told of the commissioning of women to preach the gospel on Easter morning. Jesus met the women and said, "Be not afraid, go and tell my brethren." "This act of the Savior shows that he approved of women preaching and not only women but also men, and, if he had opposed it, he never would have commissioned a woman to preach the first resurrection sermon that was ever delivered in the presence of men" (36).

Finally, those who wished to justify women's preaching and prophesying reminded modern Christians that they were living in the dispensation of the Spirit. The day of Pentecost ushered in a new economy captured in the prophecy of Joel as quoted by Peter. One of its most salient characteristics was the promise that "your sons and your daughters shall prophesy." This was "woman's equal warrant with man's for telling out the Gospel of the grace of God." "To prophesy" was not "merely to foretell future events, but to communicate religious truth in general under a Divine inspiration." Prophecy was not special prediction or the miracle of tongues, which passed away with the apostles. The Holy Spirit's perpetual presence in the church implied "the equal perpetuity of His gifts and endowments" (Gordon: 911–12).

Arguments Against Change

The conservative leadership of the churches responded to these arguments in many ways, writing long documents and going to great length to defend the status quo. For our purpose I will divide these writings into three groups:

First, there was the defense from biblical authority. In examining Paul's prohibitions Cyrus Cort refused to make exceptions. Even if we do not understand "the grounds or the propriety of his emphatic prohibition of women praying or speaking in Christian assemblies," this is Paul's teaching, "in the most explicit and didactic terms." Whether we can explain it or not, we know that whatever is clearly scriptural is right and for the best interests of society (129). Paul was progressive in many things, "the most liberal of all the Apostles." He vindicated the right of Gentile converts to become part of the New Testament church without following Jewish law. If Christianity was going to depart from the established customs with regard to women, "St. Paul would have been pre-eminently the one to enunciate and emphasize the new departure" (124). However, we find that he did not do so. "Paul did not need to live in our day in order to know the mind of the Spirit, and that the rule he gave is permanent in its nature, because it is based on reasons that are permanent" (Knowlton: 334).

> There are people who say: If Paul would live today and in America he would speak differently. He wrote his instructions on the background of his age with its conceptions of inferiority of the female sex. Such apostolic teachings, they say, must be taken in an historical sense. Now this interpretation would be all right in the mouth of a champion of modern theology; but one who does not want to give up the formal principle of the Reformation, namely that the Holy Scripture is source and rule of all faith and practice cannot afford to take that view. If we can not believe that in a question like the one here under consideration Paul, under the guidance of the Holy Ghost, said something that is true and binding to-day just as well as at the time of the founding of the church, then we are on dangerous ground. (Neve:412)

Those who argued from biblical authority had particular ways of responding to pressures for change. A woman's claim that she was called by God to be a minister of the gospel was condemned by Robert Dabney as a perilous perversion of the true doctrine of vocation. "The same Spirit who really calls the true minister also dictated the Holy Scriptures. . . . the Spirit calls no person to do what the word dictated by him, forbids. The Spirit cannot contradict himself" (2:100). Indeed, the only way anyone can do or teach something contrary to Scripture is to sustain the claim by a miracle. All who claim supernatural inspiration must prove it by supernatural works. And when any of those "preach-ing women" work a genuine miracle they can "stand on the ground of Deborah or Anna" (Dabney 2:97). Furthermore, all those who are called by the Spirit know that the call is "never complete until the believing choice of the brethren has confirmed it." The community must try the spirits to see whether they are of God. But, inasmuch as the community has no rule apart from Scripture, the answer is clear. The word teaches that God does not call a woman and, therefore, the community can never confirm her ministry (Dabney: 2:101).

According to Stephen Knowlton, Scripture gave two specific reasons why women had to be subordinate: one was the order of creation and the second was her weakness in paradise. God did not create the man for the woman, but the woman for the man. Female subordination was not a passing custom; it was grounded in creation. If a woman insisted upon speaking in public assemblies "where all stand upon a common level," she thereby denied any subordination to the other sex (331–32). The second reason was that the woman—not Adam—was originally deceived "in the transgression." "Perhaps," wrote Knowlton, "this implies that woman having taken the lead once, and made such bad work of it, there is a special fitness that she hereafter march in the rear. She made a little speech once that was the world's undoing: now let her keep silence" (332). Building upon the scriptural principle of subordination, Robert Dabney argued that no woman could ever be a preacher. Within the New Testament church "teaching" and "ruling" went together. All preachers were called to spiritual rule, to admonish, command, censure, and even excommunicate in order to conserve the fruits of their labors. But how could a woman do this if one of her male converts included her husband, whom she was bound to obey at home? When women asked for the right to preach as lay persons, they were told that public lay preaching for men or women was not legitimate (2:103).

Both sides of the debate focused upon particular words and phrases to promote their position. For example, Dabney made much of Paul's words about headcoverings. Men were supposed to preach in public with their heads uncovered, thereby standing forth as God's herald and representative. A covered head was a dishonor to the office and the God which the office represented. But for women to appear at any public religious assembly un-veiled was a glaring impropriety. It was "contrary to the subordination of the position assigned her by her Maker, and to the modesty and reserve suitable to her sex; and even nature settled the point by giving her long hair as her natural veil" (2:104). Obviously women could not be preachers.

A second type of argument sought to celebrate the expanding role of women in the churches while denying women the right to preach in large meetings. It was an awkward position but genuinely defended. Woman was the equal of man and his help. In some ways she was inferior, but in other respects she was superior. She was his counterpart. They were not equal with regard to rule and authority, but they were equal in their respective spheres.

> A woman should not take such a part in religious meeting, as shall seem to be assuming authority; she should not be a public religious teacher; she should not put herself forward and make herself conspicuous. She is then forbidden to lead in any of the exercises of public worship. In all large and promiscuous religious meetings she would be out of her sphere to take part. In the business of the church it is not her place to deliberate, and counsel, and vote, except by courtesy. She is debarred certainly, by the Apostle from the ministry, the duties of which belong to men.
>
> Yet in ordinary social religious meetings, the instructions of the Apostle do not forbid her to take part. But they teach her to perform such part, at such times, and in such circumstances as become the subjection and modesty of her sex. ("Woman's Place in Religious Meetings": 24)

Women, therefore, should share their gifts in the church. Women had unsurpassed social powers that were especially appropriate in the "social, conference exercises of the prayer meeting." "Men are engaged for the live-long day in the distractions and toils and worldliness of business. It is hard for them to leave these for the atmosphere of the prayer meeting. Woman is shielded from many of these withering and chilling influences." The social meeting should benefit from her contributions not merely her silent worship. She could help as an active, living, speaking disciple. Although a prayer meeting was often thinly attended, it was desirable that women take active parts. "The social meeting is the becoming place for her to testify what the Saviour has done for her" ("Woman's Place": 25).

This important distinction between large promiscuous assemblies and small social or prayer meetings became a much-discussed question. When a charge was brought in October 1876 against the Reverend Isaac M. See of Newark for permitting and encouraging a woman to preach publicly and to teach in his church, it was taken before the Presbytery of Newark and the Synod of New Jersey. Reverend See argued that women were allowed to speak and teach in the smaller social meetings of the church and that there was no scriptural authority for the distinction between large and small meetings. Nevertheless the Synod insisted that inviting "women to preach at the regular public services of the Church was irregular and unwise, and contrary to the views of the Scripture and the Church order derived from them." In the same document, however, the Synod also recorded its high appreciation for the services of women in other departments of Christian evangelism and benevolence (*Case of the Rev. E. R. Craven*). The minutes of this case show that there was great effort to distinguish between the public teaching and preaching of women as ordained leaders, as lay persons in the social meetings of the church, and as lay persons invited into a Sunday pulpit (*Case of the Rev. E. R. Craven:* 13). These were difficult distinctions but ones which those who feared change sought to maintain.

Finally, a third group of arguments rejected the movement of women into new arenas of ministry by citing general social and historical reasons. Biblical interpretations notwithstanding there were other reasons why such new changes should not be allowed. Cyrus Cort wrote, "If there were any doubt in regard to the meaning of [biblical] language so plain, Church history furnishes a practical commentary." Women had never been allowed to officiate as ministers in any of the orthodox and historical denominations. Women could enter only the outer court of the Jewish Temple and were seated separately in all synagogues. Although there were a few extraordinary and exceptional cases, in "thousands of years among hundreds of millions of God's covenant people" only a few women ever took positions of significant leadership (127).

Henry J. Van Dyke, Sr., offered the argument that women dared not accept the tasks of public preacher or evangelist because of their role as mothers. The great disability of a woman for the work of ministry was "directly connected with her physical constitution, with the fact that she can be a mother, and that motherhood, with all its burdens and blessings, is her divinely appointed destiny." Everyone agreed that celibacy defrauded men and women of their rights to the sanctity of the home. If it was not good for male ministers to be alone, "it must be equally not good for preaching women to be alone." Yet, this raised a delicate point. "A child-bearing woman and a nursing mother is disqualified for the exposure and nervous strain of the pulpit and the exhausting duties of the pastoral office, by a regard for public decency, for her own health and the health of her offspring. To lay this new burden on her soul and body is a refinement of cruelty." That this argument could apply also to other occupations and professions for women was beside the point. Civilization and Christianity ought to remove the obstacles to and the burdens from marriage and teach men how to support the weak (123). Frances Willard called this the "earth-born argument." Those who denied women the ministry for physical reasons took "as a basis in this calculation the average American woman as she appears to-day, deteriorated by the corset habit and the senseless costume, of which high-heeled shoes and draperies equally hideous and unhealthful are salient features." In her natural strength the combination of mother and minister was invulnerable. If one were to select a "being on this earth who could best comprehend and most movingly depict the mystery of God manifest in the flesh, conceived by the Holy Ghost, born of the Virgin Mary, who would not say that being was a mother?" (64–66).

Yet many writers failed to see things this way. A female pastor could not leave her little children for her public tasks without "criminal neglect and their probable ruin." And if anyone tried to argue that this limitation would not apply to unmarried women, they were forgetting that marriage was the proper condition of all women. Celibacy was not a crime, but even the sphere God assigned to unmarried women was private and domestic (Dabney: 2:113). "Women's work" was the noblest and most momentous work done on earth. An evangelist might convert thousands, but the worthiness of his public success belonged fully as much to his modest mother as to himself. "The instrumentality of the mother's training in the salvation of her children is mighty and decisive; the influence of the minister over his hundreds is slight and non-essential" (Dabney: 2:114). In essence, ministry was not worth doing when compared with mothering. Some scholars combined this judgment with Scripture and noted that women were actually "saved through childbearing, if they continued in faith, and love, and holiness with sobriety." It was a promise made to all women on these conditions ("Woman's Place": 29).

Education created another difficulty for women. If the preaching ministry had any value, it ought not be opened up to the "pastor's wife" or "anyone who knows enough to talk for thirty minutes on religious subjects." We ought to keep the Sabbath ministrations for those who have received training (Seebach: 580–81). Then why not educate women for this work? It was not that simple. Women could not combine household and pastoral duties. A woman had to work near her husband's store or factory or medical practice. If an unmarried woman sought to prepare for ministry, "the education for such a sphere should begin at an age considerably earlier than that at which most women can be considered confirmed spinsters." But even if there was "a moral, healthful helpful woman permanently without family ties or the desire for them," a woman's mind was not suited for ministry.

> The quality of a woman's mind is different from that of a man. This does not mean necessarily that it is inferior. It simply means that things do not appeal to her from the same side, do not appear to her in the same light, as to man. We are not to be startled any more by saying that reason is the province of the masculine mind, intuition of the feminine. Yet this means that a woman ordinarily cannot convince a man of a thing by argument. In logical presentation of truth, she is usually a failure. Thus arises a serious question: Can a woman's preaching win and hold men in the Church? And when we consider that the great lack of the Church in all ages has been such a virile and logical interpretation of truth as will appeal to *men*, and hold their allegiance, this question assumes large proportions. The church *has* the women—has always had them; she needs the men! (Seebach: 581–83)

Robert Dabney offered one final reason to discredit the movement of women into new responsibilities in the churches. Although the concerns of church women did not spring exclusively from the secular crusade for women's rights, the preaching of women and the demand for masculine political rights were so "synchronous" that they had to be viewed as "two parts of one common impulse." And if the movement for women's rights was based upon the radical conviction that society ought to disregard all distinctions of sex and allow married women to have independent control of their property, then the logic of this "social contract" thinking had to be judged totally unacceptable. "The woman is not designed by God, nor entitled to all the franchises in society to which the male is entitled." Indeed, the consequences of this revolution would be so terrible that all marriages and children would suffer.

> This common movement for "women's rights", and women's preaching, must be regarded, then, as simply infidel. It cannot be candidly upheld without attacking the inspiration and authority of the Scriptures. We are convinced that there is only one safe attitude for Christians, presbyters, and church courts to assume towards it. This is utterly to discountenance it, as they do any other assault of fidelity on God's truth and Kingdom. (2:114–18)

Conclusion

The struggle of American church women for recognition and increased ministry during the nineteenth century was a complicated story. Most of the writings used in this paper were printed after the Civil War. Although I have no reason to believe that earlier debates used different arguments, the depth of concern and treatment of the woman question had spread to all major Protestant groups by the end of the century. A more systematic examination of each denomination might reveal confessional differences in argumentation, but that was not the purpose of this study.

Pressures for recognition and promoting women's gifts in the church were real. Advocates for change believed that this was (1) grounded in the work of the Holy spirit, (2) justified by practical considerations, (3) already happening in the mission field, and (4) acceptable because of new enlightened interpretations of Scripture. Those who defended the status quo and the subordinate position of women in the churches did not agree. They argued that (1) biblical authority prohibited these changes, (2) women's role in the church was expanding enough under proper limitations, and (3) historical, social, intellectual, or political reasons made any changes in the place of women totally unacceptable. It is a debate that continues into the twentieth century.

WORKS CONSULTED

Butler, Josephine
1892   "Woman's Place in the Church." *Magazine of Christian Literature* 6: 30-32.

Case of the Rev. E. R. Craven against the Rev. I. M. See in the Presbytery of Newark and the Synod of New Jersey.

n.d.   An eighteen page pamphlet covering a case begun in October 1876.

Cort, Cyrus

1882   "Woman Preaching Viewed in the Light of God's Word and Church History." *Reformed Quarterly Review* 29: 123–30.

Dabney, Robert L.

1891   "The Public Preaching of Women." In *Discussions: Evangelical.* 2 vols. Richmond, VA: Presbyterian Committee of Publication. This article originally appeared in *Southern Presbyterian Review* in October 1879.

"Eligibility of Women Not a Scriptural Question."

1891   *Methodist Review* 75: 287–91.

Goodenow, W. S. B.

1877   "Woman's Voice in the Church." *New Englander* 36: 115–31.

Gordon, A. J.

1894   "The Ministry of Women." *Missionary Review of the World* 7: 910–21.

"Ground of Woman's Eligibility."

1891   *Methodist Review* 75: 456–63.

Humphreys, John F.

1893   "Woman's Work on the Church." *Homiletic Review* 25: 495–99.

Kellison, Barbara

1862   *The Rights of Women in the Church.* Dayton, OH: Herald and Banner Office. This forty-four page pamphlet was written by "a member of the Des Moines Christian Conference, Iowa."

Knowlton, Stephen

1867   "The Silence of Women in the Churches." *Congregational Quarterly* 9: 329–34.

Lee, Jarena

1849   *Religious Experience and Journal of Mrs. Jarena Lee, Giving an Account of Her Call to Preach the*

Gospel. Philadelphia: no publisher. Quotations are cited from *Black Women in Nineteenth-Century American Life*, ed. Bert James Loewenberg and Ruth Bogin. University Park: Pennsylvania University Press, 1976.

Lee, Luther

1853 *Women's Right to Preach the Gospel: A Sermon Preached at the Ordination of the Rev. Miss Antionette L. Brown at South Butler, Wayne County, N. Y., September 15, 1853*. Syracuse, NY: no publisher.

Loomis, H.

1874 *May a Woman Speak in a Promiscuous Assembly?* Brooklyn: no publisher. A version of this pamphlet was also published in *Congregational Quarterly* 16 (1874).

Neve, J. L.

1903 "Shall Women Preach in the Congregation? An Exegetical Treatise." *Lutheran Quarterly* 33: 409–13.

Pfatteicher, Ernst P. H.

1899 "Woman as a Congregational Voter." *Lutheran Church Review* 18: 460–78.

Scott, Donald M.

1978 *From Office to Profession: The New England Ministry, 1750–1850*. Philadelphia: University of Pennsylvania Press.

Seebach, Margaret R.

1903 "Shall Women Preach?" *Lutheran Quarterly* 33: 579–83.

Stanton, Elizabeth Cady

1898 *Eighty Years and More: Reminiscences, 1815–1897*. New York: Schocken.

Stanton, Elizabeth Cady, et al., eds.

1895–98 *The Woman's Bible*. New York: European Publishing Co.

Torrey, Charles W.

1867 "Women's Sphere in the Church." *Congregational Quarterly* 9: 163–71.

Van Dyke, Henry J., Sr.
    1888   "Shall Women Be Licensed to Preach?" Reprinted in Willard, pp. 113–28, this article first appeared in *Homiletic Review* in 1887.

Willard, Frances E.
    1888   *Woman in the Pulpit.* Boston: Lothrop.

"Woman's Place in Religious Meetings."
    1868   *Congregational Review* 8: 22–29.

V

The Bible and American Peace Movements
Charles Chatfield

"Do not kill." "Resist not evil." "Blessed are the peacemakers." Whatever the injunctions meant to Jesus, the early church, or classical theologians,
they came to Americans from the court of King James. Whatever may be
the revealed truth or accurate translation of the Bible, its historic influence
derives from its received texts and the contexts in which they were read.
This account of the Bible and American peace movements is therefore a
study in the history of ideas rather than an essay in biblical theology or
criticism. Peace movements were loosely organized efforts to mobilize public
support; only rarely did they elicit a ground swell of public opinion. They
addressed differing constituencies and programs. Their leaders held varying
ideas about the meaning and authority of the Bible; the source of peace,
justice, and war; and the nature and destiny of humanity. Nonetheless,
peace movements in all their diversity have been grounded in some measure
upon the Bible and upon the richness of its interpretation.

Three Contesting Traditions:
Dodge, Worcester, and Just War Theory

The range of biblical peace advocacy was represented in the writings of
two founders of organized peace activity in the United States and in the
frustration of early programs. Peace societies sprang up independently in the
wake of the Napoleonic wars. The French Revolution had ushered in an era
of warfare that kept the United States in intermittent conflict for a generation. The War of 1812 was interpreted by some as a divine judgment and
scourge upon the nation for straying from its original commission. Prevalent
partisan and sectional feeling about the war dissuaded peace advocates from
organizing until, in August 1815, David Low Dodge and some friends
formed the New York Peace Society.

Dodge (1774–1852) had been reared in a Connecticut Calvinist home
where his first books were a hymnal, a catechism, and Scripture. He added
works of history and ethics and became a school teacher. After marriage he

became a successful merchant without relinquishing his interest in theological and moral issues. In 1805 he was led to examine the ethics of self-defense by violence and this led him in turn to explore the ethics of war. Drawing his norms from Scripture, Dodge concluded that Christians should abjure the violence on which states rely. Dodge regarded the Bible as a book of ordinances for a community subject to ultimate authority not of this world. "The Mediator's kingdom is, in a special sense, the gospel dispensation . . . spiritual, heavenly, and divine," he wrote (Brock, 1972:130). Those who are loyal to it must acquiesce in its laws, notably the law of love. Dodge contrasted the kingdom of Christ with earthly kingdoms and inferred the "impropriety of the subjects of the Mediator's kingdom becoming political Christians and enrolling themselves with the men of this world" (Brock, 1972:163–64). His polemic aroused rejoinders. In 1812 he prepared *War Inconsistent with the Religion of Jesus Christ*, in which he argued that war is not only inhuman, unwise, and criminal but also "unlawful upon gospel principles" (Brock, 1972:2). His analysis restated a recurrent biblical tradition.

Biblical nonresistance, which Dodge traced to the early church, has been aptly designated by Geoffrey Nuttall as "The Law of Christ" (15). It informed medieval sects such as the Waldenses and the Czech Brethren. It became identified with certain Reformation groups which emigrated to America, notably the Mennonites and the Church of the Brethren, with later pietistic groups such as the German Inspirationalists and the Renewed Moravian Church, and with nineteenth-century native sects such as the Adventists and Jehovah's Witnesses. Although it was primarily associated with the so-called peace churches (Mennonites, Brethren, and Quakers), biblical nonresistance was a waning tradition among them by the time that Dodge wrote, but it appealed to a handful of individuals from other religious communions (Brock, 1968:159–329). It was based on the authority of specific scriptural texts understood as divine injunctions. Indeed, in medieval and Reformation times it had been rooted in the return to Scripture. New Testament references underwrote the Mennonite Confession of Faith of Dortrecht, Holland, in 1632, for example. A Mennonite historian has written of his church, "Since her organization she has based her position entirely upon the Word of God. . . . 'Thus saith the Lord' was her basis" (Hartzler: 43). Nonresistance was a New Testament injunction, a matter of obeying Christ and the apostles as they were received through scriptural texts.

Put in this way, the duty of nonresistants became sharply defined. They were separated from the world by a sword forbidden to them. They had to submit themselves to government in all things except those deemed incompatible with God's law, especially taking an oath of allegiance and military service. They were confronted with an ethical dualism: there are two sets of laws, one for the world and another for the disciples of God. The state must and will fight wars; true Christians should neither willfully offend nor violently resist force. Not only did nonresistants feel prohibited by God from going to war for the state, they felt that they could not forcibly obstruct the judgment of government nor share its responsibilities. If the law of love was clear, its application was another matter. Nonresistance was only one of a complex set of motives for which peace sects suffered persecution in Europe and fled to America, but it imbued the heritage they carried. It placed nonresistant Mennonites, Brethren, and Quakers in difficult positions under colonial governments and in the Revolutionary War, when their support was required in the form of fines or service by governments that had granted them sanctuary. It created dilemmas for later nonresistants with regard to the legalization of slavery, the use of force and capital punishment to uphold the social order, and service in the Civil War. However it was compromised among the sects, the nonresistant tradition persisted and was a source of antimilitarism and peace advocacy in American thought. It was the basis for almost all conscientious objection to warfare before World War I, and it was recognized at that time in laws granting limited exemption from military service.

Biblical nonresistance was adapted to the peace impulse by David Low Dodge and a long line of successors. However, an alternative antiwar perspective can be traced to a contemporary of Dodge, Noah Worcester, and to his different philosophical and biblical roots. Worcester (1758–1837) was the founder of the Massachusetts Peace Society, the major peace organization from 1815 to 1828. He largely set the course for the following generation. A liberal Congregational minister, he had fought in the Revolutionary War, but, measuring war against Scripture, he had developed an antipathy that the War of 1812 confirmed. In the midst of it he wrote the *Solemn Review of the Custom of War*, a classic repudiation of warfare. No less biblically grounded than Dodge's tract, Worcester's work reflects more clearly than Dodge's the influence of humanism upon New England Congregationalism. It is well known that many leaders of Enlightenment thought were advocates of peace. Benjamin Franklin criticized warfare and published Pierre-Andre Gargaz's appeal for a congress of nations. Jean Jacques Rousseau also urged a federation of nations. Joseph Priestley, Thomas Paine, George Washington, Thomas Jefferson, and Benjamin Rush extended humanitarianism to peace. They valued harmony in international relations comparable with that which they assumed in the natural order. Worcester restated a prevalent sentiment but, what is more, he fused Enlightenment humanitarianism with biblical concern.

Even Dodge reflected the emphases of humanitarianism, progress, and amelioration, but Worcester amalgamated them in his theology. His position was based upon general principles of the New Testament rather than specific texts, the moral standards of Christ rather than ordinances. For liberal Congregationalists and Unitarians, biblical authority was compatible with natural law; in fact, they believed that the Bible instructs humanity in universal moral laws. Jesus was understood in this tradition to be a teacher, not a lawgiver. Worcester contrasted war with the "temper of Jesus" and with the "spirit, design, and glory of the gospel." Like Congregational divine William Ellery Channing, in whose Boston study the Massachusetts Peace Society was formed, Worcester interpreted Christianity as "only a system of divine instruction, relating duty to happiness" (Brock, 1972:14, 17, 21). Worcester wrote that society improves as it becomes enlightened, that war is a relic of barbarism and a threat to modern republicanism. His peace program included education ("to open the eyes of the people to the blessings of peace") as well as rational instruments of conflict resolution—a confederation and a court of nations. *Solemn Review* was widely circulated in the United States and England. It contributed to the formation of peace societies in both countries and outlined their programs of education and internationalism.

This interpretation of Scripture was present too in the heritage of the Society of Friends (Quakers), which was enriched in this period by the publication of older works by William Penn and William Barclay and by the fresh writings of Anthony Benezet, Thomas Clarkson (of England), Jessey Kersey, and James Mott. To the intense zeal of their seventeenth-century origins Friends added an abiding humanitarianism. Nonresistance became an established Quaker tradition for which Friends were persecuted during the Revolution, but it was broadened by an equally strong emphasis on loving service. Quakers took Scripture seriously, of course. The antiwar writings of James Mott in 1815 were scarcely distinguishable from Dodge's in this regard (Brock, 1972). But for Friends, scriptural authority was mediated by the "inner light" of individual understanding. This view was compatible with Enlightenment philosophy and was the basis on which outstanding Quakers would join Protestant liberals in a broad twentieth-century peace movement after a long withdrawal into individual pietism during the nineteenth century. Noah Worcester, organizing peace activity at the beginning of that century, may well have been influenced by his contact with Quaker views on war.

In the writings of Worcester and Dodge, alternative biblical traditions became focused on the problem of war. The societies they stimulated were frustrated in their attempt to resolve the two traditions and by the strength of a third, the so-called just war theory. Worcester's Massachusetts Peace Society, Dodge's New York Peace Society, and other groups formed about the same time became related in 1828 to the first national organization, the American Peace Society. For a decade its leader was William Ladd (1778–1841), an indefatigable sea captain from Maine. Ladd traveled widely, wrote, preached, and organized for peace. His society recruited among colleges and churches and established a regular periodical, *The Advocate of Peace*. Its agents focused attention on specific foreign policy issues fostering Anglo-American entente and opposing the Mexican War. They promoted a realistic understanding of war and advocated alternatives such as a congress of nations and arbitration. They also gave attention to domestic injustice, notably slavery. What Ladd was to the national movement, Elihu Burritt (1810–1879) was to its transnational outreach. A former blacksmith and a linguistic wizard, Burritt enlisted peace advocates, internationalists, and workers in common cause. He labored in Britain and the United States, and he founded a League of Universal Brotherhood based on individual pledges to abjure warfare.

Burritt and Ladd, like their colleagues and successors in the American Peace Society, were internationalists seeking realistic alternatives to war. They were actuated by humanitarian concerns which, they insisted, had a religious and scriptural foundation. They sought allies among other reform groups and in the churches. They were frustrated, and the major source of their frustration was public apathy. For forty years foreign affairs were a minor concern for Americans. Wars were extensions of a distant frontier. Apathy toward peace was grounded in secularism, too, and in a fatalism closely related to the dominant tradition known as just war theory.

This theory was formulated by Augustine of Hippo and, reformulated by Thomas Aquinas, has formal status in Catholic thought. Its position among Protestants has been informal but not less strong. The theory was given two formulations by Augustine. One version was expressed in his letter to Boniface during the Donatist controversy; there Augustine seemed to argue that warfare against pagans would be just. A more profound formulation was presented in *City of God*; there Augustine denied that war or any other civil institution can be intrinsically just. Assuming the now-classic dualism between the heavenly state of grace to which Christians are called and the natural state of society in which they live, Augustine sought to construct a bridge ethic, a standard on the basis of which Christians could make relative choices. He tried to bring even the state under the judgment of a standard that could not be fully achieved in the world. Warfare might be relatively justified, in this view, in terms of the merits of its cause, conduct, and consequences (Peachey).

Protestants inherited a common-sense version of just war thought. Some approached the crusading spirit of Augustine's Donatist letter, especially in defending wars against fellow Christians in Europe or the indigenous people of America. Others adopted Augustine's position in *City of God*, judging war on its secular merits. This disposition was reinforced in the United States by secularism, individualism, and fatalism. Separation of church and state in the United States strengthened a tendency to judge political policy in purely secular terms. Moreover, the highly individualistic reading of the Bible which was characteristic of Protestantism and reinforced by the culture, consecrated an ethics of personal behavior. Finally, most American Christians assumed that war was inevitable in the process of social struggle that they found recorded in Scripture, the Reformation, and their own revolution. This fatalism made it even easier to sanction conflicts such as the wars against the Indians and the Civil War. In short, although biblical rhetoric was employed in support of warfare, the dominant Christian tradition was not militant. Rather, Christians tended to accept war on secular terms, to imbue it with moral qualities of civil religion, and to relegate Christian ethics to individual behavior, all of which contributed to the public apathy that so frustrated the advocates of peace.

However, there was a second source of frustration, one intrinsic to the peace movement itself. The basic issue was whether to oppose publicly all wars or only aggressive ones. Early in its history the American Peace Society took the broad view, reflecting Worcester's thought. Increasingly, though, William Ladd became converted to absolute nonresistance from his study of the Bible, from the ambiguities of trying to isolate defensive wars, and from his association with other nonresistants in Britain and the United States. The society split into moderate and nonresistant wings. By 1837 the nonresistants passed a new constitution which pledged the society to oppose all war, but this wing itself splintered. Radicals, including Henry C. Wright, Adin Ballou, and William Lloyd Garrison, sponsored a more thoroughly nonresistant movement with which they associated the slavery issue and feminism. In 1838 they formed the New England Non-Resistance Society. Moderates reasserted their influence in the American Peace Society within a decade and maintained a broadly internationalist program, while Garrisonian nonresistants became caught up in abolitionism. The internal controversy sapped the movement and frustrated its outreach. Both moderates and nonresistant wings largely capitulated to the moral claims of the Civil War. The American Peace Society even denied the existence of a state of war, regarding it as a police action to thwart rebellion. On the other hand, nonresistants such as Wright and Garrison endorsed the war against slavery. Thus many peace advocates decried the horror of war while upholding the necessity or even the exceptional morality of the antislavery crusade. Some affirmed their personal pacifism while justifying the nation's war effort. There were few exceptions. Elihu Burritt and Jonathan P. Blanchard, treasurer of the American Peace Society, reaffirmed their opposition to war, but when Blanchard canvassed the earlier signers of Burritt's antiwar pledge he found only two or three still loyal to it. Organized and principled peace advocacy ceased for the duration.

An antiwar witness was maintained among the peace churches. Mennonites and Brethren largely refused military service but accepted alternatives such as payment of commutation fines, interpreting personal nonresistance to proscribe both fighting and resisting the claims of civil authority. Some sectarians entered the army, of course, but their communions maintained the traditional dualism separating the ethical alternatives open to Christian individuals and civil authorities. Quakers found it more difficult to develop a consistent position for several reasons: the role assigned to individual conscience in their ethical tradition, their historic antislavery witness, and their greater readiness to accept civic responsibility. Quaker responses to the demands of war ranged from participation in the army and noncombatant service to commutation through fines and absolute noncooperation. However, Friends consistently refused to allow their pacifism to be confused with political opposition to war and government, and they lobbied for exemptions for conscientious objectors. Both Union and Confederate governments made commutation possible during the war, and the Lincoln government was especially lenient with religious objectors, putting them in noncombatant service when possible and pardoning or paroling absolute resisters. Oppression existed in the North, but objectors were more seriously persecuted in the South. Nonetheless, all members of the peace churches who attempted to remain true to their traditions suffered the torments of conscience. Principled opposition to warfare was upheld at considerable cost, and the witness came mostly from those religious sects that had not been active in the antebellum peace program.

Internationalism and Liberal Pacifism

Changes in American society and religious thought in the half century following the Civil War strengthened internationalism and supplemented the grounds of absolute pacifism. A reaction to the compromised record of peace advocates during the war was exemplified by the formation of the Universal Peace Union in 1866. Its founder and leader until his death was Alfred Love (1830–1913), a Philadelphia woolens manufacturer and Quaker who identified his principled noncooperation during the war with Garrison. In fact, Love attracted remnants of the New England nonresistants. His organization interpreted nonviolence as a way of life, opposed all war, and avoided direct political involvement. Nonetheless, its leaders took positions on foreign policy and extended their concerns to domestic justice, notably the rights of labor. They worked to "remold society in a spirit of Christian love and human brotherhood," along the line of Elihu Burritt and William Ladd (Brock, 1968:926).

Similarly, the established traditions of the peace sects were virtually unchanged, although these societies were significantly altered. There was no crisis of conscience sharp enough to clarify the positions of Mennonites and Brethren as they became increasingly integrated in American society. Social and theological ferment in the Society of Friends led to the erosion of pacifist commitment in some quarters, although a Peace Association of Friends in America was formed in 1867 and in the following generation there emerged outstanding leaders such as Rufus Jones, Elbert Russell, William I. Hull, and Benjamin Trueblood. These men coupled traditional Quaker pacifism with intelligent and informed internationalism. Some of them formed an important element in the liberal pacifism that became identifiable during the First World War.

Meanwhile, the chief instrument for internationalism among peace advocates was the American Peace Society, which was reorganized after the

Civil War. Increasingly, it promoted specific programs of action. Its campaign for arbitration treaties, for example, was taken up by new organizations such as the National Arbitration League (1882) and the Lake Mohonk Arbitration Conferences (1895–1916) for business, legal, government, and religious leaders. Peace advocacy was becoming professionalized, organized to enlist specific constituencies for practical programs of action.

One such program was international law. Jurists such as William Jay and David Field contributed to its professional base, while the secretary of the society, James B. Miles, formed an American Code Committee and proselytized Europe. In 1899 the First Hague Conference convened at the invitation of Czar Nicholas II and, although called to deal with armaments and the rules of war, it developed into a conference for arbitration. The emphasis shifted to a world court and congress of nations by the time of the Second Hague Conference in 1907. Little came of that conference, but it gave American peace advocates access to an influential constituency and it authenticated internationalism. The peace cause had become respectable. It even attracted significant resources, and the formation of the well-endowed Carnegie Endowment for International Peace (1910), World Peace Foundation (1910), and Church Peace Union (1914) seemed auspicious to church and lay leaders alike. The resources were not altogether financial. They included well-formulated proposals for international organization and zeal to implement them.

The biblical sources of internationalism were less focused than they had been before the Civil War. But in this respect internationalism shared a common milieu with liberal religious thought. Darwinian in its claim for universality and progress, it was consonant with the cosmologies of Lyman Abbott, Henry Ward Beecher, and John Fiske: an immanent God was working out the salvation of all humanity through the instrument of a knowledgeable, gifted, and Christian race. The consummation of all evolution awaited only intelligent, applied moral commitment. Such a view imbued the missionary zeal of Josiah Strong no less than it elevated the vision of Andrew Carnegie. It informed the rationale of imperialists no less than that of church leaders opposed to expansionism or naval programs. Hundreds of outstanding young people were enlisted for foreign mission work by the Student Volunteer Movement under the banner of social justice and humanity no less than of evangelism. Missions and peace alike became interdenominational ventures. Thus the new Federal Council of Churches established a department of peace, and the Church Peace Union of 1914 united Protestants, Roman Catholics, and Jews. Protestant religion especially was divided by social and theological tendencies in these years. The "unusual moral idealism and superabundance of zeal," which Winthrop S. Hudson identifies with the period, bridged potentially deep chasms. It served religion in the same way it would serve the nation when, as Hudson adds, it was diverted "into the one great crusade to end war and make the world safe for democracy through military power" (323).

Social and biblical developments between the Civil War and the First World War were the roots of a liberal pacifism that became focused by the need for wartime self-definition. Its context was the social gospel response to problems of cities, labor, immigrants, oppression, and corruption through church-oriented programs of uplift. Some leaders also responded to the secular bonds of kinship that they found among immigrant and laboring people, and Christian socialists especially gave a religious basis to the morality of kinship. In the process of trying to reconcile classes, social gospel leaders discovered the roots of injustice and alienation in social institutions. They became reformers perforce.

Underlying the social gospel were two modes of thought, one scientific and the other historical. These were assumed to be complementary, but they gave the movement two distinct orientations. For many the social gospel was a melioristic version of Social Darwinism: society was gradually learning to solve its problems by cooperative and empirical approaches. For others, notably Walter Rauschenbusch, the social gospel was an expression of kingdom-of-God theology, a view that underlies modern pacifism. Its prevailing mode of thought was historical. Progress, although widely assumed, was not regarded as inevitable; and sin was faced as an enduring challenge. Sin was social, and it required organized responses from church and society. Church history as opened by Adolf Harnack, Albrecht Ritschl, and others documented the capitulation of the church to society and exposed an imperative need to recover the higher morality of Jesus. In this view, the dualism of church and state is historical, and the Christian community of the present is caught in tension between two planes of morality. Individuals are required to act in society without being claimed by it, to redeem the civil community from that social sin in which they themselves are implicated.

Writers in the prewar social gospel tradition were not preoccupied with the formal technical issues of biblical analysis—the so-called quest for the historical Jesus—any more than they appealed to the words of Scripture for literal proof. Rather, they assumed that Jesus' message was revealed in the way he lived and responded to the issues of his time. His life imbued history with a moral vision. This faith gave immediacy and power to the kingdom of God which the notion of social evolution could not match. Probably that is why a lay leader such as Jane Addams found Tolstoy's writing so compelling and why he had a considerable influence in America. Faith in the historical Jesus in this sense underlay liberal pacifism and gave it considerable plasticity, as we shall see, in the context of postwar biblical analysis.

Liberal pacifism was defined in the stress of World War I. Most internationalists interpreted the war as a crusade to remove the last obstacle to a progressive world order. Their organizations supported the Allies and at least acquiesced in American intervention. They contributed to the war effort and worked for a liberal peace settlement. Those church leaders among them who did not preach a holy crusade interpreted the role of the church as Christianizing the war effort. As under classic just war thought, they supported the war in terms of the equitable and constructive settlement they sought, and they tried to minimize its violence. Those who dissented from this role formed the nucleus of modern pacifism. They organized to publicize their alternative interpretation of the war, to oppose preparedness and intervention, to promote neutral mediation, to endorse nonsectarian pacifism, and to defend conscientious objectors. The very word pacifism lost its prewar connotations of peace advocacy and was narrowed to refer to persons altogether opposed to war. These people formed the organizations that became the core of a vital interwar peace movement: the American Union Against Militarism (subsequently the National Council for Prevention of War), the Woman's Peace Party (subsequently the Women's International League for Peace and Freedom), the Fellowship of Reconciliation, and the American Friends Service Committee. Their constituency included progressive social reformers and liberal Protestants, among them leading Quakers.

The dissident minority of liberal pacifists began to clarify the implications of their commitments. Alive to the immediacy of Jesus, they repudiated all rationalizations of his witness to love, mercy, and the absolute value of personality. Schooled in the history of the church, they denounced subservience to the state. Believing in social action, they struggled to draw a line between civil and military service in the first total war. Experienced in social analysis, they located the causes of the war in the conflicting interests and ideologies of all belligerents. Relative and pragmatic in their social philosophy, they rejected the absolute claims of the state and a doctrine of progress that would absolutize the Great War. Viewing war and injustice as related social sins, they concluded that peace and justice were the common goals of social redemption.

Such theorems as these do justice neither to the agony with which individual pacifists wrestled with the conflicting demands of the gospel and the world nor to the diversity of their conclusions. They set pacifists aside from sincere nonpacifists too neatly. They do not do justice to the continuing witness of sectarian nonresistants or of secular antiwar socialists. But they may suggest the extent to which World War I was a watershed in the development of the American peace movement. At that time the traditional nonresistance of the peace sects was supplemented by absolute pacifism grounded in contextual and historical understanding of the Bible as well as in a new perception of peace and justice.

The Limits of Internationalism and Liberal Pacifism

Internationalists differed from pacifists in their estimation of civic duty and of the possibility of constructive roles in wartime, but they were nonetheless committed to peace. Both wings of the movement had common roots and they complemented each other in the years following World War I. The wartime goals of internationalists were frustrated by the peace settlement and by the Senate's rejection of League of Nations membership. The League remained a tangible symbol of an alternative force, but it ceased to be a political option. In their search for an alternative program internationalists were divided between the ideas of outlawing war and joining the world court. Their division was adroitly exploited by isolationists. Meanwhile, peace advocates of varying persuasions cooperated to increase public awareness of international issues, to educate the public in the conflicts of interest at the root of war, to challenge the trappings of militarism, and to promote disarmament and the idea of international organization. They tapped widespread disillusion with the First World War, and they tried to transform it into sentiment for constructive peace programs.

Japanese invasion of Manchuria in 1931 challenged international order and provoked demands for diplomatic sanctions. The League of Nations was ineffective in the crisis. It was essentially irrelevant in the Spanish Civil War, the Italian invasion of Ethiopia, and the German remilitarization. The goal of an independent international authority gave way to the objective of a collective alliance against aggression. Internationalists joined with pacifists in support of a revision of United States neutral rights to trade but for different reasons. The former sought to make it possible for the government to cooperate in collective economic sanctions without participating in them; the latter wanted to keep the nation uninvolved. Even collective sanctions failed to materialize. There was no platform above the flood, no authority higher than force.

The limits of internationalism yielded the logic of World War II. Toward the end of 1942 the executive secretary of the Department of Research and Education of the Federal Council of Churches, F. Ernest Johnson, wrote that "to a large and influential portion of the Protestant leadership war had become anathema before the blow fell at Pearl Harbor." Johnson was a restrained critic of religious pacifism, and yet he concluded, "The influence of the spoken and written word, unsupported by vested interest of any kind, has perhaps never been so strikingly demonstrated. . . . Christian pacifism became an indubitably authentic movement, the influence of which is felt in the religious life of America now that we are in the war" (354).

The central organization of religious pacifists was the Fellowship of Reconciliation (F.O.R.), founded in 1915. Its leaders promoted peace action and pacifism in denominational conferences and individual congregations. They were active in the Y.M.C.A. and the Federal Council of Churches. They produced the outstanding periodical of the social gospel in the period, *The World Tomorrow*, and they had access to other religious journals, notably the *Christian Century*. Pacifists published a convincing pamphlet literature and an array of treatises on war and international affairs, devotional guides, and works of biblical and theological scholarship. They recruited leaders in the ministry, the church press, and the seminaries. They addressed

Protestant opinion at a time when the problems of peace and war were as important to it as any other issues, and their arguments were as informed as they were evangelical.

Kirby Page (1890–1957) and John Nevin Sayre (1884–1977) exemplified pacifist leadership in 1922 when they called together twenty-four ministers and lay people to discuss the responsibility of churches in war. A committee including Page, Harry Emerson Fosdick, and William P. Merrill, president of the board of trustees of the Church Peace Union, penned "The Churches' Plea Against War and the War System." Signed by 150 prominent members of the clergy, it was the first proclamation by representative Protestants and Catholics that the spirit of war is antithetical to that of the gospel. It was followed by many others.

The Methodist Episcopal Church took the earliest and most adamant stand of the major denominations. In 1924 its General Conference passed a report condemning war and promising to "create the will to peace" (DeVinney: 125). An active Commission on World Peace was organized, and after a decade of advocacy the General Conference of 1936 pledged not to endorse, support, or participate in war (a position reaffirmed when the northern and southern wings merged in 1939). The Disciples of Christ was not a pacifist sect; however, founder Alexander Campbell had said that Christianity and war were mutually exclusive, and outstanding church leaders had agreed. A number of pacifists labored within the denomination, and by 1934 they carried a resolution in the church convention which pledged Disciples to "disassociate . . . from war and the war system" (DeGroot).

Denominational peace fellowships usually affiliated with the F.O.R. They included American Baptists, Methodists, Episcopalians, Universalists, Unitarians, Lutherans, Presbyterians, and Congregational-Christians. Various opinion polls revealed growing opposition to religious endorsement of war and sympathy for conscientious objectors. By 1934 Walter Van Kirk, secretary of the Department of International Justice and Goodwill of the Federal Council of Churches, had amassed a large collection of statements by religious groups and leaders who renounced war. His compilation, *Religion Renounces War*, was an act of repentance addressed to Roy Abrams's collection of World War I statements, *Preachers Present Arms* (1933).

Liberal pacifism made a significant impression upon the Protestant clergy by 1931. Its leaders included not only prominent ministers but also distinguished teachers and scholars in leading schools of theology. With their help a theology of liberal pacifism was developed that was based upon the biblical and historical orientation of the prewar period. The theology of liberal pacifism was developed at a time when some social gospel pastors had begun to look critically at the liberal tradition. They were disconcerted by its failure to effect reforms and by its emphasis on ethics apart from religion. Harry Emerson Fosdick wrote that religion was "intellectually chaotic, ethically confused, organizationally antiquated" (1927:390). Reinhold

Niebuhr, then a young pacifist in Detroit, complained that liberal religion had fallen into "the superstition of automatic progress" and was lost in "a fathomless sentimentality" (1926). What was the outlook of those who rejected nonresistance, criticized liberal religion, and yet preached social reform and pacifism to the churches? Liberal pacifists found in the Bible a record of God revealed in history through the life of Jesus. They believed that Jesus was relevant to all time precisely because his teaching was a religious response to his own historical situation. They saw in his life a revelation—an understanding—of God as Father, of persons responsible to one another and to God, and of love as the proper relationship among individuals and between them and God. They believed that Jesus' personal religious experience resulted in concern for people and therefore in social action. Jesus' response revealed the terms of the kingdom of God and required Christians to work for justice in the spirit of love and therefore to renounce violence. The religious views of liberal pacifists derived from their biblical understanding. They agreed with John Nevin Sayre that the personality and teachings of Jesus could at last be "disentangled from the misrepresentations of centuries" and the imperfections of the Gospels themselves (n.d.).

Harry Emerson Fosdick, professor of practical theology at Union, and Henry J. Cadbury, professor of divinity at Harvard, acknowledged the perils of modernizing Jesus. They subjected the categories of biblical thought to analysis and showed them to be merely temporal: the Bible's language reflects an antiquated world view, but its temporal phrasings describe enduring human experience. Fosdick wrote that it was now possible to distinguish somewhat between religious experience and its theological formulation, between the life of Jesus and the doctrinal concerns of the Apostles (1924:54–63, 91–130). This view was succinctly paraphrased by Reinhold Niebuhr: "Jesus does not make the principle of love true. He helps to give it potency" (1929). Pacifists felt no less under the authority of Christ on this account; on the contrary, they were excited by the prospect of a new understanding of him. They were especially impressed by his personality and the historical circumstances surrounding his life. Kirby Page stressed both aspects in *The Personality of Jesus* (1932). He had been much impressed by Vladimir G. Simkovitch's *Toward the Understanding of Jesus* (1927), an attempt to view Jesus as a Jew and to understand his religious revelation in terms of its historical context.

In his response to his historical situation, pacifists argued, Jesus revealed that God presides over history but that He has created an order in which universal moral rules apply. God could not have given human beings freedom without making them subject to an orderly universe, because freedom of choice implies the will to accept consequences. Humanity has the freedom to choose but not the freedom to disturb God's order. That is the theological meaning of the frequent pacifist assertion that means and ends are so intimately related that it is impossible to get a cooperative world by destructive methods. Given a system so tightly bound, with God apparently hobbled by the nature of the purpose, in what sense could pacifists hold that God acts in history? The answer to this question is the fundamental assertion of liberal pacifist theology: God acts to redeem human beings not by saving them from the consequences of their actions but rather by bringing them to an understanding of the moral grounds of their being. Pacifists meant by God's love this relationship to human beings and also this manner of reconciling them. The sacrificial life of Jesus paralleled the loving creation of God.

The actual realization of God's way in history is the kingdom of God. "Christianity means the release of love into human life," wrote Vida Scudder "It can never be satisfied till love governs institutions and governments as it governs persons" (244). She did not mean that governments would eventually be governed by love and would thus satisfy Christians. She meant instead that the demands of God's love will always disturb complacency and inspire social reform. In this respect liberal pacifists departed from an evolutionary notion of the kingdom: "Justice and brotherhood are not the automatic and inevitable results either of evolution or of revolution" (Fellowship of Reconciliation). Even in the realization that the kingdom will never be realized on earth, "men should hope and strive for an endless approximation to it" (Tittle, 1939:14–15). The kingdom was transformed from a blueprint of the future into an ideal, as Ernest Freemont Tittle wrote, a "flying goal, an ever new heaven, and ever new earth" (1933:307–8). As A. J. Muste put it, "the very 'tension' in the moral life . . . without which men relapse to the animal level, exists only if the impossible demand of the Gospel is laid upon them" (Muste). Faith validated itself in never-consummated social progress.

Pacifists preached the social gospel so ardently that critics often ignored the personal religion from which their reform impulse stemmed. The center of their attention was Jesus' religious experience. They shared the Quaker-like view that the kingdom of heaven is in us as it was revealed in him. Thus, prominent pacifists rejected the doctrine of inevitable progress and yet retained the doctrine of the kingdom by positing it as a self-validating social ideal. They took sin seriously and yet retained the idea of the kingdom within individuals by describing it as latent goodness that can be realized. At the "inmost heart" of their message, as John Nevin Sayre wrote, is the faith that even in an industrialized, urbanized, internationalized world, "personality . . . still counts" (1931).

It was one thing for liberal pacifists to urge that social and economic injustice could be ended and war abolished. It was quite another thing for them to define the means of even modestly realizing the kingdom. Critical in this attempt was their distinction between force and violence and their emphasis on the valid use of force. Force or compulsion that issued in violence was inadmissible because it contradicted the ends of a cooperative social order where individual personality is respected. Once admitted, this distinction proved to be tenuous and troublesome. It split the Socialist Party in 1934; it divided the Fellowship of Reconciliation in 1933–34; and it led Reinhold Niebuhr to repudiate pacifism altogether in 1939. At issue in each case were the ethical limits of pacifism.

In the 1920s pacifists worked increasingly with the labor movement and the Socialist Party. They founded the Fellowship for a Christian Social Order. They developed a realistic appreciation of social conflict and coercion and had to reevaluate the ethics of force. Some of them distinguished between violent and nonviolent coercion. They learned to think of nonviolence as a way of living and also as a technique of social action. In 1934 the ethics of violence debate symbolized a conflict for power in the Socialist Party. The dominant faction, led by Norman Thomas and supported by leading pacifists, was challenged by both a conservative old guard and a radical wing. Overtly they divided over the party's position on international and class war. Pacifist Devere Allen had written the Declaration of Principles, which posed the issue. It restated the party's 1917 opposition to war and advocated war resistance, but it endorsed a general strike and government under workers' rule in the event of a capitalist collapse. Passed by a majority of the party, the declaration occasioned division from which socialists never recovered.

The F.O.R. wrestled more successfully with the issue in 1933–34. Its regional secretaries and members had become directly involved in labor struggles, and, in fact, one faction urged that violence might be justified in the interest of justice. The issue was taken to 6,395 members in 1934. Balloting defined the Fellowship as an organization of Christian pacifists who sided with workers and the underprivileged and would use the methods of love, moral suasion, and education on their behalf. A majority of members also would sanction nonviolent coercion for social justice. Only a tiny faction would endorse violence. The F.O.R. was reorganized under the leadership of John Nevin Sayre, Harold Fey, and subsequently A. J. Muste. For the first time it explicitly based pacifism on a distinction between violence and nonviolent force. Reinhold Niebuhr rejected the formula. He resigned from the council because it had made nonviolence an official test of pacifism. "We probably all recognize the terrible possibilities of violence," he wrote. "We regard an international armed conflict as so suicidal that we are certain we will not participate in it" (1934a). But that was a pragmatic evaluation, not an absolute judgment. Decisions regarding social action must be made not only in the light of religious ideals but also on a political basis.

The crisis of the F.O.R. had been a crucial time for Niebuhr. The period had begun for him with *Does Civilization Need Religion?* (1921), in which he had interpreted religious insight dialectically in a kind of naive dualism that illuminated paradoxes inaccessible to logic. Religion offers civilization exactly that kind of resource, he concluded. Christians must believe in the reality of love, but they must develop keen insight into the sway of force and must understand that love will inevitably be compromised. For the next five years Niebuhr ventured into the ethics of reform. *Moral Man and Immoral Society* (1934) extended his notion of religion in tension with civilization but introduced a distinction between the absolute demands of love and the relative demands of justice as criteria appropriate to individual and social ethics respectively. Niebuhr explored the use of power in the interest of justice. He accepted coercion and rejected violence on relative, pragmatic grounds: force would be good to the extent that it is nonviolent and is employed in the interest of peace and justice. From 1934 to 1941 he applied the dialectical principle of ethical analysis to contemporary issues, slicing through liberal and conservative shibboleths and cutting into ethical paradoxes. At the same time he worked out a theology of history, finding in the Bible both the language and the substance of that duality which he attributed to the nature and destiny of humanity (1941). For Niebuhr the revelation of Christ lay less in his response to a historical situation than in his disclosure of humanity's essentially historical condition. Individuals under Christ's revelation would know a compromise when, in the interest of justice, it had to be made: responding to the demands of both the ideal and the possible, they would not confuse the categories of their choice. Although he resigned from the F.O.R. council in 1934, Niebuhr remained a member because he agreed with its objective of peace. Even though he agreed with the organization on the ethics of nonviolent action, he disapproved of limiting ethical choices arbitrarily. He was increasingly inclined to link pacifists with other liberals whose optimism and absolutism seemed to him unrealistic, ignoring the fact that reforming pacifists had criticized liberals too, and largely for the same reasons. It seemed to him that the crisis of 1933–34 had issued in an arbitrary kind of pacifism that was in danger of becoming socially irrelevant.

Ironically, perhaps, in the half decade following Niebuhr's break, liberal pacifists developed a literature of nonviolent social action. Richard Gregg provided the fullest exposition in *The Power of Nonviolence* (1934). From his personal experience with Gandhi, Gregg explicated the relation of pragmatic and idealistic considerations in the mahatma's movement and applied it to Western contexts. Other pacifists contributed to the analysis and pressed it beyond the familiar labor struggle to civil rights. Persons familiar with this literature organized the Congress of Racial Equality in 1942. CORE remained close to the F.O.R., developing the body of thought and experience that became available to Martin Luther King in 1956. However, liberal pacifists were primarily concerned with international peace in the half decade following the 1934 crisis. As warfare enveloped Asia and Europe, the broad coalition of peace advocates divided over appropriate American strategy. The division was gradual. Pacifists and internationalists united in a massive Emergency Peace Campaign to educate the public to world realities and to promote international economic and political reform, but at the same time they competed for public support on the issue of neutrality. Pacifists promoted increasingly strict neutralism while internationalists advocated ever more explicit collective security. By the end of 1939 the two wings presented clear alternatives: strict neutrality or all aid short of war to the Allies. For two years more the churches were as divided on the issue as was the nation.

With the outbreak of war in Europe, Niebuhr resigned altogether from the F.O.R. and derided his former colleagues as victims of illusion. They, in turn, drew closer to traditional, nonresistant pacifists in the peace churches in order to avoid the isolation they had felt in World War I. The wartime positions of the churches reflected the influence of both liberal pacifist and Niebuhrian analyses. The war was justified as a realistic response to conflict for a relative good—international peace, and denominational leaders contributed significantly to the public movement in support of a postwar international organization. With minor exceptions churches eschewed the crusading spirit. However justified this war might be in terms of relative political ethics, warfare was wrong in the light of scriptural standards. Donald B. Meyer summarized the position of Protestant interventionists: "Any identification of a political course with the name of Jesus Christ was heresy; the crusade psychology had no place in politics, because of the nature—the true and proper nature—of politics" (387). Fighting, no less than conscientious objection on at least religious grounds, was regarded as an ethical option for individuals. The distinction between religious and political criteria of ethical decisions made it possible to absorb a pacifist reading of the scriptural and historic church witness against war without institutionalizing pacifism. The effect was to reinforce the just war ethic governing individual political choices.

Challenges to Just War Ethics

In the generation following World War II the traditional sanctions of just war thought were reexamined in the light of several developments: the advent of nuclear warfare, a fresh assessment of the role of Christians in the world and of biblical insight, opposition to war in Vietnam, and an elaboration of ethical nonviolence. Scorching light at Hiroshima and Nagasaki eclipsed the war it epitomized. World War II had been total, and despite some objections to "massacre by bombing," massive destruction had been justified under the doctrine of military necessity. Even the use of atomic bombs was at first widely accepted. Then, total war was equated with nuclear warfare and was condemned: such destructive means negated proportionately just ends. The tenets of just war seemed anachronistic indeed. Church diplomats who had worked for postwar peace faced the threat of nuclear war and a breakdown of international order. They responded with statements condemning war. The first assembly of the World Council of Churches at Amsterdam in 1948 declared that war is contrary to the will of

God. The National Council of Churches, denominations, and church leaders in the United States echoed the cry, apparently challenging the credibility of just war thought.

Just war doctrine was the special heritage of Roman Catholics. It was consonant with internationalism and, in fact, the Catholic Association for International Peace was formed in 1927 on that assumption. Its president, Charles G. Fenwick, criticized American neutrality policy for obscuring the moral difference between aggressors and their victims. International order could be secured only by the rigorous consistent application of just war principles, he wrote. Not all Catholics had agreed with Fenwick in the 1930s. Some of them argued that just war under modern conditions was virtually unthinkable. Three significant statements of that view were penned by Franziskus Stratmann, John K. Ryan, and Caprian Emmanuel. Pacifism was advanced in Catholic circles through Dorothy Day's Catholic Worker movement, which sponsored the formation of Pax (and in 1940 the Association of Catholic Conscientious Objectors). However, liberal pacifism did not become a significant element among Catholics; modern war, not just war criteria, was the primary issue of discussion. The Japanese attack on Pearl Harbor and German aggression seemed to satisfy the requirements of the doctrine for the overwhelming majority of Catholics. As late as November 1944 there were only eighty-seven of them in the Civilian Public Service.

Following the Second World War, Pius XII urged a rigorous application of just war criteria, including the doctrine of proportionality, which he said ruled out atomic, biological, and chemical warfare. John XXIII stimulated Catholic and Protestant peace advocates with his letter, "Pacem in Terris" (Gremillion: 201–41). His appeal was echoed by Pope Paul VI in a dramatic 1965 statement to the United Nations. That same year Vatican II examined war closely, condemning the arms race, calling for an effective international authority, and urging international economic reform. At the same time it declared that as agents of security and freedom, members of armed forces were contributing to peace. It opposed total war but affirmed the right to defense as a last resort. The Roman Catholic bishops of the United States also denounced unlimited war in 1968. The positions of Stratmann, Ryan, and Emmanuel had become orthodox.

However, the equation of nuclear with total war and its condemnation on just war terms posed three kinds of problems. First, it produced a sharp ethical paradox, because the right to defense was upheld to justify the will and capacity to use weapons that were viewed as intrinsically immoral. Second, modern ideology and technology further effaced the long blurred moral distinction between offensive and defensive warfare. Third, as Robert Batchhelder has shown, religious leaders minimized the possibility of constraining war in terms of its objectives. The Korean War raised this possibility to the level of strategic theory before many church leaders thought about it. Reinhold Niebuhr implied in 1955 that limited warfare would revivify just war thought. He argued that nuclear pacifists had replaced an absolute theological injunction against warfare with a politically absolute notion of total destruction. The problem was with absolutism. Political choices remained relative, Niebuhr insisted, and the Korean War showed that the pursuit of wars with limited goals and means remained a real possibility. For the many Protestant leaders who followed his lead, therefore, opposition to nuclear warfare did not in itself erode just war ethics.

A fresh challenge to just war thought per se was mounted in anticipation of the Amsterdam conference in 1948, when a group of pacifists put together *The Church, The Gospel and War* (Jones). Amsterdam agreed with them that war is incompatible with the teaching of Christ and that just war was "challenged," but it could only describe alternative positions and call upon theologians for clarification. In response the F.O.R. created the Committee on the Church and Pacifism, from which evolved the Church Peace Mission of 1950. It was supported by the peace churches and denominational peace fellowships. It published a series of pamphlets criticizing the "nuclear pacifism" of the Protestant majority. It sponsored regional and national meetings, sermon competitions, missions to seminaries, and for a decade focused discussion on the theological and biblical grounds of just war thought. Meanwhile, the European Continuation Committee of the Historical Peace Churches and the International Fellowship of Reconciliation answered Amsterdam's call for theological discussion, becoming engaged in dialogue with Niebuhr and Bishop Angus Dun (*The Christian and War*, 1958).

Specifically, the pacifists applied an individual ethic to a collective situation. Rejecting Niebuhr's dualism between individual and social ethics, they argued that there is a more important tension—between what ought to be and what is the case. They acknowledged that the church has a responsibility to improve human life, but they insisted that the church also exercise a prophetic role: to expose and challenge the roots of war and injustice in the perversion of personality and ethics. Paul Tillich echoed their point later from a different theological orientation: "I see human nature determined by the conflict between the goodness of man's essential being and the ambiguity of his actual being, his life under the conditions of existence" (Reed: 31). The pacifist authors had interpreted this dilemma in the light of scriptural example, concluding that Christians owe individual and collective witness to the prophetic will of God as revealed in Christ.

They extended their prewar biblical interpretation, but Mennonite scholar John Howard Yoder developed a fresh one. In reply to Niebuhr and in the light of Karl Barth and Oscar Cullmann, Yoder grounded peace advocacy in eschatological hope rather than on the historical Jesus. Liberal pacifists had interpreted the historical revelation of Christ almost as a moral vision, so that their conclusions were compatible with many of Yoder's but he wrote from the Mennonite tradition, arguing that a nonresistant community has a social role. The church is necessarily separate from the state because its revelation is distinct and its role is to witness to that revelation, wrote Yoder. Christian individuals cannot accept responsibility in the state because they respond to eschatological hope rather than to practical considerations. That is the condition of having a higher relevance, a witness to the "ought" governing both individual and social relations. In this sense the kingdom of God is an indwelling standard of judgment, not an evolving condition, and it dwells in the Christian community. Yoder wrote:

> The fundamental duality with which the Christian speaking to the environing society must reckon is not the difference between church and state as social institutions, nor between interpersonal relations on the face-to-face level and large group relations or between legalism and "playing by ear,"—although these differences will ultimately be involved—but the difference between faith and unbelief as the presuppositions of his ethical message. . . . Outside the circle of faith, the presupposition cannot be the commitment of the individual spoken to and challenged, but only Christ's objective claim on him. (1964:29)

The difference between a "Christian ethics for Christians and a Christian ethic for the state is therefore due to duality . . . of responses" (1964:32). Christians must speak to the state not to improve it, although that might follow (and is in fact the main motivation of liberal pacifists), but instead in order to be Christian.

Yoder's biblical ethic was delivered to the nonresistant believers. Later it would be received also by evangelical radicals who achieved collective identity at the end of the Vietnam War and who understood "the church's biblical identity as a new community that is a sign of the kingdom in history, an alien society of God's people whose life and action is intended to play a prophetic and decisive role in the world" (*Post-American*).

At the height of the Cold War the task of focusing just war thought on theological and biblical issues was especially important because Christian communions generally accepted the ideology of a free and moral world on the defensive. By 1962 there were some who felt that the discussion had "about beaten the blood out of the turnip" (Church Peace Mission: 2). More to the point, by that time ethical concerns were being focused on concrete action, as nonviolence was applied to civil rights and as a coalition of SANE and the Committee for Nonviolent Action protested nuclear testing.

A few years later ethical concerns were focused on the war in Vietnam. In 1966 Protestants, Catholics, and Jews were about evenly divided for and against the war, but a minority of religious leaders were mobilized in opposition to it. The Clergymen's Emergency Committee for Vietnam was formed the year before in close relation to the F.O.R., and it was followed by the International Committee of Conscience on Vietnam and the Clergy and Laymen Concerned about Vietnam. Peace advocates from both pacifist and nonpacifist traditions combined to oppose the war. The F.O.R. formed a national coalition of pacifist clergy and gave staff support to nonpacifist organizations. It established international connections, including a strong liaison with antiwar Buddhists. The American Friends Service Committee was active along similar lines, especially making connections with North Vietnam. A Catholic committee on Vietnam issued an appeal from 850 distinguished Catholics, and other religious pacifist groups joined the cause, motivated largely by scriptural norms.

Meanwhile, the war was reevaluated in just war terms. Because the statements of the National Council of Churches were couched in that vein, they chart the erosion of just war sanctions. The National Council acknowledged its respect for legitimate authority, for example, urging negotiation and candor upon the administration. As the government lost credibility, legitimate authority itself became an issue. The National Council called for restraint in the waging of war, but escalation and indiscriminate bombing violated the rule of proportionality. Even so ardent a proponent of just war analysis as Paul Ramsey agreed that attacks upon the society itself were unjust. The National Council did not put the war in terms of aggressors and defenders, viewing the conflict as complex and assuming that peace required authentic options for the North. The increasing acceptance of this view weakened the just cause claims for the war. Indeed, strong reservations about the nation's course were generated among the churches, and these broadened the base of the antiwar movement. Churches were not prophetic in their war opposition, though. In large measure this was because their judgment was couched in just war categories. Catholic critic Michael Novak illustrated the problem in his very critique of the Roman Catholic record. He interpreted just war on the basis of the contingency and relativity of moral judgments, the qualities which he applied to his analysis of traditional church forms. If the religious community failed to lead opposition to the war, as Novak implied, it was largely because it was plagued by that sense of complexity and ambiguity which for both Novak and Niebuhr lay at the core of just war analysis.

Conscription raised special problems. Virtually all Protestant denominations had accepted the legitimacy of religious conscientious objection but had not provided for selective objectors. Seminary students were heavily involved in the organized resistance and, with many faculty members, opposed the war on political as well as religious grounds. Indeed, a substantial number of objectors rejected the specific war rather than all warfare. By 1968 the Lutheran Church in America and the American Catholic bishops upheld an individual's right to object to a particular war on the grounds of its injustice. Modern just war thought had come full course. A generation much influenced by Niebuhr's ethical thought had outreached his conclusions. The Vietnam War itself was attacked as a product of absolutistic ideological thinking, and individuals opposed it on the basis of relative values and probable consequences. In the 1960s for the first time in history, peace advocates of all persuasions—biblical, humanitarian, and realist, pacifist and nonpacifist—were united against a specific war.

Controversy over the war accelerated another development in the peace movement, the theory and organization of nonviolent action. Early expositions of nonviolence had been couched in New Testament terms, although they were prompted by the need felt by liberal pacifists to show social results that traditional nonresistance did not offer. The study of Gandhi's work between the world wars was a catalyst for theories and experiments in the United States. Pacifists such as A. J. Muste and Martin Luther King labored under the aegis of both the mahatma and the Christ. Nonviolence seemed to offer a way of reconciling the demands of peacefulness and justice, which Niebuhr had juxtaposed. It seemed to relate Christian and secular ethics at a time when the Fellowship of Reconciliation and the International Fellowship were seeking to become more inclusive. Nonviolence was given its fullest Christian interpretation by William R. Miller. Drawing upon a wealth of historical and contemporary experience, he offered nonviolence as a social process consonant with the biblical revelation of the "bedrock of ultimate reality"—the need for "healing and integrating the solitary man within himself, in relation to another and in groups—all in relation to God and through God's active, unselfish, redeeming love" (32).

Miller's work was eclipsed by the war in Vietnam and the application of nonviolence to new perceptions of justice. The thaw in the Cold War had made possible a demythologizing of the free world, a tendency accelerated by currents of domestic reform and by a growing awareness of a global division between rich and poor. Analysis of the Vietnam war and its conduct strengthened the perception of structural anomalies in national and international systems that underlay dependency and inequality. This coincided with the rise of liberation theology, especially in Latin America. The result was to equate systemic injustice with war as instruments of destruction and deprivation. The phrase "structural violence," used to describe this equation, conveyed the moral force of the insight. It provided a focus for the reorganization of peace advocates when the antiwar movement dissipated in the 1970s. As they identified with the dispossessed of the world and with movements for political and social liberation, they transferred the debate over just war ethics to reform and revolutionary movements.

The implications of nonviolence and liberation were debated in denominational and ecumenical conferences and journals, in the F.O.R.'s *Fellowship* and pacifist circles. They were expanded in books such as John Swomley's *Liberation Ethics* (1972), Robert McAfee Brown's *Religion and Violence* (1973), and Peter W. Macky's *Violence: Right or Wrong?* (1973). The latter was a distinctly Christian perspective on systemic violence, and Macky included an examination of the biblical tradition and the church debate. Brown related war to structural injustice and critiqued the traditional positions of Christians, stressing their roles as peacemakers and focusing upon problems of racism. Swomley developed an ethic accenting freedom as the political corollary of love. He addressed the process of transforming repressive social structures, arguing that the use of violence either to maintain or to overthrow social systems reifies oppressive relationships and sanctifies authoritarianism. He tried to fuse a Christian interpretation of ethics with a Marxist analysis of social conflict in such a way as to offer both hope and involvement in the cause of social justice, to deny ethical sanctions to both violence and war. New perceptions on human liberation have had a profound impact on Catholic thought (Gremillion).

Retrospective

The traditions of nonresistance, ethical pacifism, and just war thought have not been static doctrines. A typological or exegetical treatment would obscure their historical variety and common ideals. It would minimize the drama of people wrestling with the demands hidden in their assumptions. Peace advocates of all persuasions have lived out the terms of the human condition, straining the tension between "the goodness of man's essential being and the ambiguity of his actual being."

The Bible and American peace movements have interacted for over a century and a half. Outstanding peace advocates almost without exception have been motivated by values rooted more or less consciously in Scripture. As they have clarified their values and applied them, many peace advocates have refined their understanding of the Bible. Obedience to the law of Christ has been transmuted into discipleship under both the historical and eschatological revelation of Jesus. Humanitarian concern has been linked to the radical position taken by Jesus in relation to the messianic hope of the Jews. It has been lifted by awareness of systemic barriers to brotherhood. The goal of bringing political choices under the judgment of Christian values has been complicated by the sense of relativity and ambiguity so characteristic of our century. American peace movements were occasionally catalysts and often contexts for reorientations of biblical understanding. The tensions between individual and society, church and state, essential goodness and actual compromise have been strained more severely by choices for war or peace than by any other social issues. Biblical ethics has profited from the strain.

WORKS CONSULTED

Abrams, Roy H.
    1933   *Preachers Present Arms*. New York: Round Table
                    Press.

Bainton, Roland H.
. 1945   "The Church and War: Historic Attitudes toward
                         Christian Participation." *Social Action* 11 (January
                         15, 1945): 8–10.

1960   *Christian Attitudes toward War and Peace.* Nash-
                         ville: Abingdon Press.

Batchelder, Robert C.
1961   *The Irreversible Decision: 1939–1950.* New York:
                         Macmillan.

Brock, Peter
1968   *Pacifism in the United States from the Colonial
                         Era to the First World War.* Princeton: Princeton
                         University Press.

Brock, Peter, ed.
1972   *The First American Peace Movement.* New York:
                         Garland.

Brown, Robert McAfee
1973   *Religion and Violence.* Philadelphia: Westminster
                         Press.

Church Peace Mission
1962   "Evaluation of Past CPM Activities." In Church
                         Peace Mission papers, Swarthmore College Peace
                         Collection, Swarthmore, PA.

DeGroot, A. T.
1935   *Christianity is Pacifism.* Indianapolis: Department
                         of Social Education and Action, United Christian
                         Missionary Society.

DiVinney, James Marion
1928   "Attitudes of the Methodist Episcopal Church to-
                         ward War from 1910 to 1927." S.T.D. thesis,
                         Temple University School of Theology.

Fellowship of Reconciliation
1935   "The Message and Program of the F.O.R." Typed
                         copy in the F.O.R. papers, Swarthmore College
                         Peace Collection.

Fenwick, Charles G.
1937   *A Primer of Peace.* Washington: Catholic Associa-
                         tion for International Peace.

Fosdick, Harry Emerson
1924   *The Modern Use of the Bible*. New York: Macmillan.
1927   "Recent Gains in Religion." *The World Tomorrow*. 10: 390–93.

Gregg, Richard
1934   *The Power of Nonviolence*. Philadelphia: Lippincott.

Gremillion, Joseph
1975   *The Gospel of Peace and Justice: Catholic Social Teaching Since Pope John*. Maryknoll, NY: Orbis Books.

Hartzler, Jonas Smucker
1922   *Mennonites in the World War*. Scottdale, PA: Mennonite Publishing House.

Hudson, Winthrop S.
1965   *Religion in America*. New York: Scribner's.

Johnson, F. Ernest
1942   "The Impact of the War on Religion in America." *American Journal of Sociology* 48: 353–61.

Jones, Rufus
1948   *The Church, The Gospel, and War*. New York: Harper.

Macgregor, George H. D.
1936   *The New Testament Basis of Pacifism*. London: James Clarke.

Macky, Peter W.
1973   *Violence: Right or Wrong?* Waco, TX: Word Books.

Meyer, Donald B.
1961   *The Protestant Search for Realism: 1919–1941*. Berkeley: University of California Press.

Miller, William Robert
1964   *Nonviolence, a Christian Interpretation*. New York: Schocken Books.

Muste, A. J.
    n.d.   "Letter to a Theological Student Resigning from the Fellowship of Reconciliation." Typed letter in the Muste Papers, Swarthmore College Peace Collection.

Niebuhr, Reinhold
    1926   "Does Religion Quiet or Disquiet?" *World Tomorrow* 9: 220–221.
    1927   *Does Civilization Need Religion?* New York: Macmillan.
    1929   "Christian Pacifism." *World Tomorrow* 12: 234.
    1934a   *Moral Man and Immoral Society.* New York: Scribner's.
    1934b   "Why I Leave the F.O.R." *Christian Century* 51 (January): 17–19.
    1941   *The Nature and Destiny of Man.* New York: Scribner's.

Novak, Michael
    1964   *A Time to Build.* New York: Macmillan.

Nuttall, Geoffrey
    1958   *Christian Pacifism in History.* Oxford: Basil Blackwell.

Page, Kirby
    1932   *The Personality of Jesus.* New York: Association Press.

Peachey, Paul
    1963   "Church and Nation in Western History." *Biblical Realism Confronts the Nation,* ed. P. Peachey. New York: Fellowship Publications.

Post-American
    1975   Editorial. *Post-American* (October-November): 3.

Reed, Edward
    1965   *Pacem in Terris.* New York: Pocket Books.

Sayre, John Nevin
    n.d.   *Towards a Christian International.* New York: Fellowship of Reconciliation.
    1931   *News Letter of the F.O.R.,* October.

Scudder, Vida
1924   "Christianity: Conservative or Revolutionary?" *World Tomorrow* 6: 244–45.

Simkovitch, Vladimir G.
1927   *Toward the Understanding of Jesus.* New York: Macmillan.

Stratmann, Franziskus
1931   *The Church and War: A Catholic Study.* New York: J. P. Kennedy and Sons.

Swomley, John
1972   *Liberation Ethics.* New York: Macmillan.

Tittle, Ernest F.
1933   "A Protestant View of Religion," *World Tomorrow* 16: 307–8.
1939   *Christians in an Unchristian Society.* New York: Association Press.

Van Kirk, Walter
1934   *Religion Renounces War.* New York: Willet, Clark.

Yoder, John Howard
1955   "Peace Without Eschatology?" *Mennonite Quarterly Review* 29: 101–21.
1964   *The Christian Witness to the State.* Newton, KS: Faith and Life Press.

VI

The Bible and the Black Churches

Peter J. Paris

The importance of the Bible in the black churches cannot adequately be grasped apart from an understanding of the broader cultural context in which blacks have sought to live—those mythic forms through which blacks projected a positive valuation of their humanity, their ideals, and their struggles. Their interpretations were neither isolated from nor the mere products of the psychological, social, economic, and political forces to which the race had long been subjected; but they have manifested the transcendent spirit of an oppressed people capable of creative self-understanding in spite of adversity.

The primary locus of the race's self-interpretation has been the black churches. The churches represent the last surviving institutional link with the antebellum past and continue to be the only major institutions completely owned and controlled by blacks themselves. The histories of the race and of the churches are interrelated, and any attempt to separate the two necessarily distorts them both. It is not surprising, therefore, that histories of the race isolated from the function of its enduring institutions result in studies of social disorganization. Similarly, studies of the black churches isolated from the race as a whole result in analyses of religious pathology. The integral relationship between the black churches and the race as a whole reveals a fundamental principle that is at the heart of black religion: there is no radical cleavage between the religious and the secular dimensions of life. The many anecdotes in the black community illustrating the positive relationship between the experience of Saturday night and Sunday morning point to this fact. In his study of religious and secular forms of music in the black community James Cone has argued that "the Blues and the Spirituals flow from the same bedrock of experience, and neither is an adequate interpretation of Black life without the commentary of the other" (111). A similar kind of unity between religion and culture characterizes the black religious experience.

The unity of religion and culture in the black community does not imply a similar closeness between the black churches and the wider

American culture. In fact, black religious leaders have usually viewed white culture as alien and racist. Thus, the black churches belong to the family of the "prophetic religions of liberation," which Vittorio Lanternari has described (v). Though he did not undertake a full study of the black churches in America, his evidence suggests that the modern prophetic religions of the oppressed comprise no lunatic fringe but signify the quest of the human spirit for salvation whenever it is threatened. The conflict that he describes between the cultures of the indigenous peoples and the colonial powers is similar to that which has characterized the black and white cultures in America. Like the prophetic religions that Lanternari describes, the black churches are institutional embodiments of religious and political freedom (Wilmore: 708). Their historical emergence represented a religious independence movement the political implications of which were not fully perceived by the alien culture, though it readily discerned some of its dangers.

In separating themselves from the white churches, blacks were attempting to create an alternative to the enslavement they had experienced within the segregated white churches. The movement towards independence was motivated by the desire to construct a world of their own. Not surprisingly, this independence was understood differently by blacks and whites. The former viewed it as a necessary condition for racial pride, racial solidarity, and racial advance. The latter understood it as black preference for their own religious practices, which the whites considered subordinate to their own. Consequently the black churches have always understood their relationship with the white churches in a way quite different from that in which blacks as a race have viewed the relationship between themselves and whites. On the one hand, the black churches have a long history of independence from the white churches but, on the other hand, the races have been related in a structure of domination and dependence, that is, white over black. Though victimized in many ways by the control and subjugation of whites, blacks discovered in their churches the means for developing a positive understanding of themselves. There they have been enabled to discern their capacity to act in the midst of extreme constraints and to demonstrate their ability not only to transcend those repressive conditions but also to experience the resiliency of the human spirit when life itself is threatened.

Joseph Washington has argued persuasively that the religion of the black churches has always existed apart from mainline white Protestantism because of the latter's racial policies (1964). If this is true, the black churches of the contemporary period are heirs to a religious tradition different from that of white Americans. I suggest that there is a black Christian tradition that has been normative for the black churches and for the black community and that is distinguished from the Western Christian tradition by its nonracist appropriation of the Christian faith. In this tradition one discovers a distinctive hermeneutic that joins certain biblical assumptions about humanity with the struggle against racism. Although blacks were introduced to Christianity by the Western Christian tradition, they quickly extricated the gospel from its racist entanglements. In the Bible, blacks found a perspective on humanity that was wholly different from that which they experienced in the teachings and practices of white Americans. The universal parenthood of God implied a universal kinship of humankind. This is the basic proposition of the hermeneutic designated as the black Christian tradition. The black churches have always discerned this doctrine to be the bedrock of the biblical perspective on humanity, and they have given prominence to biblical passages that make it unequivocally clear. Furthermore, this hermeneutic has enabled the Bible to speak both constructively and critically to every violation of the principle of kinship.

The discovery of this perspective in the Bible was of paramount significance, providing blacks with their most powerful weapon of opposition to white American racism. Ironically, both white racism and black opposition to it appealed to the biblical sources for their respective justifications. But eventually white racism became defensive, finding it both theologically and morally difficult to negate the basic tenets of the black Christian tradition. Thus the white Christians found this tradition to be a major threat to a cultural ethos that had been founded, nurtured, and promoted by belief in the racial superiority of whites over blacks; but the black churches made this newly discovered hermeneutic a way of life. Being black no longer was viewed as a curse but as a gift from God. The discovery of the biblical understanding of universal human equality provided not only theological grounds for opposing racism but also a means of evaluating the authority of the Bible itself. Accordingly, the black churches have never hesitated to disavow any interpretation of Scripture that would attempt to legitimate racism, slavery, or any other form of human bondage. One can conclude that there have been no sacred scriptures for blacks apart from the hermeneutical principle immortalized in the black Christian tradition.

For black Christians this hermeneutical principle was neither a theological abstraction nor an eschatological hope but was a lived experience. Racism has never found asylum in the black churches. They have always been united by their common belief in the fundamental hermeneutic of the black Christian tradition, the universal parenthood of God and kinship of humankind. However, the black churches have differed in the implications for social action that they draw from this hermeneutic, and these differences are important because the preaching and reception of the gospel are filtered through them, resulting in several different strands of the black Christian tradition: pastoral, prophetic, reformist, and nationalist. Each typifies forms of action and life that were shaped, refined, and preserved by the churches. Each had its beginning in a particular historical period and, although modified by time and circumstance, survives into the present. In the following analysis, we will consider each strand in turn, setting forth its salient characteristics and the way in which the Bible is appropriated by one of its prominent representatives.

The Pastoral Strand

The pastoral strand is clearly the oldest since its historical roots lie deep in slavery. W. E. B. DuBois contended that this strand took the place of the priests or medicine men in traditional African culture (342). It aimed at comforting the sorrowful and instilling hope in those standing on the brink of despair. Its awareness of the sociopolitical impotence of blacks caused it to focus on the eschatological rewards of heaven and eternal life, which also functioned as a critique of the status quo. In nurturing the virtues of humility, patience, and good will, this strand has frequently been mis-understood as encouraging a spirit of submission to racism. DuBois thought that it at times departed from genuine (though docile) honesty by incul-cating habits of deception aimed at manipulating those who dominated blacks (346).

Black ministers who may be classified as representatives of this pastoral strand view themselves as servants of the sacred and of all people who are in need of ministry. Insofar as they consider the structure and spirit of the American nation to be harmonious with the truths of the Christian Gospel, they serve both the nation and the church with equal fidelity and reverence. While they admit that moral corruption might invade the thought and practice of both the nation and the church, they shun any notion that either has become totally corrupt. Rather they believe that the source of such immorality lies in a minority who assuredly will be conquered by the majority in due time. Generally they view nation and gospel as essentially united. They emphasize the similarities and continuities that exist between the nation and the Christian churches. While they reveal no interest in amalgamating the white and black churches, they view both as custodians of the same nonracist message and both as charged to be faithful to that message at all times. They abhor conflict and insist that all problems be resolved in a spirit of peace and good will and with the quickest possible dispatch lest the nation and the church be brought into reproach. In times of great adversity these ministers encourage endurance and patience, which are considered historical attributes of eschatological hope. It is not surprising that they well know how to get along with their enemies with minimum overt conflict.

A prominent contemporary representative of this tradition is Joseph H. Jackson, whose pastoral concerns are foremost in all of his preaching, lecturing, and policy making. Jackson believes in the quest for civil rights but has always insisted that it be carried out in a spirit of good will. He refuses to judge America itself or any of its structural systems as agents of racism. Rather, he places the blame on individuals who betray the public trust by practicing racial segregation and discrimination. His love of race, nation, and church is equally distributed. He abhors racial chauvinism and is quick to blame blacks for not taking advantage of the opportunities at hand instead of begging whites to assist them in their own development. His criticism of the civil rights movement is clearly stated:

> Many civil rights organizations and leaders have taken on an anti-church attitude, anti-religious disposition, and carry on anti-Christian propaganda. Some are anti-democracy, oppose the freedom of speech, and have resorted to picketing churches. While we must always be for civil rights with all our soul, mind and strength, we must not leave our people as the helpless victims of those who would use them for selfish purposes and who would labor to keep them in chains. We must always oppose discrimination and segregation in every form and work for first class citizenship with all our might. But we must labor incessantly to give our people Christian assistance, Christian fellowship, and Christian guidance in this hour of crisis. (National Baptist Convention, 1963:207)

The pastoral concern made explicit here is also present in his discussion of civic responsibility. Here he bases his reflections on the Exodus in order to demonstrate his position that the defeat of segregation is not an end in itself since it is not equivalent to freedom. He feels that it is possible to win the battle against segregation while losing the battle for freedom. Deliverance from bondage must lead citizens to assume responsibility for their own growth and development. Reflecting on the crossing of the Red Sea and the death of the Egyptians, he concludes that since the Hebrews no longer had any masters against whom to express their hostility and envy, they finally started blaming those who had led them out of bondage. "They had been delivered from the chains of Egypt but longed for the customs and flesh pots of the old land of bondage" (National Baptist Convention, 1963:207). While Jackson is aware of the bondage in which the children of Israel lived for several centuries and while he eloquently preaches about their miraculous liberation, he gives no attention to the political nature of it. Rather, he emphasizes the morality of the Israelites as the cause of either victory or defeat. In this respect he equates their condition with that of black Americans and places the burden of responsibility on them (as was true of the Hebrews) to shape their own destiny subsequent to their liberation.

The cross of Christ is also a central symbol in Jackson's thought. He admonishes theologians, preachers, and laity to put the cross back into the gospel, the church, and the everyday lives of Christian people. He contends that the cross of Christ is good news to the poor and the needy, to the weary, the lonely, and the dying. He vividly portrays this message in a sermon in which he sets the cross of Christ in opposition to the Sermon on the Mount. He gives an example of a poor dying woman who was not comforted by the preacher's reading of portions of the Sermon on the Mount. But when he read John 3:16, she was comforted by the assurance that God's salvation is not dependent on what she had done (National Baptist Convention, 1970:75).

Jackson has always opposed all forms of direct protest confrontation, because he believes that it generates hatred and malice. He believes that as citizens we owe unqualified allegiance to the American nation. As Christians we must be true prophets, bringing about change by practicing a higher form of virtue based on higher principles. Such a position does not set one against the state. "Jesus at no time threw himself against the petty laws of the Roman Empire. He said, 'Render unto Caesar the things that are Caesar's, and to God the things that are God's'" (1967:35). In his treatise against nonviolence in the civil rights movement, Jackson cites Matt 5:31–32, "Ye have heard that it was said by them of old time, Thou shalt not kill; and whosoever shall kill shall be in danger of the judgment. But I say unto you, that whosoever is angry with his brother without a cause shall be in danger of the judgment" (1967:35). According to Jackson's analysis, nonviolence may be defined as a nonphysical attack. Hence it does not reach the ethical standard proclaimed by Jesus. Jackson calls for a greater morality than that of nonviolence, a morality that would reflect a positive attitude of the actor towards the nation, democracy, the rights of others, and respect for law and order.

Jackson also argues that the love of Jesus is not the same as that proclaimed by the advocates of nonviolence. He says that it is not a love that punishes, antagonizes, and forces enemies to change their minds. Rather it is the kind of love that Paul demonstrated in 1 Corinthians: "Love suffereth long and is kind" (Jackson, 1964). Jackson utilizes the text of Josh 17:14–16 to base his proclamation that people should have a vision that demands struggle and hard work. The children of Joseph had complained that they, being a great people, were not given enough land. Jackson states that Joshua did not dispute their claim. He knew that a hill is never enough if one has the vision of a mountain. And so he answered them, "If thou be a great people then get thee up to the wood country and cut down for thyself." Jackson comments that Joshua was telling the people to take command of their own future and shape it for themselves. They would find no prepared place for them in the mountain; they must build one themselves out of their own vision and strength. Jackson hastens to relate this message to black Americans who, he believes, had all the necessary conditions for racial advance at hand:

> In a social struggle we must build when we get to the right spot. We are now at the right spot to build a strong, healthy, and democratic society. We have the records of some economic, cultural, and scientific achievements to encourage us. We have some of the most far-reaching legal supports in the field of civil rights, supported and passed by the Supreme Court and the Congress of the United States of America. . . . The ballot has been extended to more citizens than ever before in the history of the country and the ballot is the strongest and most powerful weapon that any citizen can receive . . . . Already there is enough capital passing through the hands of Negroes to make a great and powerful economic force if organized and properly directed. We are at the

right spot to become creative. This is our task and our responsibility. Any further delay
in this noble venture must be laid at our own doors. (1976:215)

Here the emphasis is on production, development, and progress
wrought by the vision and labor of the people themselves. As Joshua told the
people that they should build if they would be great, so Jackson felt compelled in many of his sermons, addresses, and policies to reiterate that message. Jackson and many others in this strand of the tradition seek to force
blacks out of their state of self-pity and despair into the realization that they
are children of God and hence are expected to assume responsibility for
their own destiny. In this form of preaching, the notion that God helps those
who honestly try to help themselves is a traditional adage. This form of the
tradition emphasizes the primacy of God's love as the good news for the
weary and the downtrodden.

William Holmes Borders is illustrative of one who combines the pastoral and the prophetic strands. His sermon "Handicapped Lives" is a good
example of the pastoral tradition. After reflecting on the handicapped lives
of George Washington Carver, Charles Moseley, and a blind paper boy,
Holmes proclaims the fact that God uses weak and handicapped persons to
prove his power. He admonishes all to work within their limitations
whether they be physical, social, racial, or economic. He then recalls the
death of Lazarus as an opportunity for Jesus to prove himself master over
the grave; the immortal poetry of Paul Lawrence Dunbar, dead from
tuberculosis by the age of thirty-five; the slave music of the Jews in Babylon
(Psalm 137).

> "How can we sing the Lord's song in a strange land?" (See Psalm 137:1, 3, 4). How can
> slaves shout for joy? How can we be happy chained in slavery? How can the clink of
> iron chains be converted into musical harmony? How can your heart sing when your
> body sags under fetters of iron? How can a mocking bird sing with a broken wing?
> How can a rabbit run with a broken leg? How can we sing—miles from home with a
> dagger in our hearts? Some do best under a handicap. (Philpot: 21)

The imaginative skill of Borders is clearly portrayed in the following passage
from the same sermon, and it illustrates the way in which many black
preachers bring the Scriptures to life in their congregations.

> I imagine Paul spread himself before God saying, "I am your servant; you are my God.
> I am tortured and pained without end. I have done all I know. I have preached 'pray-
> er.' I have preached 'power.' I have preached 'ability.' Now I am caught with a thorn
> in the flesh which I can't master. I prayed once. I prayed twice. This is a third time. I
> need a personal answer. When it stormed, you sent an angel. When I was in Philippi,
> you rocked the jail. When I was trapped, you let me down over the Macedonian wall.
> When I was headed for Damascus to raise hell, you blocked the traffic. When I was
> stoned, you saved me. I need a personal answer to my plea. You made my body. A
> master mechanic knows his product. I have the faith in God, and you have the power."
> (Philpot: 23)

Borders concludes the sermon with an ode of praise to Paul who, in spite of his handicap, accomplished great things for God and in the Christian tradition stands second only to Jesus himself. The call and challenge to blacks to actualize their potential in spite of their adversities is an integral part of the pastoral tradition. Time and again blacks are admonished to remember God and his power and protection. As he liberated the Israelites so also will he liberate blacks. Borders and others have frequently turned to poetry to illustrate God's protective care:

> The children of Israel were a lost and flung-down people.
> Away from home, down in the land of Egypt.
> Salt was sprinkled in the open wounds of these slaves,
> For they were hard pressed and driven like cattle.
> They moaned, and God heard their groans,
> For slavery hurt His heart.
> The Almighty dipped His pen in the ink of eternity
> And wrote Israel's Emancipation Proclamation.
> . . . .
> Israel got hungry. The angels cooked some manna,
> On the big gas range of glory.
> They dropped it down, properly seasoned and salted,
> Wrapped in heavenly packages.
> Israel got thirsty, Moses melted the rocks;
> A spring bubbled cool water.
> The children shouted around the spring,
> Some stooped down and lapped water. (English: 74)

Thus, the pastoral strand of the black Christian tradition is characterized by a posture of quiet and moderation in its encounters with racism. It tends to be optimistic in outlook and ever cognizant of the need for blacks to seize the opportunities at hand and to construct a way around obstacles and adversity.

The Prophetic Strand

The prophetic strand of the black Christian tradition is rooted in antebellum opposition to slavery that predates the official abolitionist organizations. Soon after the birth of the independent black churches in the early nineteenth century, blacks began to protest slavery through moral suasion. The prophetic strand is the locus of some of the finest rhetoric in American history and the source of some of the most persuasive arguments against human enslavement and oppression.

Unlike the pastoral strand, the dominant characteristic of the prophetic is that of criticism, subjecting the prevailing institutions, beliefs, and practices to scrutiny in order to uncover their racist bias. This strand assumes that the nation has the will to correct its practices and beliefs when its errors are pointed out. Hence its style of criticism is constructive. Unlike the pastoral strand, it neither affirms nor celebrates the past uncritically but subjects all events, deeds, and actions to rigorous evaluation in accordance with the principles of the black Christian tradition. It diligently seeks to reveal the contradictions inherent in the life of the nation and to clarify the moral dimensions of those contradictions and to urge their resolution. It insists that only those with moral sensibilities, utilizing moral means, can effect the kind of moral redemption needed. Its primary aim is to explain the gravity and urgency of the problem to all who have ears to hear and to pressure those in power to resolve the problem that, it believes, will destroy the nation if permitted to persist. Those who struggle against the moral problem of racism struggle not for the salvation of the race alone but for America as well. The prophetic style results in political action governed by the principle of racial self-fulfillment. Richard Allen, Frederick Douglass, W. E. B. DuBois, James W. C. Pennington, and Martin Luther King, Jr. are some of its most prominent representatives. Let us now examine a number of sermons preached by Martin Luther King, Jr. as a representative of this prophetic strand in order to discern how he employed the Scriptures.

In a sermon entitled "A Tough Mind and a Tender Heart," King used for his text "Be ye therefore wise as serpents and harmless as doves" (Matt 10:16). The sermon begins with a statement that Jesus knew the value of blending opposites. Since he knew that his disciples would face all kinds of difficulties in a hostile world, he told them, "Behold I send you forth as sheep in the midst of wolves," and then he gave them the text of this sermon as a formula. While it is difficult to imagine a person having the combined qualities of a serpent and a dove, this is precisely the kind of person Jesus was seeking. That formula is then employed as a descriptive principle for assessing the virtues of the toughminded person as one who is perceptive and imbued with firmness of purpose and commitment. Alternatively, he described the problems inherent in softmindedness: gullibility, praise of ignorance, a disposition to laud half-truths, prejudices, and falsity. Softmindedness pervades the society and is considered one of the basic causes of racial prejudice. But King said that we must not be content with the mere cultivation of toughmindedness: "The gospel also demands a tender heart. Toughmindedness without tenderheartedness is cold and detached" (4). He proceeds to analyze the opposite of tenderheartedness—hardheartedness— stating that such a state lacks compassion, the capacity to love. Further, it tends to view others as objects to be manipulated. He then introduces additional biblical passages to show that Jesus condemned those who did not have a tender heart, such as the rich fool and Dives. King then joins the dialectic in a synthesis: "Jesus reminds us that the good life combines the toughness of the serpent and the tenderness of the dove. To have serpentlike qualities devoid of dovelike qualities is to be passionless, mean, and selfish. To have dovelike without serpentlike qualities is to be sentimental, anemic, and aimless. We must combine strongly marked antitheses" (6).

King admonished blacks to combine these two qualities in order to move toward the goal of freedom and justice. He criticized the pastoral strand, judging it historically to have been too softminded. "Softminded individuals among us feel that the only way to deal with oppression is by adjusting to it. They acquiesce and resign themselves to segregation" (6). He drew upon Exodus symbolism in order to condemn those who fear deliverance. "When Moses led the children of Israel from the slavery of Egypt to the freedom of the Promised Land, he discovered that slaves do not always welcome their deliverers. . . . They prefer the 'fleshpots of Egypt' to the ordeals of emancipation." King was not gentle with those who stood in the prophetic strand of the black Christian tradition. In fact he accused them of preferring their own comfort and safety to freedom for their children. Further, he accused such persons of cooperating with the racist system by passively accepting it. King condemned those blacks who are hardhearted and who advocate violence and hatred. Again he drew upon biblical imagery to support his own position: "A Voice echoing through the corridors of time, says to every intemperate Peter, 'Put up thy sword'" (7).

Finally, King showed how the text supported his philosophy of nonviolence and opposed the other traditions.

> A third way is open in our quest for freedom, namely, nonviolent resistance, that combines toughmindedness and tenderheartedness and avoids the complacency and donothingness of the softminded and the violence and bitterness of hardhearted. My belief is that this method must guide our action in the present crisis in race relations. Through nonviolent resistance we shall be able to oppose the unjust system and at the same time love the perpetrators of the system. (7)

The sermon ends with a claim that the attributes of toughmindedness and tenderheartedness inhere in the nature of God—the former expressed in his justice and wrath and the latter in his love and grace. The sermon expounds the importance of both attributes in God and the need we have at various times to see one or other side of the Divine. We need to see God's justice in the face of the giants of injustice, and we need to experience his love in times of adversity, disappointment, and defeat.

In a sermon "On Being a Good Neighbor" King used as his text the query of the young lawyer, "And who is my neighbor?" (Luke 10:29). Once again we find him using his text as a means of describing the evil implicit in the human situation in addition to pointing the way for its resolution. After showing the way in which Jesus rejected the temptation to engage in an abstract theological debate but rather chose to illustrate the nature of neighborliness in a concrete way by telling the story of the Good Samaritan, he concluded that neighborly virtue is altruism. That concept served as the organizing principle for the rest of the sermon. Altruism is discussed according to the three ways in which King discerned its appearance in the story of the Good Samaritan: universal altruism, dangerous altruism, and excessive altruism.

First, the Samaritan's capacity for universal altruism is seen in his refusal to limit neighborly concern to race, religion, and nationality. The tribalism of the Old Testament, ancient Greece, and the practices of the American society are contrary to the spirit of the Samaritan. Those who are tribally centered, nationally centered, or racially centered ignore all who stand outside of those boundaries. Second, the Samaritan risked his life to save another. The road to Jericho was a dangerous one and those who passed by on the other side might have been afraid to stop. Similarly, many in our own day are afraid to take a stand for a variety of reasons. King praised Albert Schweitzer, Abraham Lincoln, and black civil rights workers who have not been motivated by thoughts of personal safety but rather by the moral issue at hand and its implications for the future. Finally, the Samaritan possessed excessive altruism. He went the second mile. He did more than duty required. King called for similar virtue in our day. While laws are necessary for regulating human behavior and are urgently needed to rid the land of racial segregation, King was fully aware of the fact that they alone would never bring about the kind of society we require, one characterized by neighborly relations at both the intergroup and interpersonal levels. Laws will effect desegregation, but a spiritual transformation necessitates an inner change, which alone can guarantee genuine interpersonal relations and expressions of compassion that cannot be regulated by legal codes.

King related his text and its interpretation directly to the civil rights movement and to the person of Jesus. The latter embodied the three forms of altruism revealed in the Good Samaritan, and those who participate in the civil rights movement are called "to obey the unenforceable" (28).

> A vigorous enforcement of civil rights laws will bring an end to segregated public facilities which are barriers to a truly desegregated society, but it cannot bring an end to fears, prejudice, pride, and irrationality, which are the barriers to a truly integrated society. These dark and demonic responses will be removed only as men are possessed by the invisible, inner law which etches on their hearts the conviction that all men are brothers and that love is mankind's most potent weapon for personal and social transformation. (28–29)

The Good Samaritan and Jesus manifest neighborly love, which alone is the aim of the struggle against racism.

As we have seen, King usually took a text as a basis for organizing his thought about contemporary problems. The sermon "A Knock at Midnight" is another such. Here he used Luke 11:5–6: "Which of you who has a friend will go to him at midnight and say to him, 'Friend, lend me three loaves; for a friend of mine has arrived on a journey, and I have nothing to set before him'?" The sermon begins with a focus on midnight—midnight in the parable and midnight in our world today. In the first section King described the midnight in the social order widened by war and the threat of war and midnight in our psychological and moral orders. Second, he discussed the

search of modern persons for hope and love and the expectation of many
that it can be found in the church. The third part of the sermon attends to
the response given to the one who knocked asking for three loaves. Here
King discussed the disappointments many experience who knock on the
doors of the church seeking the bread of social justice. At this point King
related the text directly to the immediate concerns of blacks for civil rights.

> Millions of American Negroes, starving for the want of the bread of freedom, have
> knocked again and again on the door of so-called white churches, but they have usu-
> ally been greeted by a cold indifference or a blatant hypocrisy. Even the white
> religious leaders, who have a heartfelt desire to open the door and provide the bread,
> are often more cautious than courageous and more prone to follow the expedient than
> the ethical path. One of the shameful tragedies of history is that the very institution
> which should remove man from the midnight of racial segregation participates in
> creating and perpetuating the midnight. (56)

King discussed the disappointment of those who approach the church
asking for the bread of peace during wartime or seeking the bread of
economic and racial justice. He did not spare the black church in this
respect; rather he said that two types of black churches have failed to
provide bread: "one burns with emotionalism and the other freezes with
classism" (58). King ended the sermon on a note of hope based on the fact
that every midnight looks forward to the dawn. That the slaves had hope is
evidenced in their songs. The Supreme Court decision of 1956 ended the
twelve-month ordeal of midnight experienced by blacks of Montgomery,
Alabama.

Thus, King is a good example of the prophetic strand of the black
Christian tradition. He employed scriptural texts for the purpose of
describing the nature of evil, the direction in which humanity should move
in order to overcome the destructive forces, the way in which Jesus
embodies the good, and the manner in which the civil rights struggle is
commensurate with the life of Jesus.

The Reform Strand

The reform strand was born during Reconstruction and is, therefore,
the most recent. Both the brevity of the period and the subsequent
disfranchisement of blacks seriously limited its development. This strand is
closely related to the prophetic strand, its chief difference being that its
thought and action approximate the American political process. It is goal
oriented and unafraid of compromise. It prefers to reach a portion of its
goals rather than none and is thus the most pragmatic of all. Representatives
of this strand of the tradition assume that religious thought and political
action are not the same thing and that the points of contact are necessarily
tenuous. The imperfect nature of humans prevents anyone from fully
embracing the truths of religion, which are grounded in the perfect will of

God. This theological position does not weaken their involvement in social action. They uphold the belief that since all human action is necessarily tinged with imperfection, it need not adhere rigorously to any absolute principles of action. Hence there is freedom for pragmatic decisions. These leaders engage in a minimum of philosophizing and theologizing and expend immense energies calculating effective means to reach limited, concrete goals. They enjoy a high degree of confidence that their actions will be successful and that their judgments are true. Repeatedly these representatives remind their followers that God is on their side and that, therefore, they cannot lose the battle. The Scriptures are constantly employed as a source of assurance. Let us illustrate the use of the Bible in this tradition by focusing on the preaching of Adam Clayton Powell.

Whenever Powell preached at Abyssinian Baptist Church, he made it clear that he spoke as a congressman, a leader in Harlem, and as a minister of the gospel. Since he saw no conflict among these roles, he was never reluctant to discuss from the pulpit his stand on any particular community or political issue. For example, in the opening sentences of a sermon entitled "Ye Are Not Your Own," he said, "I speak today as a minister of this historic church, and as one of the community leaders, and in my capacity as chairman of the Committee on Education and Labor in the House of Representatives of the United States Congress" (89). As a congressional representative and leader of Harlem, he stated his support for the school boycott, which he hoped would become national. Then he went on to say:

> And finally, I speak as the minister of this church. I tell you in the language of Paul: What? Know ye not that your body is the temple of the Holy Ghost which is in you, which ye have of God, and ye are not your own?
> For ye are bought with a price: therefore glorify God in your body, and in your spirit, which are God's. (1 Corinthians 6:19-20). (90)

Powell proceeds to expound on the dictum "Ye are not your own" by proclaiming that the final voice in all matters of community, home, and church life is not conscience, the president, the mayor, or anyone but God. Recognition of God as the final voice results in a sense of inner peace and security. Powell argues that those who do not acknowledge the voice of God as final arbiter may enjoy temporary success, but eventually they will be brought to destruction. He recalls David's envy in Psalm 73 of the prosperity of the wicked; envy that ceased after he went into the temple and discerned their final outcome.

> It is soul-soothing, and mind-easing, and spirit-strengthening to know that the final voice is in God. . . .
> In these days the voice of finance, industry, capitalism, money may seem to have the final word. But the final voice has not yet spoken: the voice of Him who holds the world in the hollow of His hand, where the cattle upon a thousand hills belong to Him; the voice of Him who lives upon the horizon, where everything is within His vision. In

these void days, the voice of dynamic progress may claim to have the final word. The voice of Him to whom a thousand years are but a day has yet to be heard.

In these days the voice of force, the tread of marching men, the searing of the skies, the intercontinental missiles may seem to have the final say. But the voice has not yet been heard from Him who hath put down the mighty and exalted the humble.

In these days the voice of white backlash may claim to have the final word, although it is speaking rapidly with less authority. But the final word will one day be spoken by Him in whom there is no east or west, who out of one blood made the entire world, who is classless and raceless. (92)

In a sermon called "The Courage to Repent," Powell urges the nations to repent. The sermon opens with a description of the statue to Servetus in Geneva, which was erected as a monument of repentance by the followers of John Calvin. Powell portrays with abhorrence the prevalence of self-righteousness. Not many will look back to the evil deeds of yesterday and say, "I have sinned against heaven and in Thy sight, O God." He continued, "People say that 'man may repent, but how can a nation?' I reply that public opinion, which is the mood of the masses, can be fashioned into either self-righteousness or humility and sorrow. This is the trouble of our world since World War II—an absence of any sense of common guilt. The world wants peace without repentance" (96). Powell acknowledges the difficulties of repenting and beginning anew. "Habits, thoughts and emotions establish their own patterns" (97). But Jesus demonstrated in the story of Nicodemus and the woman found in adultery that in the light of sincere repentance new beginnings are always possible. The sermon ends with Powell's recounting a dream in which he traversed the world and saw a new monument—a monument of repentance.

> In South Africa there was one set up and it had
>   the word "SHARPEVILLE" on it.
> In Russia there was one set up in Moscow and had
>   the word "HUNGARY" on it.
> In England it had the word "SUEZ."
> In Germany it had the words "SIX MILLION JEWS."
> In France the word "ALGERIA."
> In America it had the word "NEGRO." (98)

Like most black preachers, Powell was fond of demonstrating the relationship of the biblical message to the black situation by use of analogy. This is clear in a sermon "Walking Under A Cloud," based on Exodus 40:34–38. It was preached in the same week that the Supreme Court began hearing arguments in the case *Brown* v. *Board of Education*. Powell considered the problem of racial segregation in the nation's schools to be an evil greater than the nuclear bomb. The sermon focused on the symbolism of clouds. The "legalized cloud of segregation" comprises a paramount moral problem for the nation and the world. Since the cloud is the sign of an oncoming storm, Powell predicted that as the cloud of hindrance was removed for the people of Israel, so would the cloud of segregation be removed for black Americans (157).

Powell condemned capital punishment in a sermon entitled "The Injustice of Justice," arguing against the death penalty because it is not a deterrent to crime and because evidence shows that criminals spared from death after a period of imprisonment have better records than others. He cited scriptural injunctions to support his position, for example, the sixth commandment, Matt 5:38–39, and Matt 25:40.

Powell's message characteristically focused on the success that attends the efforts of the children of God. He demonstrated his ability to employ Scripture masterfully in a sermon "What A Day To Live In," based on Galatians 2:20, "I am crucified with Christ."

> There is nothing that the world can do against the people of God that will cause God to forget them as long as they "reverence him."
> He hath scattered the proud.
> The day of dictators in high places and in low places has passed. Nobody has sensed this more sensitively and completely than the black mass: that there will always be unity among men and women who are not proud and arrogant but in their humility will stand together.
> He hath put down the mighty.
> No person ever ruled this world for a considerable period through force and power and might and arrogance. Those who would seek to destroy the sons of God always end in self-destruction.
> Not by might, not by power, but by my spirit, saith the Lord.
> Let us make the world safe for what is right.
> He hath exalted them of low degree. (184)

In the same sermon Powell stressed the way in which the lowly have always been the agents of conquest over forces of inequality and injustice. "The men and women of history who have brought to this world any semblance of social progress, and substituted humanity for inhumanity, have in the main been barefoot prophets—men clad in rags, wandering in the desert, all souls proclaiming their protests from the depths of slavery. This is our racial and religious heritage" (184). Powell contended that Paul had this in mind when he wrote to his friends in Corinth "that God hath chosen the weak of the world to confound the mighty" (185). He went on to show that the Bible promises to care for those who follow him, to clothe and to feed them (Luke 12:22, 31; Ps 84:11; Ps 37:25). This sermon was integrally connected with the proposed legislation of the War on Poverty, which at the time Powell was busy guiding through Congress.

In a sermon, "Brotherhood and Freedom," Powell argued that the black church from its inception "has waged a ceaseless battle against the Hebrew-Christian doctrine of the inequality of man, believing instead that such a covenant ran counter to the plan of redemption" (232). He praised the black churches in general and Abyssinian Baptist in particular for keeping the faith when all others eliminated blacks from the Lord's plan. A significant flight of imagination, considerable rhetorical skill, and the use of allegory enabled Powell (like many other black preachers) to conclude that Jesus has blessed the black church in a unique way.

> When the Master saw His many Black children wronged, when he viewed the denial of His blessings to His flock, He must have addressed the founders of the Negro church thus: "upon this rock I will build my church; and the gates of hell shall not prevail against it. . . . I will give unto thee the keys of the Kingdom of heaven." (Matthew 16:18–19.) (232)

The sermon forcefully proclaims white Christianity's corruption as a result of its denial of Christ in its practice of racism. But it affirms the black church as the faithful agent of Christ and therefore a necessary instrument for the redemption of America and its churches.

The Nationalist Strand

The fourth strand in the black Christian tradition is the nationalist, which had its beginnings in the colonization movement before the Civil War. Perhaps its most characteristic feature is its spirit of cynicism and disillusionment. America is viewed as a place where blacks will never be treated justly. Advocates of this tradition consider racial injustice inevitable as long as blacks are controlled by whites, and consequently they advocate some form of racial separation to allow the race to gain the necessary control over its own destiny. Many of its prominent representatives have called for the founding of a black nation (either in Africa, America, or some other place) and have been self-consciously ideological, aiming at teaching blacks the truth about themselves, their history, and their contemporary situation. They anticipate the dawn of a new day when blacks will be self-sufficient and separate from those bent on their subjugation. Self-determination is the basic ethical and political principle underlying their thought and action. The principle of national sovereignty is believed to be a necessary condition for racial justice. Whenever the advocates of this principle have become racially chauvinistic, they have been in danger of betraying the racial equality implicit in the black Christian tradition. They have usually claimed that God is black, thus bestowing divine worth on their positive valuation of the black race.

While the other strands of the tradition often address themselves to whites as well as to blacks, the nationalist strand always speaks solely to blacks. Prominent exponents of this style have been Henry McNeil Turner, Marcus Garvey, and Albert Cleage. Let us examine Cleage's sermons in order to discern the way in which he uses the Bible to support his nationalist perspective.

The text for his sermon "Fear Is Gone" is Genesis 1:27, "So God created man in his own image." The opening paragraph states the intent of blacks to live as creatures of God. "'So God created man in his own image.' (Genesis 1:27) This is the essential Christian message which gets so mixed up in the minds of people. God created us in his own image. We intend to live as beings created in the image of God, and everything we do in the church should be designed to help us live that way" (11). The rest of the sermon is a description of the dawn of black consciousness throughout the land, enabling blacks to affirm themselves and their interests with dignity and pride. Cleage interprets all such trends as the beginning of a black nation in a white world. The black consciousness movement implies that blacks no longer wish to be a part of the white world, which they designate as corrupt and hostile. Consequently, whites can no longer exclude them. Rather, they aim at controlling their own world and shaping their own destiny. At the end of this sociopolitical treatise, Cleage proclaims that the black church "must free our minds, strengthen our bodies and unite our people." Then he concludes with a reminder of the text and its challenge: "This is the task of the church because God created us in his own image and as children of God we must walk with pride and dignity. We are going to be free by any means necessary" (20). In other sermons Cleage used this scriptural verse to prove that God is black. He argued that if God created the human person in his own image, then we must look at the human in order to see God's image. If people are white, black, brown, red, yellow, it follows that God must be some combination of all. Since, in America, one drop of black blood makes one black, then according to American law God is black.

Cleage believes that the black nation is the kingdom that Jesus, the black messiah, intended to build on earth. His sermon "A Sense of Urgency" is based on the text, "Behold, the hour is at hand" (Matt 26:45). Much of the sermon is a description of Jesus as a black nationalist trying to bring a nation into being. Cleage believes that Jesus went to Jerusalem to found the black nation and that he later chose to die in order that the nation might live. The eating of bread, drinking of wine, foot washing, the betrayals—all symbolize important elements in nation building.

> The hour is at hand. And the hour is the hour of building a Black Nation. Some of us, if need be, must die. Anytime we forget that we must be willing to die, the Nation is through. Because anybody can oppress us if we're afraid to die. We have to have a basic commitment to build a Black Nation. And this we will build on the teachings of Jesus Christ, Black Messiah. (31)

Cleage deletes the writings of St. Paul from the canon because he believes that Paul's emphasis on individualism has corrupted authentic Christianity. In a sermon entitled "An Epistle to Stokely" he attempts to demonstrate that the Christianity Stokely Carmichael repudiated is an aberration constructed by white racists. Cleage believes that Christianity is essentially and historically a black man's religion, and he reinterprets the basic stories of Israel in that light. His analysis leads him to conclude, "There is no question about Abraham and the beginning of the Nation Israel being very

closely related to Africa, the Egyptians, and to Black people" (39). Cleage
sees a close similarity between contemporary black nationalists and Jesus.
Both rejected the institutional expressions of religion by founding movements rather than churches. Here his allegorical style rises to prominence.
The "Epistle to Stokely" is based on the text Mark 3:27, "But no one can
enter a strong man's house and plunder his goods, unless he first binds the
strong man; then indeed he may plunder his house." Cleage relates this verse
to the contemporary situation in this way: "When they draft all of the cream
of our young men, whether they kill them in Vietnam or put them in the
penitentiary, they have bound our strong men. Then indeed they may at
their will and at their pleasure plunder our house" (46).

Similarly, Cleage relates many scriptural passages directly to the black
condition. Psalm 62:3 ("How long will you set upon a man to shatter him,
like a leaning wall, a tottering fence? They only plan to tear him down from
his dignity") is related to the enemies of the black nation today. "How long
will they continue to oppress and to exploit and to do all the things they
have been doing? How long will they continue to use violence in an effort to
destroy us?" (48) Cleage has no difficulty in showing the relationship of
Scripture to the contemporary black situation because God's task in both the
Old and New Testaments has been that of rebuilding the black nation.
Cleage interprets the verse "How can we sing the Lord's song in a strange
land?" to mean that blacks should not act the fool for white people but rather display dignity and respect for themselves and their traditions, for those
qualities comprise the cornerstone of black nationhood (52–53).

Cleage strongly asserts that anything that makes blacks proud is good
and anything that reduces their dignity is bad. And he believes that God's
will is precisely that—restoring dignity and self-respect to black people (55).
Hence, Cleage proclaims black people "God's chosen people." The command
is to love one another regardless of what the enemy does and with the confidence that the ultimate victory is God's. Cleage reminds his parishioners
that Jesus' task coincided with the building of a black nation. "In his efforts
to build a Nation out of the corruption and disunity of Israel, he constantly
faced the people's conviction that anything they might do would be futile,
because they felt that it was impossible for Israel to ever become a Nation
again. Jesus called men to decision saying, 'He who is not with me is against
me. He who does not gather with me, scattereth'" (60).

Cleage spurns all references to individualism in the New Testament,
considering them to be evidence of the decay of nationhood and the final
attempts of a colonized people to secure some individual benefits from their
relationship with the Roman oppressor. Cleage portrays Jesus' walking from
village to village, preaching, teaching, and healing, as part of the struggle of
building a black nation. Jesus is viewed as a revolutionary zealot in opposition
to the scribes and pharisees who collaborated with Rome. Cleage reminds us
that when Jesus began his ministry he went to the temple and read from

Isaiah. It was an offense and the people tried to kill him. "His ministry began in violence and conflict, just as it ended in violence and conflict" (62). After John the Baptist (also a zealot) had been imprisoned, Cleage tells us that Jesus assumed the leadership of the movement. When John's disciples came to inquire about his credentials for leadership, Cleage quotes Jesus as saying, "Tell John the things you see. I am building the movement by freeing and healing men that the Black Nation may be reborn." More importantly, Cleage says that the dictum "He who is not with me is against me" is as crucial for the black nation today as it was in Jesus' day (62).

Cleage's preaching demonstrates the humanity of Jesus in contrast to the theology that, he believes, views much of Jesus' life as a ritualistic preparation for a mystical act of redemption. He is convinced that our interpretation of his message depends on what we think he was doing. Since Cleage believed Jesus to be a nationalist, everything in his life is interpreted in that perspective. Thus, the triumphal entry into Jerusalem is viewed as a nationalist demonstration in which the focus is not on Jesus as a person but on the emerging new nation. Hence the cries, "Blessed be the kingdom of our Father David, that is coming" (76). Cleage depicts the 1963 march on Washington as the same sort of triumphal march as Jesus' entrance into Jerusalem.

In the Shrine of the Black Madonna, the meaning of all the Christian symbols is explicated in the framework of black nationalism. In Cleage's own words:

> Make it clear when people come into the church that they are coming into a Black Nation. Make it clear that the sacrament of communion is the sacrament whereby we symbolize the simple fact that for the Nation we must be willing to sacrifice even ourselves, even to have our bodies broken and our blood shed. The sacrament of communion is not some little empty thing whereby individuals are guaranteed a place in Heaven. It is the symbol that unites us in the Black Nation.
> So the Resurrection that we celebrate is not the Resurrection of the physical body of Jesus, but the Resurrection of the Black Nation which he started, the Resurrection of his ideas and his teachings. (99)

Similarly, all of the parables, miracles, and teachings of Jesus are interpreted in such a way as to show their immediate relevance to the liberation of blacks and the building of the black nation.

Thus, the nationalist strand of the black Christian tradition interprets Jesus as a zealot and allegorically shows how his thought and action relate directly to the black nationalist struggle against racism. Jesus was not a racist in spite of his identification with a specific group of people. Black nationalism does not necessarily imply a racist perspective, and, in the thought of Cleage, all racism is evil.

Conclusion

The way in which the Bible has been appropriated by the black churches is not a simple matter. It is a mistake to view the black churches as homogeneous institutions; they are as diverse and complex as the people and their experiences have always been. This is not to imply that there is no common ground among them, but the richness of the subject matter is lost if one focuses only on that which they have in common. A careful analysis of the black churches reveals many forms of religious thought and practice.

The main objective of the pastoral strand is to comfort and to console those who are battered by life's adverse circumstances and to assist in their recovery and continued development. The chief goal of the prophetic strand is to create a normative basis for its social criticism and its redemptive potential for both races. The reform strand aims primarily at giving its people hope in the future, assurance that their struggle is just, and confidence of victory because of God's unquestioned support of their efforts. And the nationalist strand concentrates on the task of building the race into a nation by instilling in all blacks racial pride, solidarity, and a new world perspective.

The Bible is utilized whenever it is helpful in verifying and justifying the aims of the various strands of the black Christian tradition. Scriptural passages, interpreted in the light of these strands, lend the weight of sacred authority to these perspectives. Whenever Scripture is interpreted from the perspective of some tradition other than the black Christian tradition, it fails to speak meaningfully to black people. In fact, it is experienced as alien, irrelevant, insignificant, and even false. Thus the interpretive framework is more basic than the Scriptures themselves because it alone guarantees meaning. In fact, there are no sacred Scriptures for blacks apart from the hermeneutical principles by which they are received and transmitted.

It should not be difficult for anyone to discern the reasons why the black churches rarely engage in doctrinal controversies regarding the Bible. The Bible in itself is not the concern of the black churches. The specific perspectives on race relations are their fundamental concern, and hence those perspectives have been the basis for considerable conflict, which has had significant implications for the use of the Bible in the black churches.

WORKS CONSULTED

Cleage, Albert B., Jr.
    1969   *The Black Messiah*. New York: Sheed and Ward.

Cone, James H.
    1972   *The Spirituals and the Blues*. New York: Seabury Press.

DuBois, W. E. B.
    1970   *The Souls of Black Folk*. In *Three Negro Classics*. New York: Avon Books.

English, James W.
1973   *The Prophet of Wheat Street: the Story of Wil-
                        liam Holmes Borders, a Man Who Refused to
                        Fail.* Elgin, IL: David C. Cook.

Jackson, Joseph H.
1964   *Many But One: the Ecumenics of Charity.* New
                        York: Sheed and Ward.
1967   *Unholy Shadows and Freedom's Holy Light.*
                        Nashville: Townsend Press.

King, Martin Luther, Jr.
1968   *Strength to Love.* New York: Harper and Row.

Lanternari, Vittorio.
1965   *The Religions of the Oppressed: A Study of Mod-
                        ern Messianic Cults.* New York: New American
                        Library.

National Baptist Convention
1963   *Record of the 83rd Annual Session, September 3–
                        8, 1963.* Nashville: Sunday School Publishing
                        Board.
1970   *Record of the 90th Annual Session, September 8–
                        13, 1970.* Nashville: Sunday School Publishing
                        Board.

Paris, Peter J.
1978   "The Moral and Political Significance of the Black
                        Churches in America." In *Belief and Ethics: Es-
                        says in Ethics, the Human Sciences, and Ministry
                        in Honor of Alvin Pitcher,* ed. W. W. Schroeder
                        and G. Winter. Chicago: Center for the Scientific
                        Study of Religion.

Philpot, William M.
1972   *Best Black Sermons.* Valley Forge, PA: Judson
                        Press.

Powell, Adam Clayton, Jr.
1967   *Keep the Faith, Baby.* New York: Trident.

Washington, Joseph R.
1964   *Black Religion: The Negro and Christianity in the
                        United States.* Boston: Beacon Press.
1966   *The Politics of God.* Boston: Beacon Press.

Wilmore, Gayraud S.
    1972   *Black Religion and Black Radicalism: An Exami-
                    nation of the Black Experience in Religion.* New
                    York: Doubleday.

Dorothy Day and the Bible

William D. Miller

During the afternoon session of August 6, 1976, Dorothy Day was to respond to a paper, "Women in the Eucharist," at the Catholic Eucharistic Congress at Philadelphia. Although the city was at that moment racked with alarms and rumors over the outbreak of legionnaire's disease, a sizable crowd had gathered to hear her. Most attending the congress—priests, nuns, and lay persons—knew of Dorothy Day and her Catholic Worker movement. Many thought of her as a prophet. She was now in her eightieth year and beset by the infirmities of age. Many in the audience felt that her future speaking engagements would surely be limited, and her appearance seemed to confirm their concern. She was frail, as one who had come from a sickbed, and the transparency and fragility of old age were upon her. However, these signs increased rather than diminished the dramatic impact she had always registered on audiences. Her eyes, with their unusual slant, seemed larger and more luminous, and as always she was garbed in clothing that probably had come from the bins of the New York Catholic Worker house.

Despite her years of public speaking and the assurances of those who heard her that she had an unusual gift for this form of communication, she always approached a platform with a trepidation approaching terror. A week before the congress she had written to a friend that she was looking forward "with such dread to the Eucharistic Congress when I speak Aug. 6 (Hiroshima Day) that I can plan nothing" (Letter to W. D. Miller, July 28, 1976).

With taut lines in her white face she began, and as usual she did not try to conform to the format prescribed for her but spoke directly of those convictions of her heart that had been the unquenchable flame of her life for half a century. Conceivably, she might have launched a well-tailored polemic on some aspect of the position of women in the Catholic church, but she did not. She spoke of the love of God and of the necessity of taking that love to all creation. She wanted to express, she said, her own experience of the awakening of that love. "My conversion began . . . at a time when the material world began to speak in my heart of the love of God." She thought of a passage in St. Augustine's *Confessions* that she had read at the time. "What is it I love when I love Thee?" Augustine had written, and then, as she explained, he had gone on to list all of the beauties of creation that delighted the senses. She had lived by the sea at the time, and it was its beauty, the sense of wonder and of awe it produced in her, and its ability to sustain life that "spoke to me of a Creator who satisfied all our hungers."

She talked of the church: "It was also the physical aspect of the Church which attracted me. Bread and wine, water (all water is made holy since Christ was baptized in the Jordan), incense, the sound of waves and wind, all nature cried out to me." She said her love and gratitude to the church had increased with the years. "She taught me the crowning love of the life of the Spirit." But the church had also taught her that "before we bring our gifts of service, of gratitude, to the altar—if our brother have anything against us, we must hesitate to approach the altar to receive the Eucharist. 'Unless you do penance, you shall all perish.'"

And then, having invoked a truth of Scripture, she reminded her hearers and the managers of the congress that there, on August 6, they had not registered a sign of penance, of sorrow for the event that had occurred on that day some thirty-one years ago. "And here we are on August 6th, the day the first atomic bomb was dropped. . . . There had been holocausts be-fore—massacres. After the First World War, of the Armenians, all but forgotten now, and the holocaust of the Jews, God's chosen people. When He came to earth as Man, He chose them. And He told us 'All men are brothers,' and that it was His will that all men be saved, Japanese, Jew, Armenian." The Lord, she said, "gave us life, and the Eucharist to sustain our life. But we have given the world instruments of death of inconceivable magnitude." She concluded: "Today we are celebrating—how strange to use such a word—a Mass for the military. . . . No one in charge of the Eucharistic Congress had remembered what August 6th means in the minds of all who are dedicated to the work of peace. Why not a Mass for the Military on some other day?" Even now, could not they all regard that Mass and all other Masses that day as an act of penance, asking God's forgiveness for all desecrations of life—of creation? (*The Catholic Worker*, September 1976).

This brief address was typical of the talks she had for forty years been giving to audiences ranging from a few people in the main room of some Catholic Worker house of hospitality to august assemblages of church leaders. Her theme was one from which she seldom departed: the love of God for all of creation, the oneness of creation, and the necessity for an immediate and radical transformation of the social order so that the love of God for all humankind could again become believable to the masses of the world who feel themselves alienated from that love. For, as she would have affirmed, all persons (however disorganized, mad, or enraged by what appeared to be the growing malignancy of a determined history) want to believe. And what they want to believe in is not the final triumph of nothingness but the completion of love, the completion of community in an everlasting ecstatic moment—in God.

This was the woman who on past occasions had appeared to rebuke church authorities for what she considered to be their failure to fulfill the gospel spirit in dealing with the world of history, yet who in her heart was utterly loyal to the church. It was she who, with several young helpers, had tremulously pushed her way into New York's Union Square, jam-packed with communists assembled there for a May-Day rally; she was selling the first edition of *The Catholic Worker,* a tabloid priced at a penny a copy—which still sells for a penny. The paper announced that it would be a Catholic voice for the poor, for all who were victimized by prejudice and the outworn dogmas that structured the nation's political and social system. It would be an *authentic* Catholic voice, seeking to cut through the bourgeois accretions that had all but obliterated the spiritual center. Its guide would be the church of tradition, the lives of the saints, and the papal encyclicals, especially those that dealt with the social order.

It was she who for nearly half a century had, with her many devoted associates, succored in Catholic worker houses of hospitality those debilitated and deranged outcasts from society who had escaped the net of institutionalized ordering. It was she who had taken the inflexible position that all war was contrary to the gospel; that the capitalistic system, with its emphasis on profit and its consequent deification of things at the expense of true human creativity, was antithetical to true freedom. It was she who saw in the mushrooming complexities of the object world the growth of a Caesardom that was destroying the dignity and self-consciousness of the person, a view that was expressed in a phrase she frequently used, "Holy Mother State." Dorothy Day was a radical who did not look to history's process, to forms and institutional arrangements to solve the human problem, but who looked to the truths of the timeless life of the spirit.

So unaccustomed is the contemporary mind to seeing religion—or the idea of the spirit—as a force that can be made active in a world shattering into a mad and brutal impersonalism that the idea itself is radical beyond all others. The traditional role of the liberal reformers has been the redirecting of history's process, not the transformation of the process. They have been obsessed with the accumulation and organization of facts in the hope that the morbidity of erratic change will give way to the hum of an eternal and steadily accelerating progress. In the view of Dorothy Day and the Catholic Worker movement, it is this quest for the objectifiable that has prompted the increasingly grandiose visions of structural order (the totalitarian state) and, more insidiously, has stripped us of freedom. This quest has imposed upon us the necessity of conforming to an ever-increasing multiplicity of mechanical interactions; by so conforming, we have lost the contemplative dimension of existence in favor of one that could be called the historical dimension, where sense is deified and the idea of the spirit has been lost.

As Dorothy Day said at the congress, it was "the crowning love of life of the Spirit" which came first and by which all else was ordered. The central fact of existence should not be history's process, with individuals holding on in whatever places they find most tolerable; it should be a turning to a life of active love that finally would redeem and end history. The revolution of Dorothy Day and the Catholic Worker movement was a personalist revolution. It was not to be waged for a political or social organization in the customary dress of slogans, banners, and the exciting call of fighting one more battle to rid the new idea of all its enemies. On the contrary, it was to be a revolution that began by "putting on Christ." It proceeded toward community rather than fragmentation. It meant the primacy of the subject rather than that of the object. It was a revolution that began with the person but that had all of creation as its object.

This is the position of the woman whose reputation and influence has steadily increased through the years so that she has been placed by many into an almost magisterial role in the church. This role had been assigned to her by Catholics looking for a new vision and a new life in their church; it had come from members of other religious bodies who felt that they had found in Dorothy Day someone who affirmed truths that did not admit of sectarian labeling. She has elicited a wondering and bemused approval from those who professed to have lost faith. "If I were a praying man," wrote a retired professor who once had been high in the councils of his field, "I would say a special prayer for you and your vocation every night. As it is, a day seldom passes without my thinking of you and your work—and being thankful that the crazy human race can still produce some people like you and your fellow Workers. Sometimes when I think of you and this dying world, I weep like Jeremiah" (Catholic Worker papers).

The first three decades of Dorothy Day's life were her wandering years. She was born November 8, 1897, at Bath Beach, Brooklyn. When she was six, her father, a sports writer, took the family to California. They were there just over a year when the great San Francisco earthquake occurred, burning the plant of the newspaper for which the father wrote. The Days then moved to Chicago, where they lived in modest comfort and in the warmth of the family. For Dorothy, this community was made up of her mother and father, two older brothers, a little sister, and a baby brother. Her father was always a remote person, someone who worked at night and slept during the day and for whom she seemed to have developed no especially strong ties of affection or dependency. Her mother was an efficient and intelligent woman, the center of graciousness and order in the family. With a scholarship based on test scores, Dorothy went to the University of Illinois at Urbana when she was sixteen, just as World War I was beginning. At college she went her own way, missing classes, staying up all night to read Fyodor Dostoyevsky, Jack London, and Upton Sinclair, and otherwise working for pennies a day with which to buy a meager amount of food.

In her autobiography, *The Long Loneliness*, she describes her changed attitude toward religion: "I felt . . . that religion would only impede my work. I wanted to have nothing to do with the religion of those whom I saw all about me. I felt that I must turn from it as from a drug. I felt it indeed to be an opiate of the people and not a very attractive one, so I hardened my heart" (41). On the other hand, the Marxist slogan, "Workers of the World unite! You have nothing to lose but your chains," seemed to her "a most stirring battle cry. It was a clarion call that made me feel one with the masses, apart from the bourgeoisie, the smug, and the satisfied" (4). The one source of human warmth in her life was her friendship with the daughter of a well-to-do Chicago merchant, Rayna Simon. Rayna, an intense and vital person, nourished Dorothy with food and a sensitive appreciation of her young friend's hunger for friendship. Rayna, cause-driven herself, went on to become a dedicated communist, dying tragically in Moscow in 1927 (Sheean).

Dorothy left college in June 1917 to follow her parents in a move to New York City. There she got a job as a reporter for the socialist *Call*, and for several months she breathed the exhilarating air that came from being nineteen in New York at a time when a new cause was born amidst the catastrophe of World War I. She took a room on Cherry Street near the Manhattan Bridge in the midst of the Jewish community; she interviewed Trotsky for the *Call*; and on March 21, 1917, at Madison Square Garden, "I joined with those thousands in reliving the first days of the revolt in Russia. I felt the exultation, the joyous sense of victory of the masses as they sang . . . the worker's hymn of Russia," described by the *Call* the next day as a "mystic, gripping melody of struggle, a cry for world peace and human brotherhood" (Day, 1952:63). In April 1917 she left the *Call*—fired by the editor, probably because the young reporter's five dollar-a-week salary was more of a drain on the financial reserves of the *Call* than it could stand.

Unemployed, she joined a group of Columbia University students who were going to Washington to demonstrate against the war. Returning to New York, she found a job on *The Masses* as an assistant to Floyd Dell, who described her as "a charming young enthusiast, with beautiful slanting eyes" (Miller: 47). That summer, while the war raged, she and her radical friends talked and dreamed of the new socialist society that would rise after the war. In November *The Masses* was suppressed, and Dorothy, again unemployed, went to Washington to join a group that was going to picket the White House for women's suffrage. She was jailed for two weeks, again returning to New York when she was released. That winter she lived an aimless life—a Greenwich Village bohemian. She did a little writing and sought the companionship of her artist-radical friends. That winter she began to hang around the Provincetown Playhouse, where Eugene O'Neill was beginning to carve out his career as a playwright. On winter nights after a play practice, she would join the players in the back room of Jimmy Wallace's saloon at Fourth Street and Sixth Avenue, just around the corner from the Provincetown Playhouse. It was in this room, called by its denizens the "hellhole," that she listened one night to O'Neill reciting Francis Thompson's "The Hound of Heaven." Thirty years later, in his *The Moon for the Misbegotten*, O'Neill fashioned a character, "Josie," a composite who had at least one of the characteristics of Dorothy Day.

The next seven years of Dorothy Day's life, from 1918 to 1925, are years that she prefers not to talk or write about. She briefly trained to be a nurse, gave it up, married, and went with her husband to Europe, where in Italy she wrote a novel. Apparently leaving her husband, she returned to America in 1921 and took up life in Chicago. Her days there were disordered, and seeking to break with that life she went in 1923 to New Orleans and got a job reporting for the New Orleans *Item*. Her assignment was to take a job as a taxi-dancer on Canal Street and write stories about the girls.

In the spring of 1924 the manuscript of the novel she had written in Europe was published by Boni and Liveright, the firm that was bringing out the works of many of the young writers who would so brilliantly illuminate the literature of the postwar era. Then came a telephone call telling her that the manuscript had been sold to a movie producer for five thousand dollars. This heartening augury of a significant breakthrough into the higher levels of literary renown was misleading, but the money was real. With her fortune she returned to New York and began again to associate with her communist, anarchist, and literary companions. She bought a small beachcomber's cottage on Raritan Bay among a community of Russian anarchists. Shortly after, she began to live with a war veteran, a somewhat iconoclastic person whose view of existence was dour.

In *The Long Loneliness* Dorothy Day has written an account of her conversion to God, and in it, for a brief moment, she tried to fathom those years between 1919 and 1927 when her life had been swept into an aimless and sometimes turbulent course. "I was making no pretensions to being a Christian at the time," she wrote. She was a radical whose rule for her own life was that of "following the 'devices and desires of my own heart.'" Sometimes it was perhaps the Baudelarian idea of "choosing the downward path that leads to salvation" (57). And further on she wrote that "the life of the flesh called to me as a good and wholesome life, regardless of man's laws, which I felt rebelliously were made for the repression of others. The strong could make their own law, live their own lives; in fact, they were beyond good and evil. What was good and what was evil? It is easy enough to stifle conscience for a time. The satisfied flesh has its own law" (82). Scattered and misdirected as her life appeared to have been, she had always possessed a sense of the sacred and, from somewhere, no matter how much she might rationalize to her own satisfaction the character of her life, she heard the call of the spirit. "Many a morning after sitting all night in taverns or coming from balls at Webster Hall, I went to an early morning Mass at St. Joseph's Church on Sixth Avenue and knelt in the back of the church, not knowing what was going on at the altar, but warmed and comforted by the lights and silence, the kneeling people and the atmosphere of worship" (82).

Malcolm Cowley, the author and critic, recalled a time (he thought it was in the spring of 1919) when Dorothy had come to visit him and his wife, Peggy, at 107 Bradford Street in the Village. As Peggy cleared the kitchen, Dorothy and Malcolm went out to shop for additional food. Cowley remembered that their course took them past St. Peter's Episcopal Chapel on Hudson Street and that Dorothy had said, "Come in with me." "So we went in," Cowley continued. "The service was the Episcopal Evening song, or something like that, and after a while Dorothy got down on her knees and prayed. I saw tears streaming down her face, and then she said, 'Don't tell anybody about this'" (Letter to W. D. Miller, August 6, 1976).

When she was training to become a nurse, she dragged herself out of a heavy sleep to an early Sunday Mass. "One day, I told myself as I knelt there, I would have to stop to think, to question my own position: 'What is man, that Thou art mindful of him, O Lord?' What were we here for, what were we doing, what was the meaning of our lives?" (Day, 1952:90). And through these years there was "always . . . the New Testament. I could not hear of Sonya's reading the gospel to Raskolnikov in *Crime and Punishment* without turning to it myself with love. I could not read Ippolyte's rejection of his ebbing life and defiance of God in *The Idiot* without being filled with an immense sense of gratitude to God for life and a desire to make some return" (1952:105).

Through it all it is clear that at the core of her being she was a seeker of love and community, and she was so sensitive and open-minded to the signs of the spirit that she intuitively moved toward a love that transcended the senses. Walking along the beach at Raritan Bay, she came to see nature as a striking sign of God, and, as she said, she began unconsciously to pray, coming to realize that she took delight in it. Then she asked herself what she was slipping into. Her communist authorities had told her that religion was a crutch for those not quite whole; it was an opiate, a delusion for those who grieved or were deeply troubled. But then, she thought, she was not unhappy. She prayed because she was happy.

On March 3, 1927, her daughter, Tamar, was born. It was an occasion of such joy that she wrote an article about the experience which was published in the *New Masses*. Several weeks later as she was wheeling her baby, she encountered a nun, Sister Aloysia, who was from a nearby home run by the Sisters of Charity. With a minimum of preliminaries she told Sister Aloysia that she wanted Tamar baptized. This statement from a radical and bohemian seemed not to have startled the nun at all. A procedure was mapped out, and shortly after Tamar was baptized. The action appeared impulsive, but like other seemingly impulsive actions in her life, it was an expression that she accepted as beyond reason or feeling to redirect. Having Tamar baptized meant that she, too, would in time become a Catholic. It also meant that it would insure the departure from her life of Tamar's father, although this contingency appeared to have been increasingly probable under any circumstances. So on a misty December day in 1927, she took the ferry from New York City to Staten Island and then made her way to the village of Tottenville, where she was baptized in its Catholic church. When it was over and she had gone to confession, there was no rapturous welling up of her spirit. She had set herself a hard course, yet she would never doubt that it had been a truthful one.

Perhaps at this point she might have written a "convert" book whose sales potential could be enhanced by a condemnation and exposure of her radical life and past friends. Not that. What she sought in the church was instruction, a way of life that would lead her into the life of the spirit. She did not want the kind of community that came from condemnation, the kind that went with banners, exhortations, and crusades, where there was always one more dragon to be slain; she wanted a community that embraced all of creation and was timeless. In becoming a Catholic she had assigned a redirection to her life, and with an inflexible determination she tried to conform to the mind of the church as it was shown to her by priests whom she had taken as her spiritual advisers. There was progress. In an article she wrote in 1932 she spoke of her spiritual contentment: "And when this morning after I made my Communion and my soul was in a very sensitive state of joy and tenderness, the idea came to me again that I should write of the different times and ways that God has sought my soul. I felt that a command had been given me and a duty laid upon me" (1932:223–24).

Dorothy Day seems to have seldom been without a sign when she required one, and ordinarily that sign always confirmed her in convictions already established. Yet, if in the fall of 1932 she felt that a duty had been laid upon her, it was not that of writing a spiritual biography. It was at this point that her profession as a Christian and Catholic encountered a crisis, and it was from this crisis that the Catholic Worker movement emerged. Dorothy Day's extravagances of action and of pronouncement—her uncompromising, unqualified pacifism, her insistence that the most abandoned of the "unworthy" poor must be fed, clothed, and given their human due, her intransigent opposition to the spirit and many of the practices associated with capitalism—have struck some as a kind of romantic escapism. But her position is not one of escape but of confrontation—a radical confrontation with the abiding question of what it means to be human.

Her crisis came in December 1932 when she went to Washington to report on the hunger marches for two Catholic periodicals, *America* and *Commonweal*. Witnessing the long lines of the hungry unemployed, she was confronted by an aching realization that her religious profession did not reach to the problem of these hungry men and women. She knew, without the aid of a computer analysis of the subject, that somehow her Christian faith had been turned aside from history, distorted in its meaning, and converted into cotton candy fluff to be smeared on all the forms of bourgeois striving that had taken hold in the world so as to give wars and the acquisition of things an aura of holiness. The communists had organized the hunger march; they could organize the world, but Christianity and the gospel spirit must stand aside from history's process. Anguished, she went to the Shrine of the Immaculate Conception to pray for a solution to the dilemma she felt. "And when I returned to New York I found Peter Maurin—Peter, the French peasant, whose spirit and ideas will dominate . . . the rest of my life" (1952:162).

What was Peter Maurin to the Catholic Worker movement? He was the founder, Dorothy Day has answered, and that is true. Peter gave Dorothy the idea, the platform, that enabled her to see her religious profession not as something that ended with herself where the world of institutions and history's process was concerned but as a profession which, if it followed true to the teaching of the gospel and to the mind of the church, could leave no part of creation untouched or uncared for. As Dorothy Day has said so many times, Peter Maurin taught a correlation of the spiritual and the material. There could be no separation of the life of the spirit from the object world. Community formation began in time. It began now—not according to the time-serving formulas of ideologies, class divisions, or racial enmities, but immediately with the other person. Community was in the opposite direction of the objectivized impulses of the bourgeois person. It was found in the spirit of the Gospels; it was found in giving and not in acquisitiveness. It began with the person next to you, but it had no ending.

With this redirected view of things, commencing with the subject rather than the object, the meaning in history could be rediscovered. Peter Maurin was a professor who professed, who dealt with ideas, and who constantly strove for what he called "clarification." He was an intellectual historian who for years had read history and especially those social thinkers of the nineteenth century whose ideas were presaging profound changes in the life of the world. He made notes on what he read and was constantly synthesizing this material in an effort to answer that final question, what does it mean to be human? Dorothy Day has called Maurin a saint and a genius. Yet, who was he, when one considers the prestigious accomplishments of America's institutionalized scholars? He had no important monographic publications; he had received no grants from any of the large agencies that direct the creative efforts in American higher learning; he ignored the canons of acceptable scholarly writing (he did not use footnotes); in fact he did not even carry a briefcase, since all of his notes and his own writings were stuffed into the pockets of the clothes he wore. He was in fact a poor man, as indifferent to the accepted amenities of dress as he was to academic style. He gave his lectures to all who would listen to them: to professors, business people, editors, even to those clay-faced individuals who sat on benches in New York's Union Square. He believed that somewhere among them would be one that would see as he had seen. Then George Shuster, editor of *Commonweal* magazine, told Maurin he ought to meet Dorothy Day.

It was this meeting and Peter's subsequent daily instruction of Dorothy that produced the Catholic Worker movement. Perhaps Dorothy was the first student who caught the meaning of his "clarification," the one who did not see his selflessness, his obliviousness to all of the allurements of the object world as a kind of comic buffoonery but as the character of the saint who lives outside of time. Later, when those ardent young people came to the Worker house to build what they thought would be a new social order, some of them felt the impact of Peter's ideas and person—Stanley Vishnewski, Marge Hughes, Arthur Sheean, and Julia Porcelli. "Peter was a poet, he was an agitator, and the gentle strong voice of truth. This was the voice of the Holy Ghost and it wasn't listened to!" Miss Porcelli once exclaimed (Interview with Deane Mowrer, 1970).

Perhaps the leaders of the church did not listen to him, but Dorothy Day did. "We have written this before, and we repeat it again," she wrote in a concluding judgment of Peter; he "was the poor man of his day. He was another St. Francis of modern times. . . . He was a man with a mission, a vision, an apostolate. . . . He was truly humble of heart and loving. . . . He was impersonal in his love and he loved all, saw all others around him as God saw them. . . . He saw Christ in them" (*The Catholic Worker*, June 1949). Maurin died at the Catholic Worker farm at Newburgh, New York, on May 15, 1949.

"Peter . . . urged those of us who followed his direction to make a new synthesis of 'cult, culture, and cultivation;' and to read history," wrote Dorothy Day in her journal sometime in 1966. It was in this phrase, so frequently used by Maurin, that there occurred the "correlation of the material with the spiritual." It meant affirming the primacy of the spirit and then a reordering of the objectivized world of an economic and political process whose values have dominated contemporary culture to the life of the Gospels. It meant in one's own life a voluntary movement into unstructured simplicity, into poverty in terms of giving up all of the technical superstructure of contemporary life that poisons creation, into the formation of agricultural communes where the person can become a creative worker and where "the worker would become a scholar and the scholar become a worker."

What was his program for Dorothy? She, being a journalist, should begin a paper to introduce Maurin's ideas into the context of daily events. In the community formed around this enterprise, Maurin would hold what he called "roundtable discussions for the clarification of thought," and the poor around them would be fed. So it all began in May 1933. The world was seething on that day. Gigantic rallies were held in Moscow and Berlin with banners, marching, and singing—all, it might be supposed, springing from an irrational and frenzied seeking for community in a world where a vision of the unity of all had been obscured by a fragmenting acceleration of history.

The Catholic Worker spoke of a revolution of person against mass ideological and so-called scientific formations, but it was no less concerned with the social question. The paper announced that it would be a Catholic voice, seeking to cut through the bourgeois accretions that had obliterated the spirit. Its center was the church of tradition, the example of the saints, and the recent encyclicals of the popes that dealt with the social order.

The paper succeeded immediately, and within five years it was claiming a circulation of over one hundred thousand. These were the depression years, and many persons were disposed to think critically of the character of the institutional forms that structured their lives, a disposition that appeared to have been true for many Catholics, religious and lay, who were unmoved by the saccharine pieties and subservience of the traditional Catholic press to the dictums of the American bourgeois establishment. What paper apart from *The Daily Worker* would at that time have taken up the cause of the Scottsboro boys, the nine Alabama blacks who had been convicted of rape and sentenced to be executed? Dorothy Day said she prayed that they would be spared because their plight was the consequence of an "antagonism which . . . is often built upon the struggles of the poor whites and the poor blacks," both of whom were "victims of industrialists who grind the face of the poor" (*The Catholic Worker*, July 1933).

As in this case, some of the phrases in the *Worker* during its first years had about them the ring of class confrontation. The issue of March 1935 declared that "while Andy Mellon fights to hang onto the few million dollars of his $81,000,000 fortune which the government claims he owes in income tax, Mrs. Mary Johnson, employed for the last twelve years by the National Biscuit Company, is out on strike because she needs more than the twenty-two and a half cents an hour which is the . . . wage to be paid her by the largest biscuit company factory in the world, in order to take care of herself and her invalid husband who has not worked for three years." Perhaps Dorothy justified such contentious phrases on the grounds that they would establish *The Catholic Worker* as a paper that defended the rights of labor, as fiercely as *The Daily Worker*. For a brief period Dorothy was elevated to a leading role in the always popular cause of anticommunism. In 1932, when she protested the treatment of the Catholic church in Mexico, there was much approval. Two thousand singing and marching Catholic high school students in New York City joined a handful of Catholic Workers in picketing the Mexican consulate. Many saw it as a stirring example of the faith militant. The Catholic Action Club of Detroit wrote to the *Worker* that its activity "in combating the . . . fanatical persecution of the Church in

Mexico deserves the most unstinted praise. You may rest assured that the forces of Catholic Action in Detroit will not lag in the struggle against the vanguard of militant atheism" (Miller: 84). But confrontations were not what Maurin was talking about. "We are to be announcers and not denouncers," he said on many occasions. It took Dorothy some time to understand that Peter's "gentle personalism," as he called it, was alien to the spirit that indulged in journalistic flourishes at the expense of "Andy" Mellon or John D. Rockefeller.

The Spanish Civil War began in July 1936, and out of this event there emerged a Catholic Worker position on war that became its most controversial—its pacifism. "Almost to a man," says David O'Brien, "the heirarchy and the American Catholic press supported the Franco side" (86). But Dorothy Day did not support Franco and her sentiments were recorded in *The Catholic Worker*. "We do not expect a glittering army to overcome . . . heresy. . . . As long as men trust to the use of force—only a superior, a more savage and brutal force will overcome the enemy. We must use his own weapons, and we must make sure our own force is more savage . . . than his own." If, "we do not . . . emphasize the law of love, we betray our trust, our vocation" (Miller: 145).

In this period the cacophony of anti-Semitism broke out in Germany, and it was a malaise from which America was not free. Both Peter Maurin and Dorothy Day possessed a special sense of the historical and spiritual contribution of Jews to culture. A number of Maurin's short essays in the *Worker* were concerned with the special role of the Jews in the plan of salvation and with the sin of anti-Semitism. In Dorothy's own life Jews had been prominent as especially close friends and associates: Rayna Simon at the University of Illinois and then Mike Gold, editor of *The New Masses* during the twenties. In one of her random notes in the Catholic Worker papers Dorothy wrote, "To be a Jew—singled out—a priestly people—unique—to be a Jew is something sacramental." In this period of Father Charles Coughlin's *Social Justice,* the Christian Front, and the Silver Shirts, the Catholic Workers organized "The Committee of Catholics to Fight Anti-Semitism." It was headed by Professor Emmanuel Chapman of Fordham University, and it published a paper, *The Voice,* to which Catholic Workers were the main contributors.

As the signs began to foretell the coming of World War II, Dorothy Day remained steadfast in her pacifism, and in the period preceding the bombing of Pearl Harbor, she and *The Catholic Worker* received much approving support. On December 7, 1941, most of this support evaporated, but for Dorothy Day there was no change. In the January 1942 issue of *The Catholic Worker* she announced that her position had not changed. "We Continue Our Christian Pacifist Stand." She saw no choice in the matter. "We will print the words of Christ who is with us always: . . . 'Love your enemies, do good to those who hate you, and pray for those who persecute and calumniate you.' We are at war . . . with Japan, Germany, and Italy. But still we can repeat Christ's words, each day, holding them in our hearts, each month printing them in the paper. . . . We are still pacifists."

During World War II, her pacifism was not a unanimously held position among the thirty or more Worker houses around the country. Many, like young John Cogley, who was one of the founders of the Chicago house, took exception to the *Worker's* pronouncement. The circulation of *The Catholic Worker* fell by half. As one priest wrote her, she had gone against "the teaching of Moral theologians and against the Archbishops and Bishops of the country who sent word to our president telling him they were in utter cooperation with him in the present crisis" (Miller: 174). The pacifism of *The Catholic Worker*, like all of its positions, did not accommodate itself to the necessity of getting along in the process of history. It has remained absolute, and—judging from the example in contemporary times of the many young men who from a conscience formed by Catholic Worker principles chose prison rather than war—it might appear that history's process has been challenged.

Dorothy Day never regarded the publication of *The Catholic Worker* or the formation of positions on public issues as the primary concern of the Catholic Worker movement. Living under the tutelage of Peter Maurin, she came to see the central truth of his teaching: that entering into history's process as a combatant was not the way to effect history's redemption. Its redemption began with the person. In *The Catholic Worker* of January 1946 she wrote an editorial entitled "Why Poverty":

> People reading *The Catholic Worker* must be confused at times and feel as they go through its pages that they are leading a sort of Alice in Wonderland life. For instance, look at the first page. One article on the strike situation, and the prevalent low wages, high prices and ugly housing conditions for the workers. And now an article by Abbe Longpre on voluntary poverty, one of the planks in Peter Maurin's platform and the most fundamental and necessary plank. Perhaps we should even call it the cornerstone of the edifice which he is trying to build, the rock on which to begin to build. The acceptance of voluntary poverty liberates men from fear, from insecurity, and puts them in the frame of mind which enables them to think. Once we begin not to worry about the kind of a house we are living in, what kind of clothes we are wearing—once we give up the stupid recreation of this world—we have time, which is priceless, to remember that we are our brother's keeper and that we must not only care for his needs as far as we are able immediately, but we must try to build a better world.

Voluntary poverty and feeding the poor—were these of themselves the instruments for building a new world where social justice would prevail? Dorothy Day was not so simplistic as to believe that feeding the Bowery's poor would alleviate starvation in Asia. No, these were the means of changing the person, of taking a new position toward creation, of making the good believable, of affecting people who would affect others, so that the starving everywhere might be made a part of the human family and raised out of their slough. And so the little group at the first Worker house on Fifteenth Street in New York began to feed the poor. In the February 1937 issue of the *Worker,* Dorothy wrote that "Every morning now about four hundred men come . . . to be fed. The radio is cheerful, the smell of coffee is a good smell, the air of the morning is fresh and not too cold." But it was heartbreaking, she said, as she passed the line on her way to Mass. "One felt more like taking their hands and saying: 'Forgive us, let us forgive each other!' All of us who are more comfortable, who have places to sleep, three meals a day, work to do—we are responsible for your condition. We are guilty of each other's sins. We must bear each other's burdens. Forgive us and may God forgive us all!"

By 1940 Dorothy Day had established the main outlines of Peter Maurin's plan of action for her: a newspaper, houses of hospitality for the poor, and a farm commune that had been established at Easton, Pennsylvania, in 1936. All the while, she had, in her articles in the *Worker* and in the many talks she was giving around the country, affirmed her love for the church and her utter disposition to live as completely as she could the life it prescribed. In one of her undated notes she had written, "As for me I love the Church who has room for saints and sinners, for the mediocre, the lame, the halt and the blind. The great diversity in the Church gave me a feeling that I was truly welcome in it and I still like the expression, 'Holy Mother Church.'" Even as she was writing this, she said, she thought of "that big warm motherly soul in Steinbeck's *Grapes of Wrath,* who sits by the side of her son who is driving the broken down truck from one field of work to another, defeated by the miseries of their lot, but not conquered, fulfilling her woman's role of keeping the family of man together, in a life which can indeed be considered a vale of tears, but a life too, filled with the most intense joys which go hand in hand with sorrow and suffering in both the natural and supernatural order."

As a Catholic, Dorothy Day looked finally and solely to the church for her instruction—for her salvation. The church was at the point of unity where all of creation found its fusion and its meaning in the eternal. It was God moving into the substance of history; it subsumed all. She believed this in a believing that was more than a pious affirmation. She believed as one who, wasting with thirst, had found the cool stream. She was truly a pilgrim of the Absolute. Yet as rich and as joyful as her conversion had been, she set her foot into the church with no clear sense of the particular pathway that it might provide for growth in the life of the spirit. Peter Maurin had provided her with an understanding of the way in which she, a Catholic, could grapple with time so as to direct its course toward redemption; he had shown her a vocation; and he had given her a personal example of holiness beyond anything she had ever before seen. Still, she seemingly retained a yearning for that sweetness and assurance that would lift her above the turmoil of time, that would give meaning and hope to the totally exhausting life that weighed upon her as head of the Catholic Worker movement.

In the priest-directed retreats of the war years she found the true end of a spirituality that would stop short of nothing but the very substance for which she sought. In a study of the Bible this assurance and strength was given to her. A retreat, as Catholics know it, is a drawing apart, away from the commands of the world so as to focus on the life of spirit. Retreats vary in time from one day to several; in character, from the informal to the rigid and austere. The Catholic worker retreats went on periodically from 1940 through 1946, and they were notable for their rigor, with fasting and silence enjoined upon the retreatants. For Dorothy Day "it was as though we were listening to the gospel for the first time. We saw all things new. There was a freshness about everything as though we were in love, as indeed we were" (1952:245). She noted again that "when we separated, it was with pain; we hated to leave each other, we loved each other more truly than ever before, and felt that sense of comradeship, that sense of Christian solidarity which will strengthen us for the work" (Miller: 187–88). Such was the sense of community that she and her Worker friends felt that she called it a "fore-taste of heaven."

What had these retreats, this new experience of the Bible, done for her? They had opened a new vision of human and divine love. Without these retreats, she wrote, "I would never have a glimpse of this mystery, an under-standing of it. I could never have endured the suffering involved, could never have persevered" (Miller: 185). She had come to a new sense of what Peter Maurin had taught her. He had emphasized the person's worth and had made her understand that the realization of this worth was bound up with the social process. "Let us make a world where it is easier for people to be good," Peter would say repeatedly. But before she had not had so clearly that transcendent sense of the worth of the person. She explained: "For too long too little had been expected of us. . . . We began to understand the distinction between nature and the supernatural . . . and we saw for the first time the incomparable heights to which man is called. We saw for the first time man's spiritual capacities raised as he is to be a child of God. We saw the basis of our dignity" (Miller: 188–89).

She had once thought that she faced the alternative of choosing be-tween earth and heaven. However, people could give the world its brightest due by living in it and using it as they should when they became aware of what God had planned for them and sought to live in conformity with that plan. She had, she said, known of all this before. She knew well the scrip-tural admonition, "Seek ye first the Kingdom of God." But the retreats involved her in a "clarification" of personal experience. After one of the retreats she wrote:

Living as we do in the midst of thousands . . . I am often reminded of our quest:
"I will arise and go about the city: in the streets and
    broad ways.
I will seek Him whom my soul loveth.
I sought him and I found Him not . . . But, when
I had a little passed by them, I found Him whom my
    soul loveth: I held Him and I will not let Him go."
(*The Catholic Worker*, December 1951)

Pondering Scripture, she believed that she saw an example in the life of Christ that had meaning for her work. She came to see Christ not primarily as a social reformer but as the exemplar of all-sufficient love. In the January 1944 issue of the *Worker* she asked questions about Christ: "When St. John was put in prison by Herod, did Our Lord protest? Did He form a defense committee? Did He collect funds, stir up public opinion? Did He try to get him out?" No, she answered, he had done none of these things. His concern was not with institutionalized forms, with the world of process and of time. His concern was to draw all to the kingdom of God wherein all of creation would be redeemed.

The retreats impressed upon her one final, transcending conviction: that all were called to be saints and that the true revolution would occur when this call was answered. At the bottom of the cover of a Worker pamphlet entitled "Called to be Saints," in her own hand Dorothy had written, "This is the retreat." To become a saint, she wrote, "*is the Revolution*," giving the phrase her own emphasis. "Too little has been stressed the idea that *all* are called. Too little attention had been placed on the idea of mass conversions. We have sinned against the virtue of hope." Had there not been, she asked, mass conversions to Naziism, fascism, and communism? "Where are our saints to call the masses to God? Personalists first, we must put the question to ourselves. Communitarians, we will find Christ in our brothers." To see people as anything less than as God saw them was to deny people their human due. Thus the "call to be saints" was the call to true humanism.

In the Catholic Worker papers there is a copy of the notes that Dorothy made on a retreat at Oakmont, Pennsylvania, given by Father Louis Farina in the summer of 1943. To quote a fragment from these notes, hastily written as they were, would fall short of providing the substance of the retreat, yet they show a part of the process of a mind and soul bent on achieving the life of spirit. The thoughts, which Dorothy rapidly notes, are those of Father Farina:

The battle against mortal sin is a hopeless one. We must attack roots, the natural motive. Then sin will be dried up. The [Chris]tian fights on this plane always. Our whole attitude towards the world must be changed. St. Paul: All things new. 2 Cor. 5:17. We must cease looking for *natural* happiness.

Like being in love. No one exists for us but the Beloved . . . Helps and aids in growing in love of God. Spiritual reading. Best is God's own book—the Bible. Church is very insistent that we read the Bible, especially New Testament. St. Jerome: "he who does not know N.T. does not know Christ." St. John Chrysostom: "The mind of Paul is the mind of Christ." He [Father Farina] recommends reading epistles weekly so we know the mind of Christ—so we put on Christ. . . .

But the Bible is not the only source of truth; there is also tradition, the living voice of the Church. The Lord never wrote anything. He sent his apostles out, not to write but to teach.

Then Father Farina discusses a further way toward holiness: that of making a radical distinction between the call to a purely natural and sense-gratified existence and that of the call to God. In her notes, Dorothy writes her assent to this differentiation: "There is a law of the flesh" whose danger was in "captivating" the person. And then she adds a thought from Scripture: "Unhappy man that I am, who shall deliver me from the body of this death? The grace of God by Jesus Christ our Lord." How to be delivered from this "law of the flesh"?

It is by denying satisfaction to the flesh that we strengthen spirit. Rom 8:13. Wisdom of flesh is death. Our flesh life and spiritual life is like white and black threads all entangled. Gradually and slowly we must take out of our lives all that is of self. Galatians 5:16, 17. . . . Put God in every action every moment. . . . All day long we can make this choice, fight this battle. . . . Even thoughts of doing good are of the Spirit. We are essentially good.

Then, apparently at the close of the day's session, she writes: "The burden of retreat is to know that sanctity [the goodness that is in all] and let it grow—to start now. And we will indeed grow. . . . The only purpose for which we were made is to become saints." Later that evening she wrote something of a personal meditation:

I made the stations of the cross. (Did St. Francis start that?) Then I took a walk, saying the rosary. While walking I picked some sweet clover which is in the back of my notebook now. As I write, sitting here at my desk in the conference room, little bugs make exploratory trips around the desk and a measuring worm paces out its way across the back of the desk. Not content with what it is finding, it has made its way back to my bunch of weeds, my sweetgrass, which is as good a sample as I know of God's sweetness.

She wrote on, thinking about her vocation:

Fr. [John] Hugo once said, quoting from somewhere, that the best thing to do with the best of things is to give them up. Well, I have long since "given up," "offered up," the field and the shore for the city slum. "Why are you staying here?" Fr. McNabb's friends asked him, he who lived in London but was forever talking about Nazareth or Social Chaos. "To get people out of here," he replied.

So, she concluded,

It is my vocation to agitate, to be a journalist, a pamphleteer, and now my time must be spent in these cities, these slums. But how wonderful it is to be out here in . . . the

midst of fields, atop a hill and to have samples of Heaven all about, not hell. I truly
love sweet clover and thank God for it. "All ye works of the Lord—bless ye the Lord."

Most of the retreats were given by Father John J. Hugo who had
adapted his retreat form from one that had been given in the 1930s by a Ca-
nadian Jesuit, Father Onesimus Lacouture. When asked about retreats,
Father Hugo suggested as a source *Applied Christianity,* his basic retreat
formula, privately printed in 1944. Father Hugo stressed the role of the
Bible in his retreats:

> As to the Bible: I can only say that our retreat, which Dorothy made many
> times, was based on the Bible. I like to refer to it as an evangelic or Gospel retreat.
> Only one book was used: the Bible. We asked each retreatant to provide himself or
> herself with a Bible, at least a New Testament. The meditations are all inspired by,
> and based directly on, biblical passages. My task in directing retreats, as I saw it, was
> simply to bring the teachings from Scripture together in a unity that would provide a
> light on the Christian pilgrimage. . . . Dorothy never tired of making the retreat,
> whose basic plan was always the same. . . . We always insisted on silence and asked
> the retreatants to spend their time—six days or more—simply meditating on Scripture
> within the compass of the plan provided. But of course they were urged to move out
> into the Scriptures generally.

Father Hugo went on to say that one of the phrases that Dorothy used many
times in *The Catholic Worker* came from the retreat: "It may be said with
exact truth that one's own love of God is equal to the love that one has for
the person whom one loves least." Of course, Father Hugo continued, "This
is but a paraphrase of 'for with what measure you measure, it shall be measured to you' (Lk 6:38)." The priest concluded: "As you know Dorothy became a Catholic without much help, especially from Catholics. I have often
felt that through our retreat she found a spirituality and a theology" (Letter
to W. D. Miller, June 24, 1977).

The retreats were not above criticism from some members of the Catholic clergy, who questioned their austerity generally and specifically their
underlying principle of opposing nature to grace. As for Dorothy, she preferred to stay out of the debate, saying that she did not know enough about
the subject to register an opinion. Yet in the retreat of 1944, she was already
planning to write a book on the retreats, and the title she chose was "All is
Grace."

In some preliminary notes on her book plan, she commented on her
choice for a title. How, she mused, "in the face of the agony around us, how
can we say those words, 'All is Grace,' when we live in the midst of a war
whose horrors confront us hourly, daily; every hour on the hour, we get
news of the battle which is being fought, men are dying of fear and loathing
and hatred when the deepest desire of the human heart is to love." But
transcending all of the horror of war, "God is love," and "There is that assent
in our hearts to the truth of this. 'What have I on earth but Thee and what
do I desire in heaven beside Thee?' My heart and my flesh cries out for the

living God, and even the longing for this consummation is a joy, a foretaste of Heaven" (Catholic Worker papers). She wrote several hundred pages of notes on the retreats, but she never published the book. A quarter of a century later she was writing in her notes that "I wish to write one more book before I die and that will be about a spiritual adventure, our retreats which began in the early forties which influenced my life and gave me courage to persevere, and . . . 'this joy no man can take from me'" (Catholic Worker papers).

To those who are accustomed to regarding the Bible as a sole and all-sufficient source of truth, requiring no ordering authority to extract the true meaning of its message, Dorothy Day's experience on the retreats, which she described "as though she was listening to the gospel for the first time," might seem curious. As a Catholic she could not have regarded the Bible as a source of truth unrelated to the teaching authority of the church. She would have seen the church itself as a living extension of the Bible into history. Had not the church woven the Bible into the very substance of its life in its liturgical prayers? Had not the church, in fact, been so zealously concerned with maintaining the inerrancy of the Bible that in its councils and through its popes it had rejected all private spiritual or mystical understanding of the Scriptures, insisting upon "interpreting Scripture according to the literal sense intended by the human author"? (*New Catholic Encyclopedia*, 2:515).

In 1943, at the time when Dorothy Day was in the midst of her retreat experience, Pius XII published his encyclical letter on the Bible, *Divino afflante Spiritu*. One phrase in the letter particularly suggests Dorothy's position with respect to the Bible: "The sacred books were not given by God to men to satisfy their curiosity or to provide them with material for study and research, but as the Apostle notes, in order that these divine oracles may 'instruct us to salvation' by the faith which is in Christ Jesus" and "that the man of God may be perfect, furnished to every good work" (*New Catholic Encyclopedia*, 2:518). Pius, of course, was referring to the nineteenth- and twentieth-century commentaries on Scripture that tended to erode its traditionally sacred character, but to such interpretations Dorothy Day gave scant attention, and she did indeed believe that Scripture would "instruct to salvation."

The retreats confirmed her in her vocation and from them she achieved a new level of spirituality, but they did not introduce the Bible into her life. Into whatever byways she had gone in the days of her youth, she had always in the first promptings of her mind and heart been a seeker, believing that there was an answer. And by possessing this belief she had already opened herself to faith and the Bible. She reminisced once in her journal (as she frequently did) that "when as a child I first found a Bible in the furnished house we had rented in Berkeley—I was probably seven—I remember to this day how I held it in my hands, and went apart into the attic where it had been in a pile of books, and sat and read with a sense of the holiness of the Book. I remember the mustiness of that little attic as I remember the smell of fresh shingles in the building going on down the street, as I remember the smell of flowers we crushed up in little bottles in trying to make some perfume for our dolls, as I remember the smell of fresh baked bread in the house" (Catholic Worker papers).

Then later, in November 1918, when she was in solitary confinement in Occoquan prison for participation in the suffrage demonstrations, she turned again to the Bible. "I read it with the sense of coming back to something of my childhood that I had lost. My heart swelled with joy and thankfulness for the Psalms. . . . I clung to the words of comfort in the Bible and as long as the light held out, I read and pondered" (1952:78). She read the Bible through her wandering years, and later she would write concerning her baptism: "I had read the Gospels, and I believed. The Word was in Scripture and the Bread on the altar and I was to live by both, I had to live by both or wither away."

After becoming a Catholic she participated in the prayer life of the church, especially the Mass, which she attended almost daily. "It was the liturgy which led us to praying the psalms with the church, leading us to an understanding joy in prayer," she said in a speech she made at St. John's Abbey at Collegeville, Minnesota, in August 1968. "It was the liturgy which brought us close to scripture with all the new translations, the New Standard Version, the Knox translation, the Phillips paraphrase (I have heard it called) and now the Jerusalem Bible, with all its notes and commentaries. The 'hard sayings' of the Gospel became for us truly a sword which pierced the heart and separated us often from family and friends" (Catholic worker papers).

In no sense was reading Scripture a pious duty for her. Reading the Psalms every morning and praying the prayers of the church at compline every evening became the undeviating and necessary custom of her life. Again, it is in her journal that one finds this life described: "I wake up feeble with age and noise and the duties of a large family around me, here in the city and at the farm, scattered over the country, at home and abroad, and communicating with me by mail." But strength returned—with a cup of coffee "and the reading of the psalms, sometimes one or two, sometimes all of the Matins and in the Divine Office, complete, or in the short breviary, fortunately made available to us all now."

Why did she spend so much of her time in reading the Psalms? It was to revive her flagging spirits, she said, "I need this 'shot in the arm' to recognize that my first duty in life is to worship, to praise God for his creation, in order to get my mind straightened out so that I can see things in perspective."

"Shot in the arm!" she exclaimed. She recalled a drug addict "who had the bed next to mine in the Woman's House of Detention where I was serving a fifteen-day sentence for refusing to take shelter during an air raid drill . . . [who] made this remark: 'When I wake up in the morning you are reading in that little book, and when I go to sleep at night you are reading it. Me—the first thing I think of in the morning and the last thing I think of at night is how when I get out I will get me a fix!'"

"'This is my fix,' I told her, and I think she understood me. What she longed for was the beatific vision which we have glimpses of in this life, but which will only come after we pass that gateway which is death" (Catholic Worker papers).

In these latter years as the world seemed to be plummeting toward some cataclysmic climax in history's increasingly eccentric process, Dorothy Day had reached an abode in the life of the spirit where the tempests passed her by. Yet the "crisis in faith" that has touched many who were closer to her had burdened and saddened her. "Sick of the church, sick of religion!" she heard at every hand.

> The desert Fathers themselves complained of it and called it *acedia:* defined in the dictionary as spiritual sloth and indifference. And the remedy for that, according to spiritual writers, is faithfulness to the means to overcome it, recitation of the psalms each day, prayer and solitude, and by these means arriving or hoping to achieve a state of well being. . . . To pray the psalms even without understanding . . . then suddenly like a sudden shower, understanding a verse comes, with the light of joy like sun breaking through clouds. (Catholic Worker papers)

She had hope. The church was suffering "from an embarrassment of riches in this time of renewal. . . . New translations of Scripture abound. In reading over Paul's Epistle to the Galatians, which carries a subhead, 'Faith and Freedom' in the New English Bible . . . I saw again how applicable it was for our own day. The turbulence of the Church today is a result of a newfound, newly realized emphasis on the liberty of Christ, and the realization, too, that we have scarcely begun to be Christian, to deserve the name Christian." Yet, "there comes a time, very often, when one must live on blind and naked faith." Still she knew "that God sends intimations of immortality. We believe that if the will is right, God will take us by the hair of the head, as he did Habbakuk, who brought food to Daniel in the lion's den, and will restore us to the Way" (Catholic Worker papers).

WORKS CONSULTED

Avitabile, Alex

1971   "A Bibliography on Peter Maurin, Dorothy Day, and the Catholic Worker." Mimeographed. Milwaukee: Marquette University Archives.

Berdyaev, Nicolas
    1939   *Spirit and Reality*. London: Centenary Press.
    1960   *The Destiny of Man*. New York: Harper Torch-book.

Catholic Pacifists' Association
    1944   *Blessed Are the Peacemakers*. Privately printed.

The Catholic Worker
    1933–   Monthly newspaper of the Catholic Worker move-ment.

Catholic Worker papers.
                  Milwaukee: Marquette University Archives. All un-published material cited in this article is from the Catholic Worker papers.

Coles, Robert
    1973   *A Spectacle Unto the World: The Catholic Work-er Movement*. New York: Viking.

Cornell, Thomas, and Forest, James H.
    1968   *A Penny a Copy: Readings from The Catholic Worker*, New York: Macmillan.

Day, Dorothy
    1932   "A Human Document," *The Sign* 12 (November 1932): 223–24.
    1933   *The Catholic Worker*. New York: The Catholic Worker.
    1938   *House of Hospitality*. New York: Sheed and Ward.
    1939   *From Union Square to Rome*. Silver Springs, MD: Preservation of the Faith Press.
    1948   *On Pilgrimage*. New York: Catholic Worker Books.
    1950   *Peter Maurin, Christian Radical*. St. Louis: Pio Decimo Press.
    1952   *The Long Loneliness*. New York: Harper.

Hugo, John J.
    1944   *Applied Christianity*. Privately printed.

Maurin, Peter
    1949   *The Green Revolution, Easy Essays on Catholic Radicalism*. New York: Academy Guild Press.

Miller, William D.
   1973   *Harsh and Dreadful Love, Dorothy Day and the Catholic Worker Movement*. New York: Liveright.

New Catholic Encyclopedia.
   1967   New York: McGraw Hill.

O'Brien, David
   1968   *American Catholics and Social Reform*. New York: Oxford.

Sheean, Vincent
   1969   *Personal History*. New York: Sentry.

Sheehan, Arthur
   1959   *Peter Maurin: Gay Believer*. New York: Hanover House.

Vishnewski, Stanley
   1970   *Dorothy Day, Meditations*. New York: Newman Press.

INDEX